AF555065

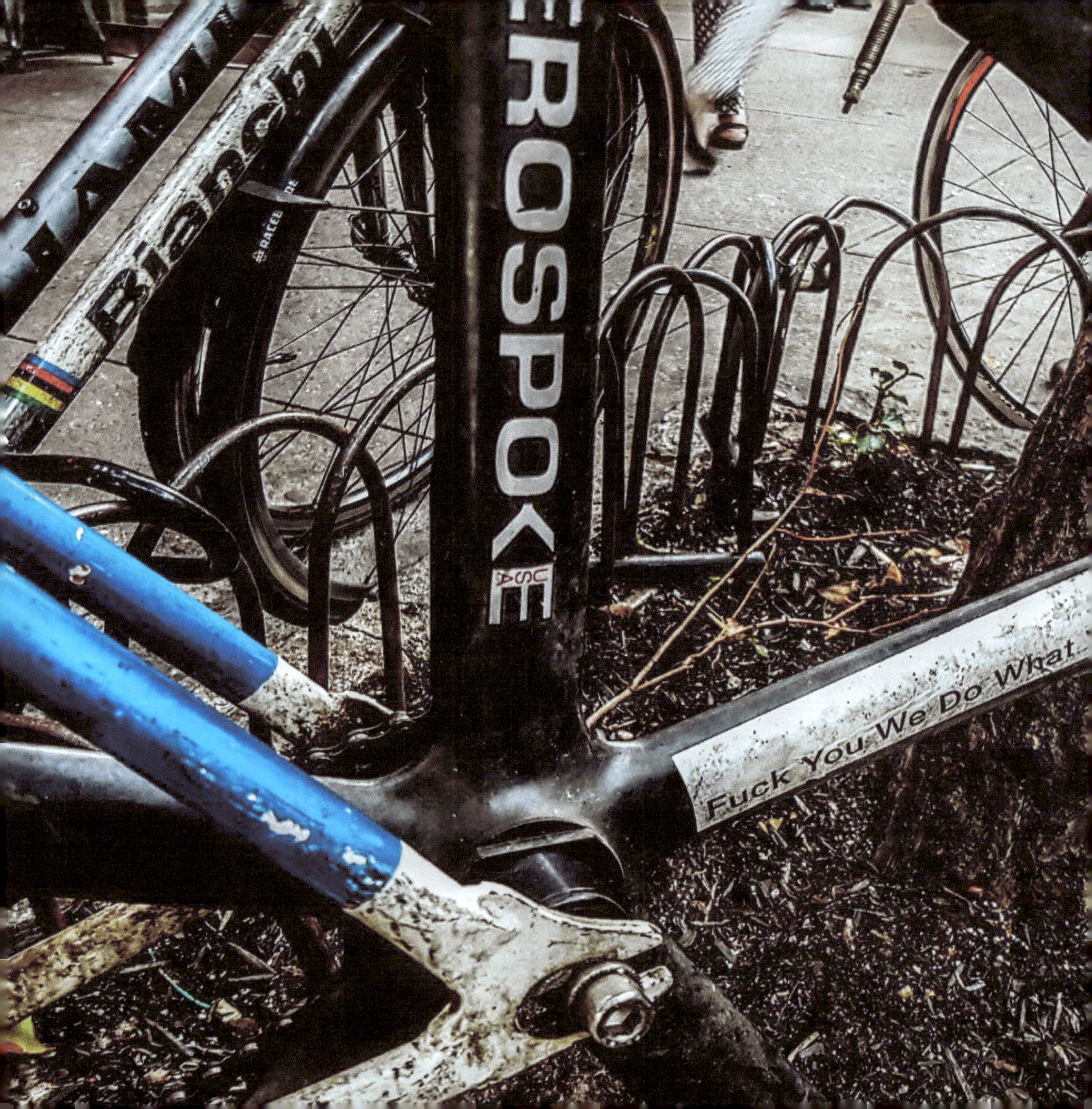
Fuck You We Do What

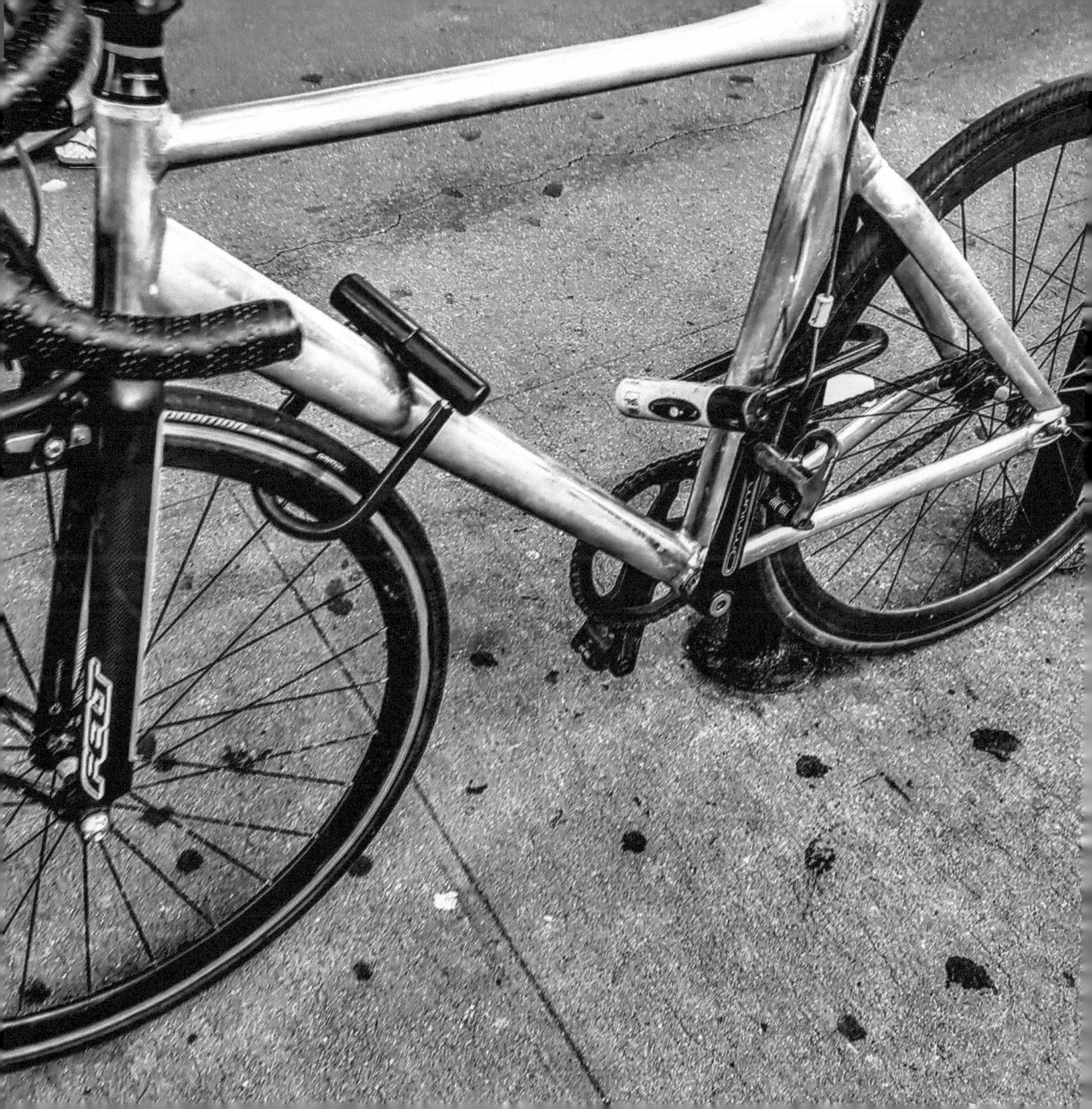
FELT

Hi-Tensile

The beater bike. An essential New York City commuting tool that needs to be useful, but undesirable. These bikes are heavy and purposefully dumbed down with electrical tape, stickers, dints and rust to appear less attractive to would be thieves.

Peeling eroded paint and beaten-up rust cover the hi-tensile steel frame tubing. Heavy duty hi-tensile steel chains then leave their tell-tale signs of abuse on the bike as they secure the dilapidated steed onto NYC street furniture. The absent owner lives in hope hour by hour, day by day, that their heavily punished and eroded transport will remain un-stolen and available to serve them for the onward journey.

To the avid bike enthusiast, the colour of the peeling paint or frame design might actually reveal a glorious past of what was once perhaps high-end race-bred beast that is now living a life of neglect as an expendable workhorse on the famous streets of New York City.

This is a photo journal, wherein I have photographed every bike I have walked past in a 24-hour period.

A Ride Iconic project created by Shane Ellis; these are the beater bikes of New York City.

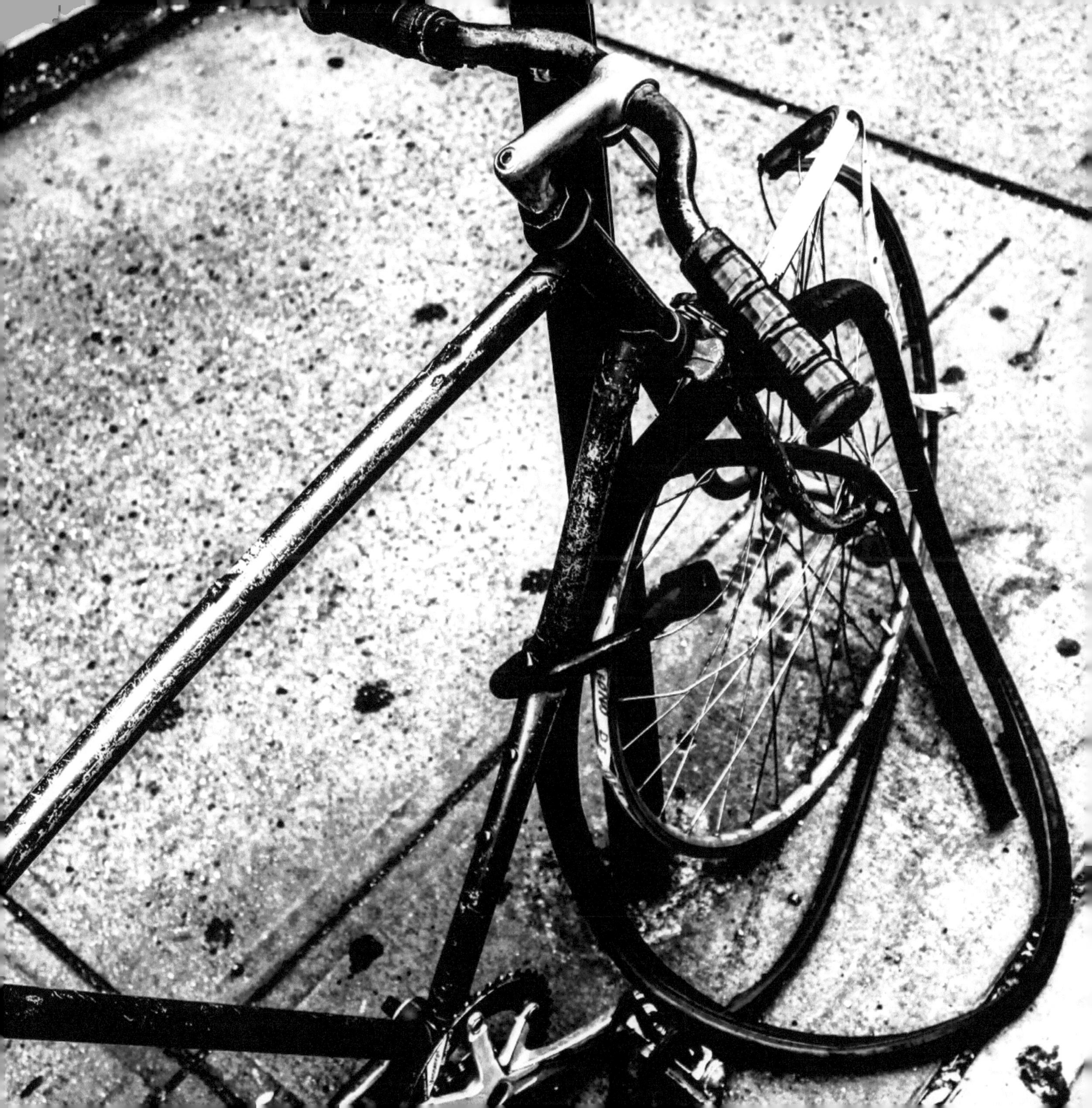

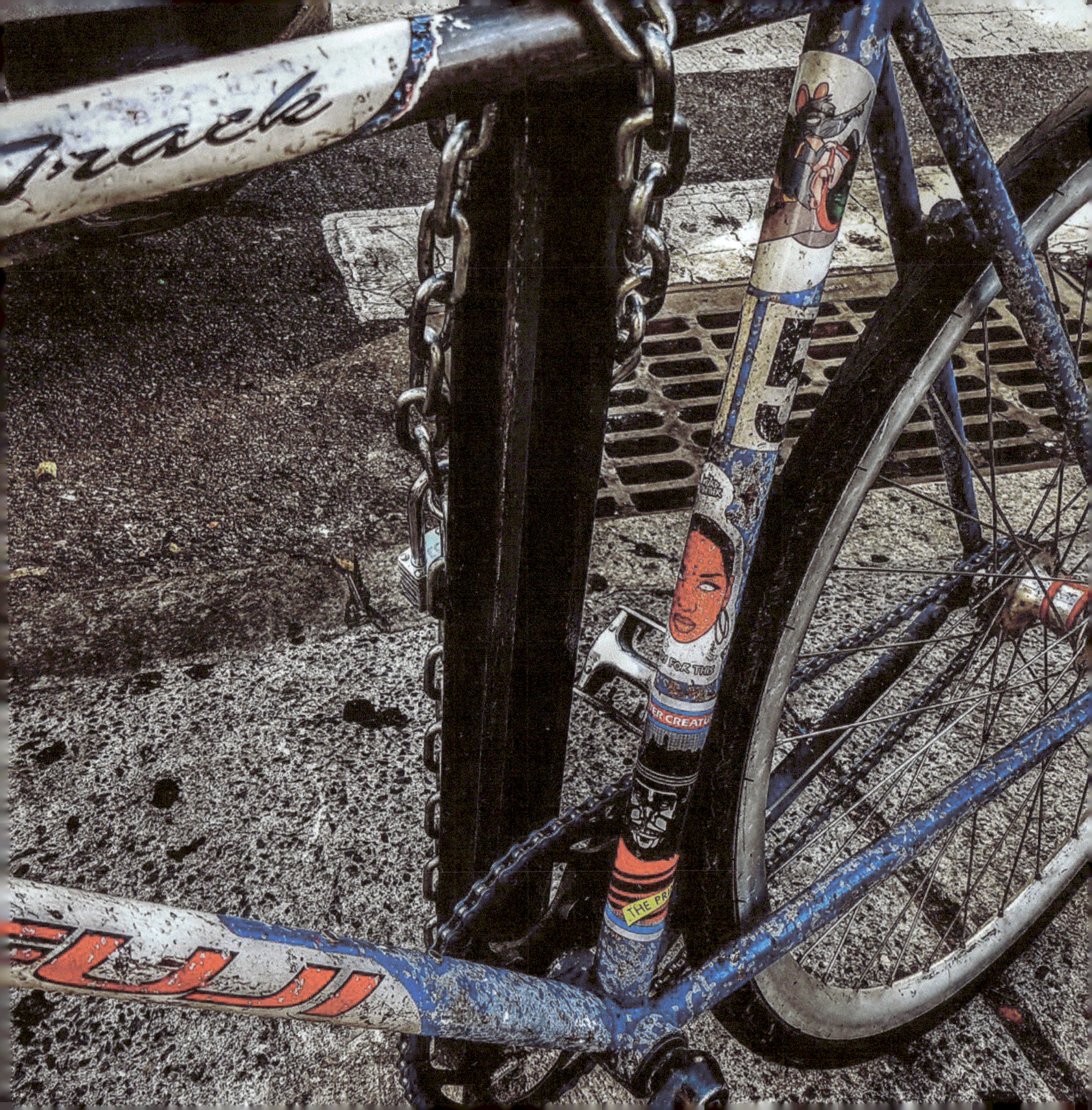

Track
FUJI

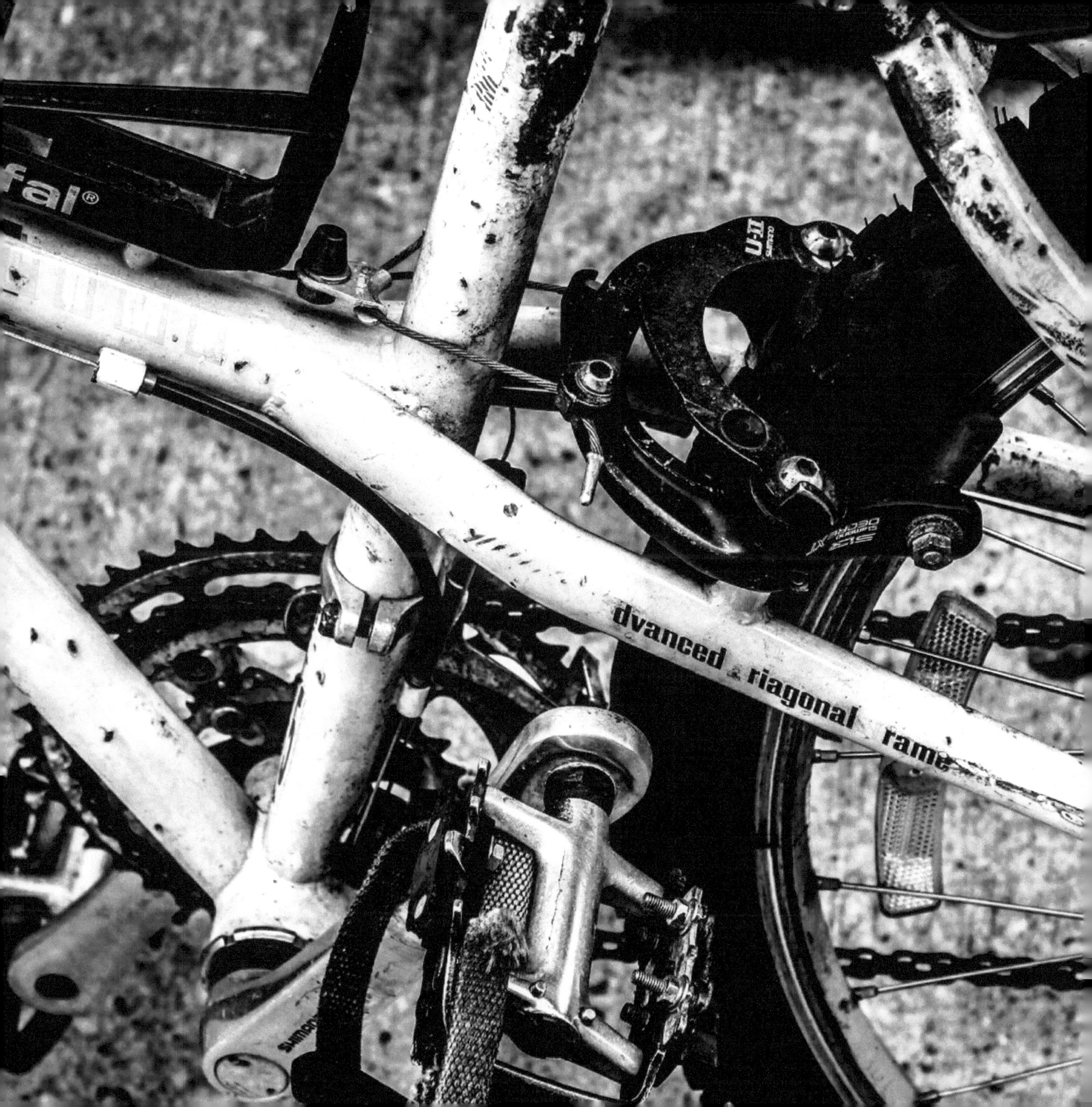
fal®
U-II
dvanced
riagonal
rame

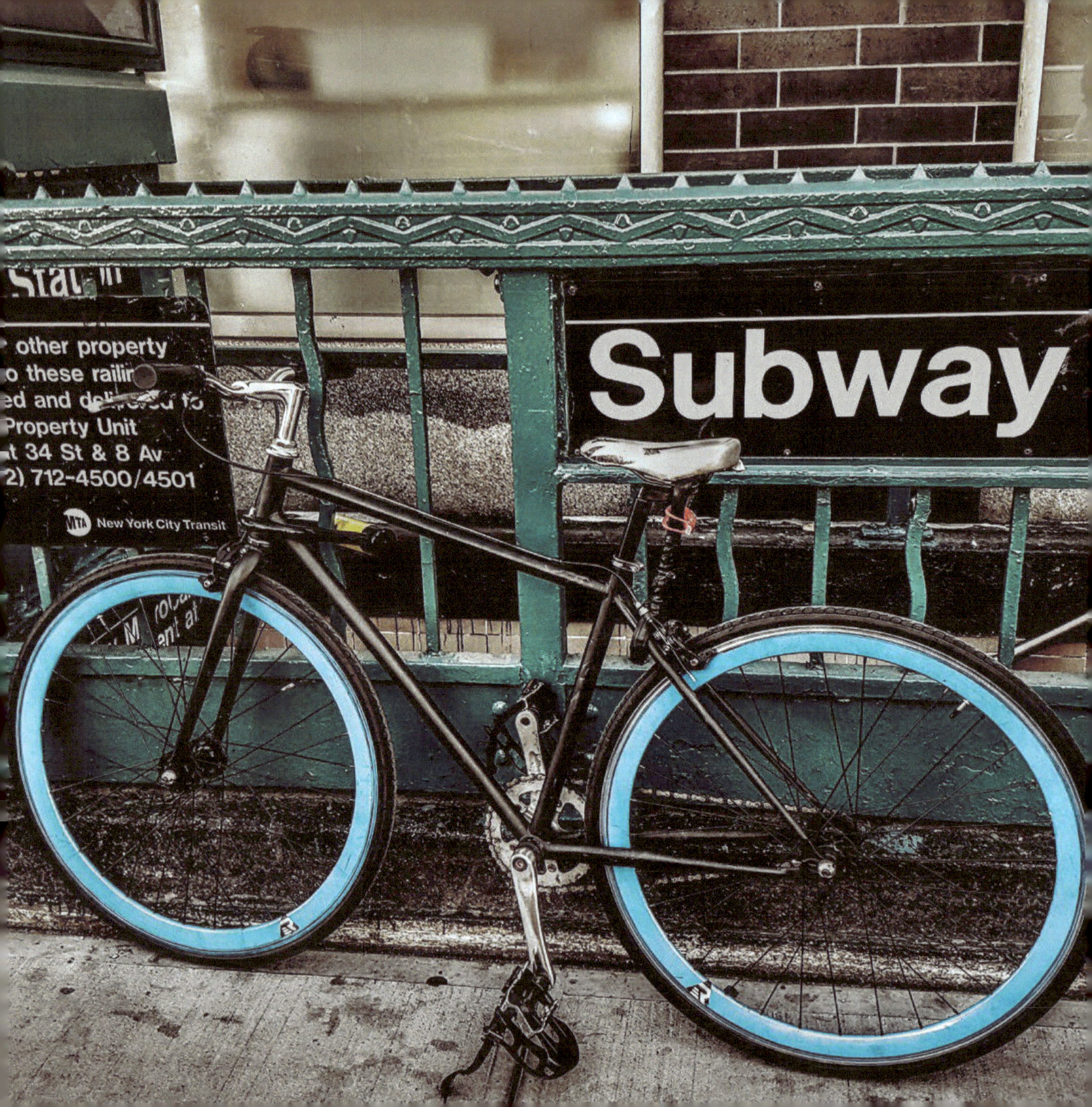
other property
Property Unit
34 St & 8 Av
712-4500/4501
MTA New York City Transit
Subway

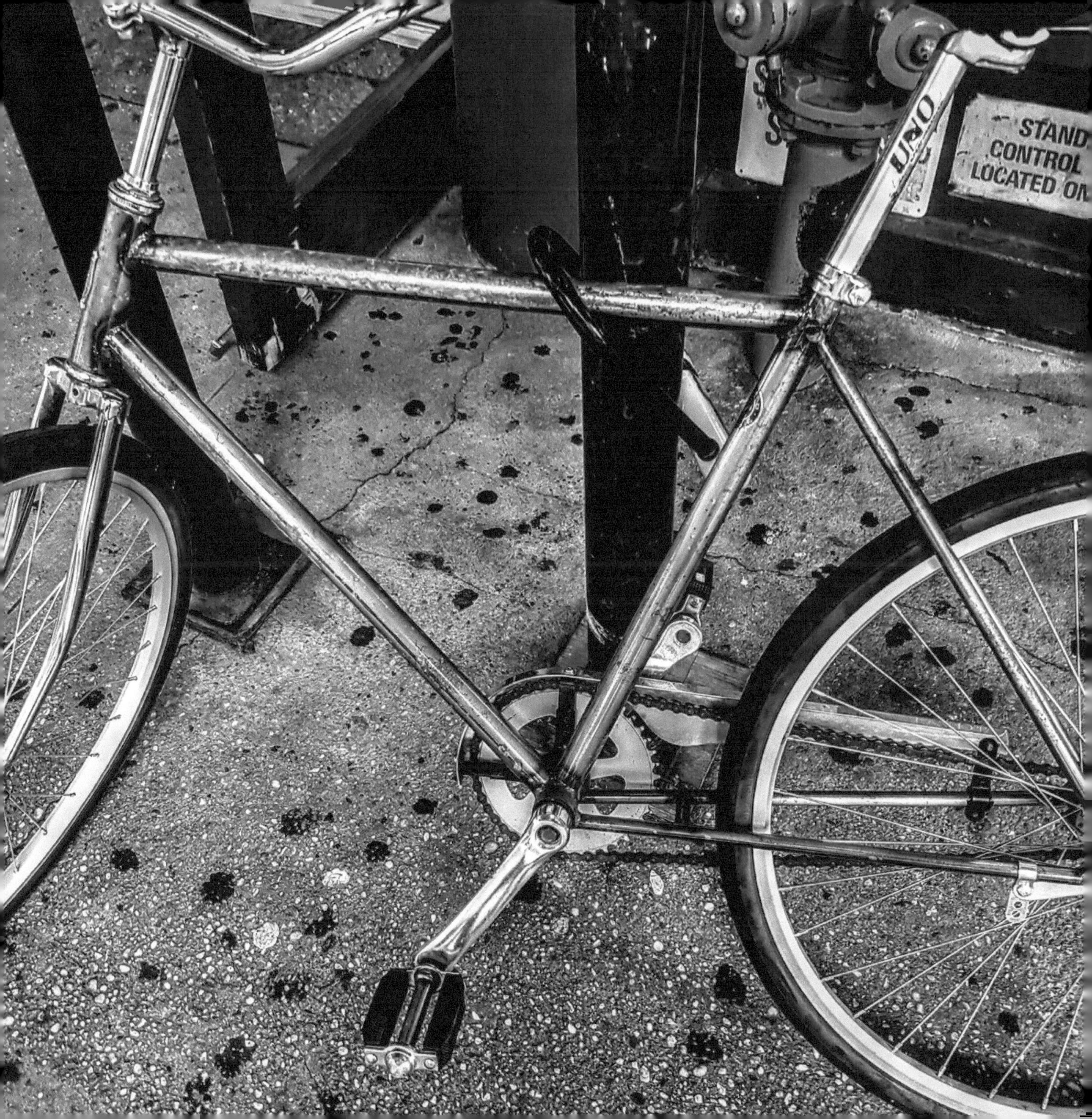
UNO
STAND
CONTROL
LOCATED

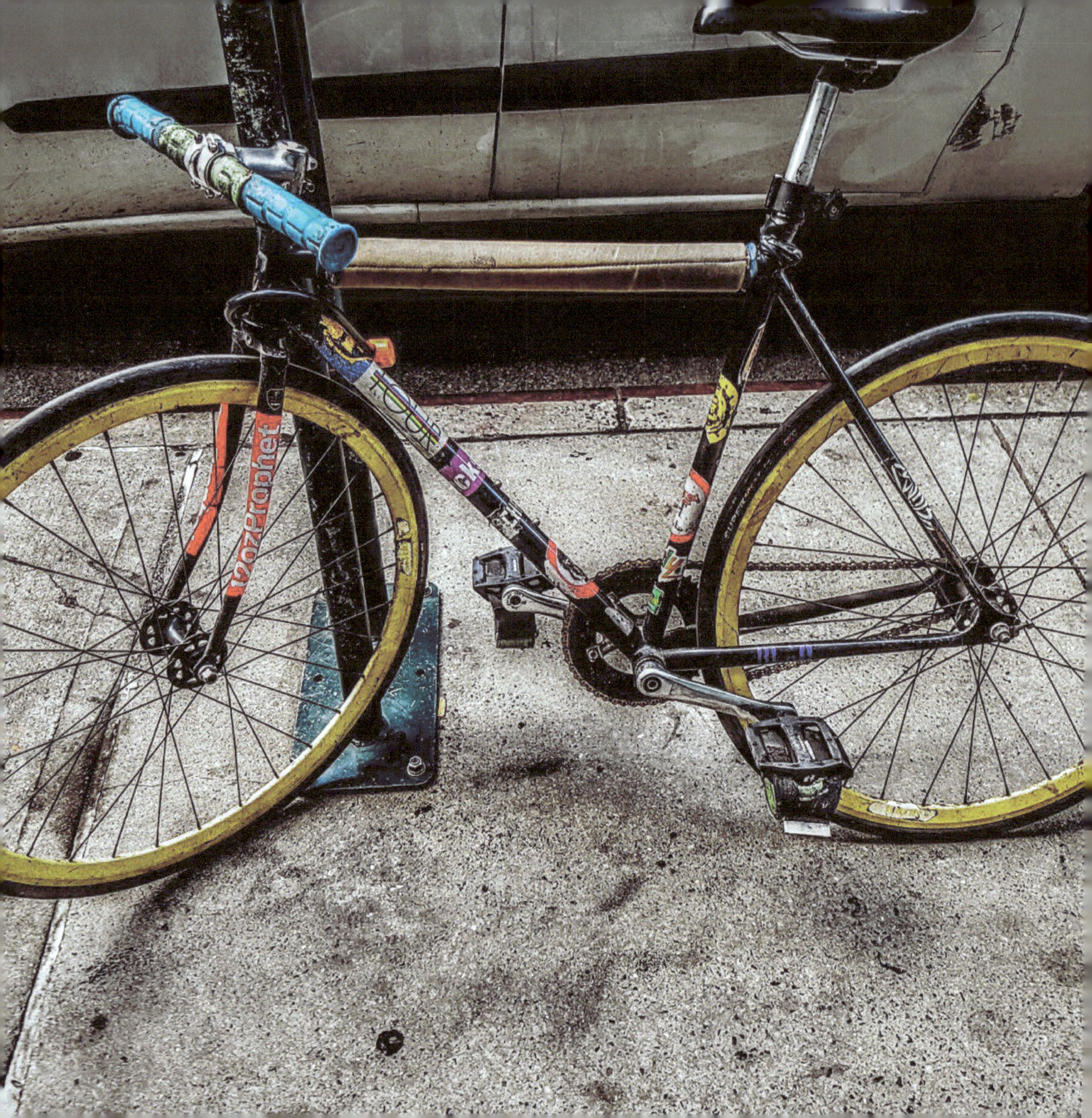
1207Prophet

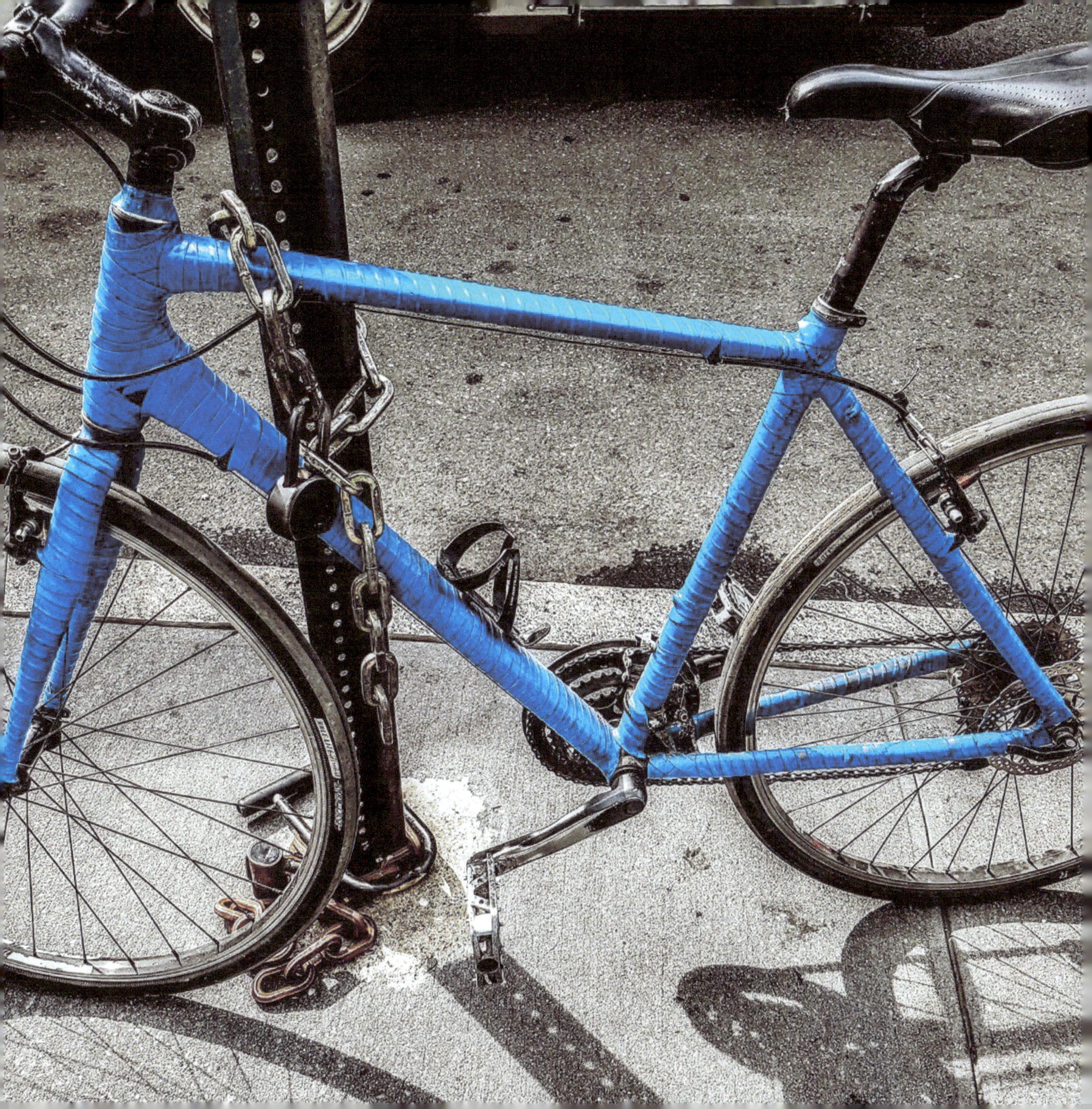

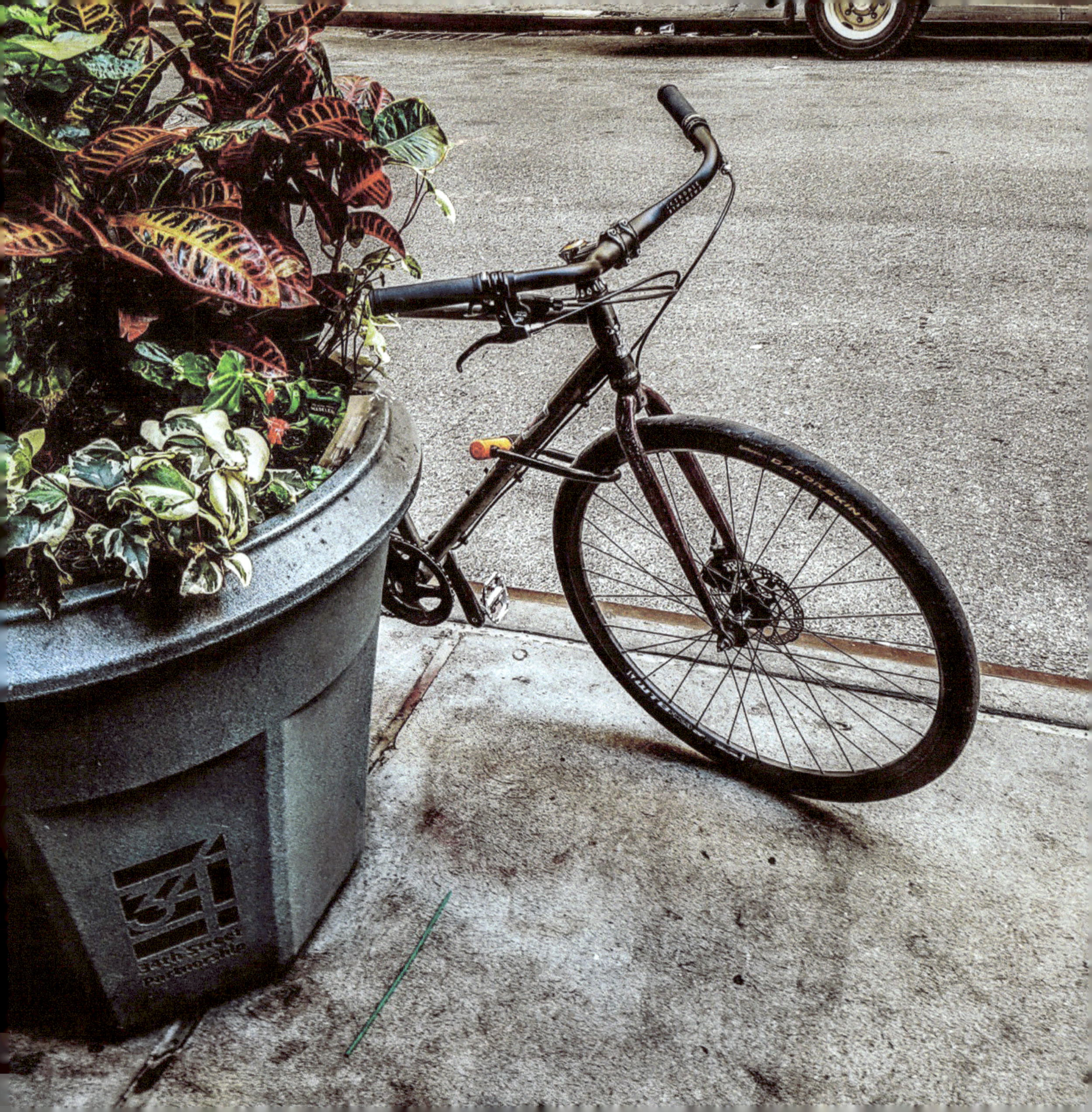
34
GATORSKIN

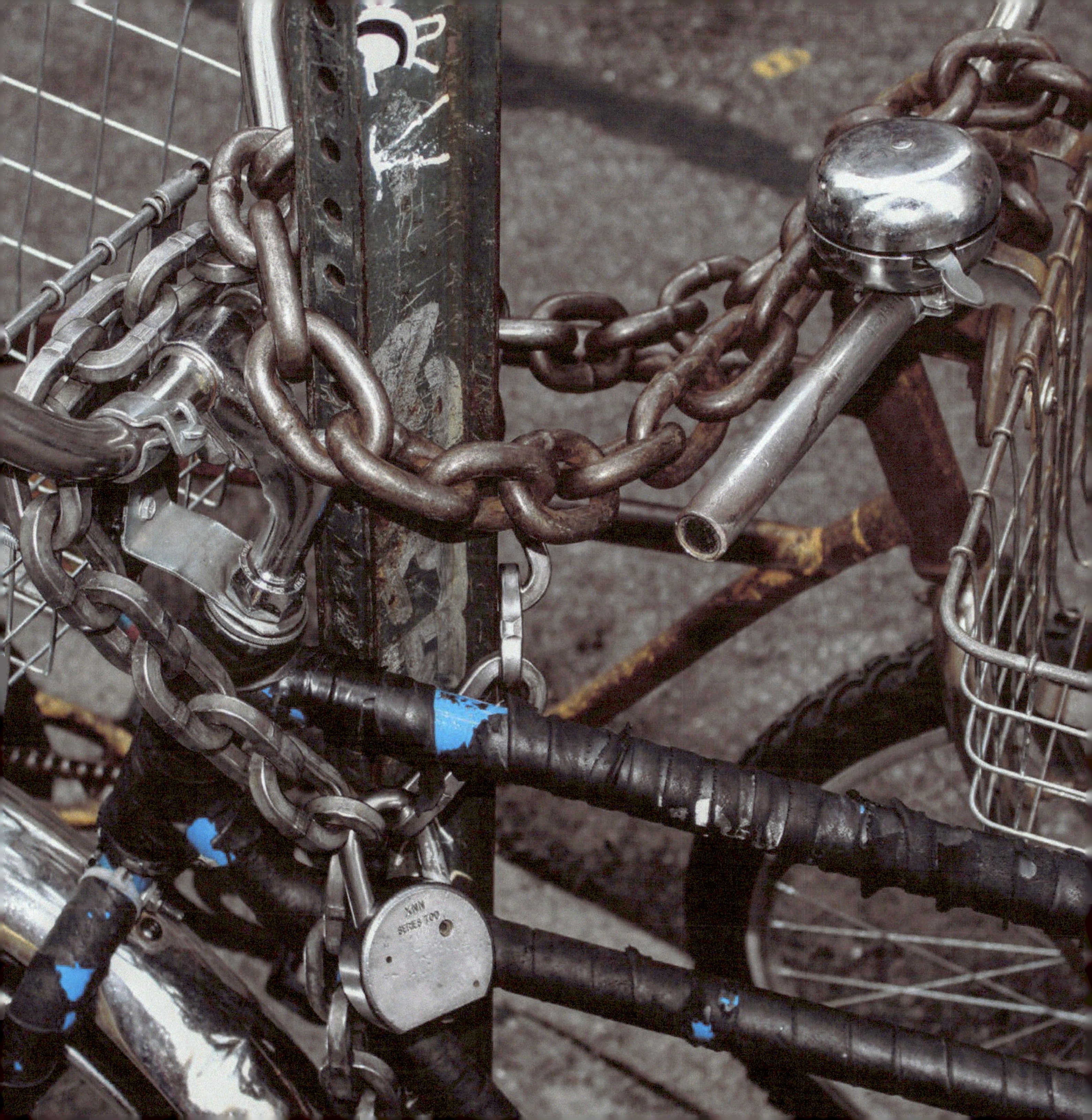

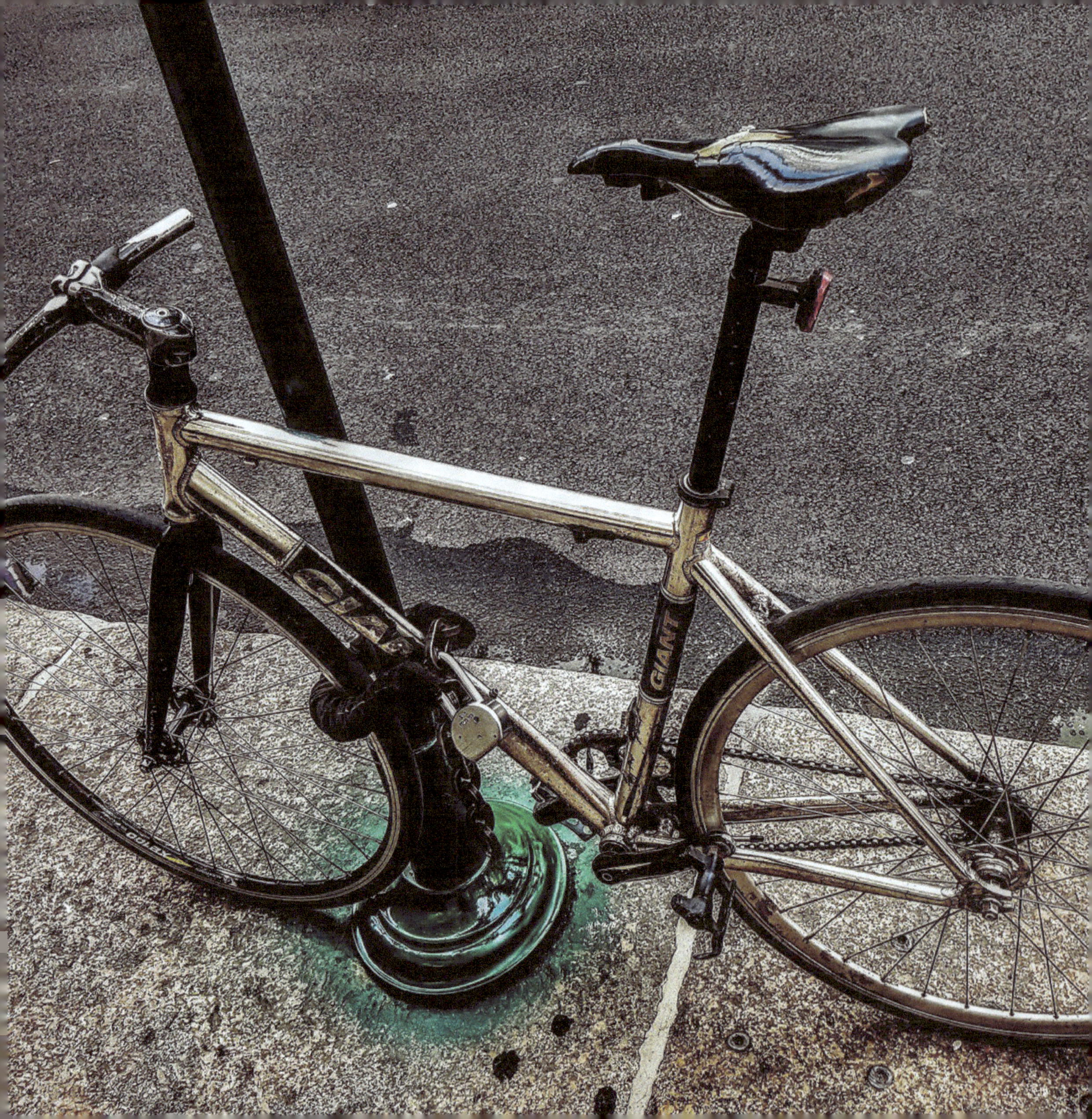
GIANT

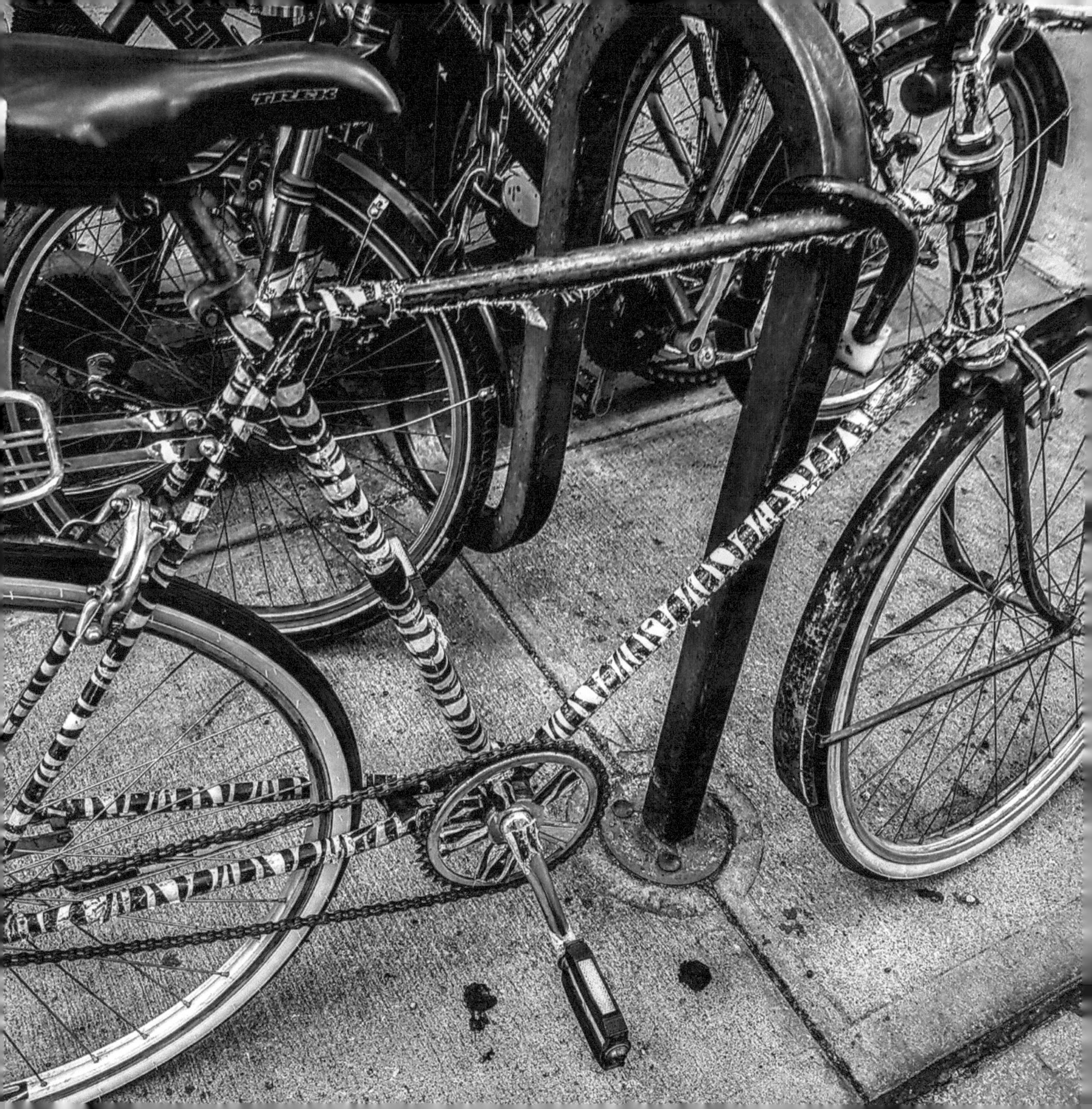
TREK

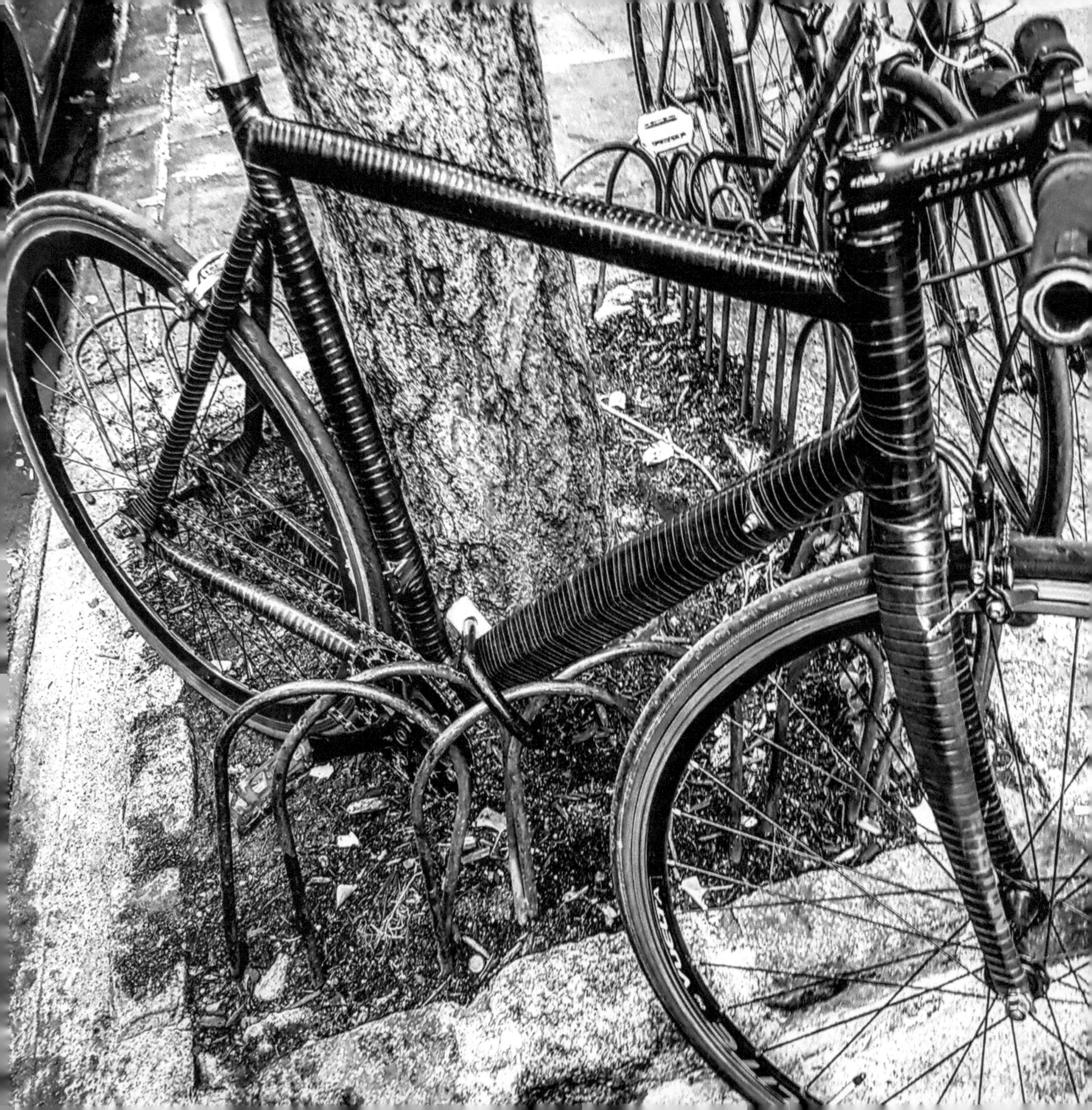

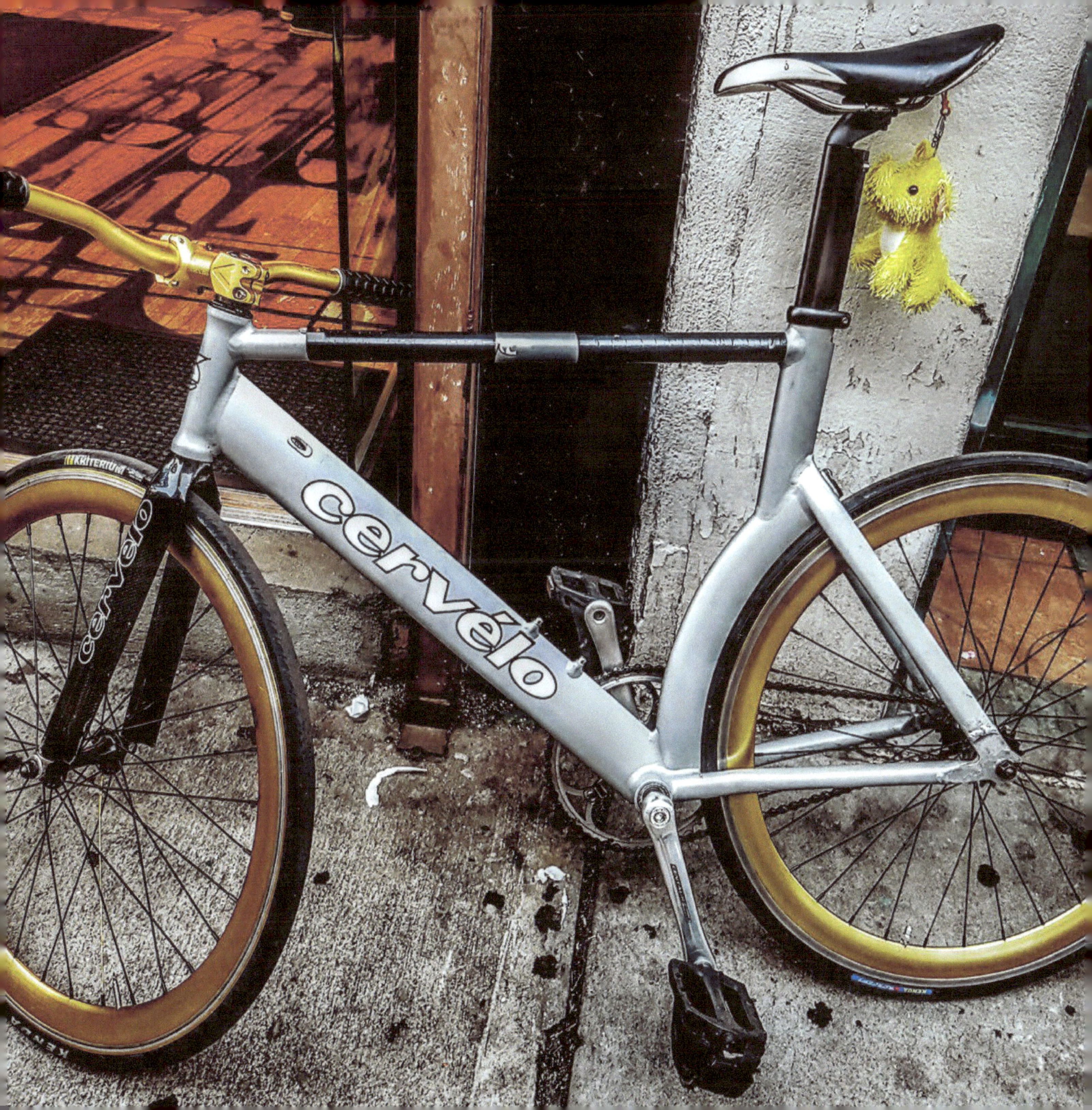
cervélo
cervélo

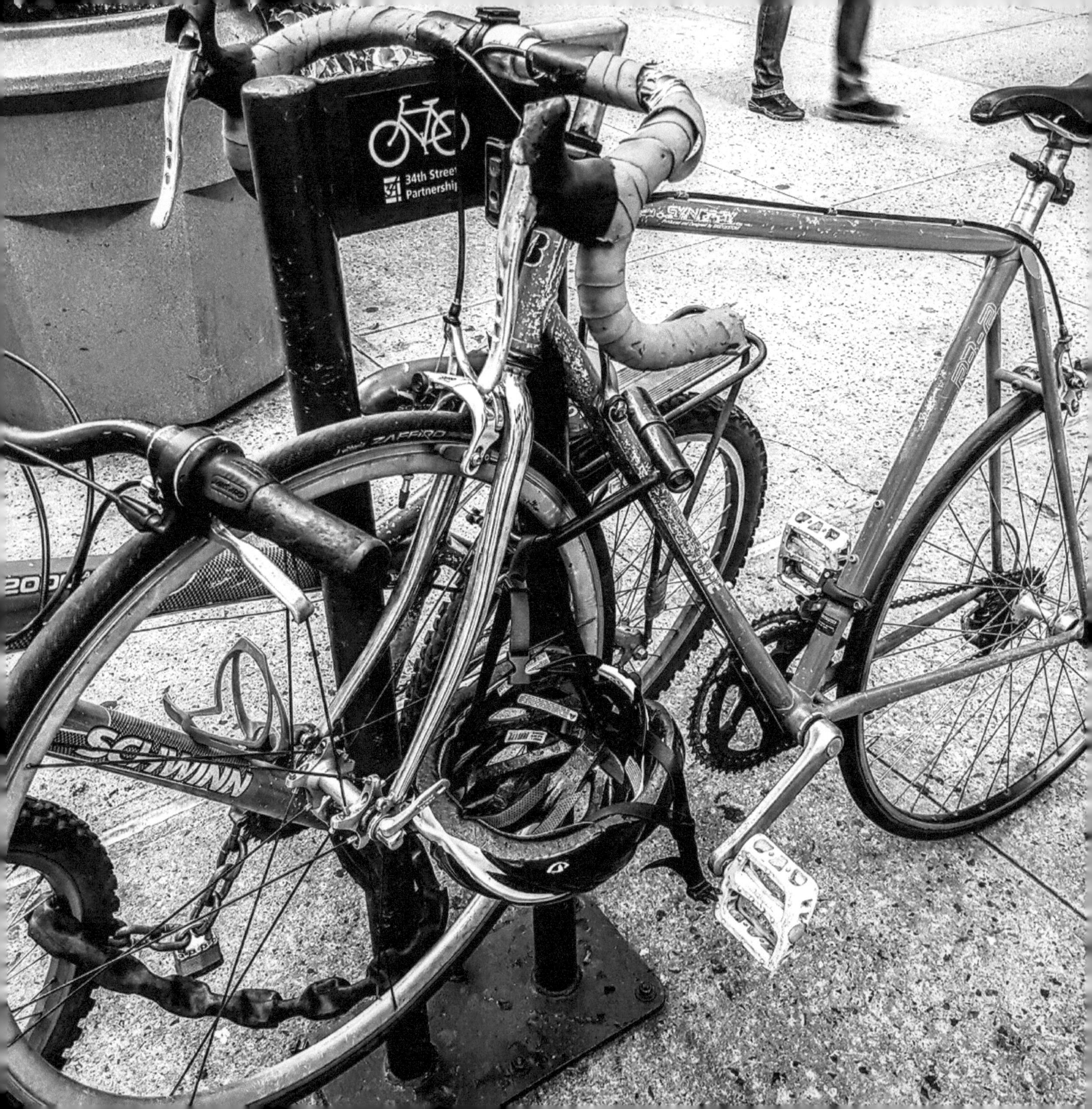
34th Stree
Partnership
SCHWINN

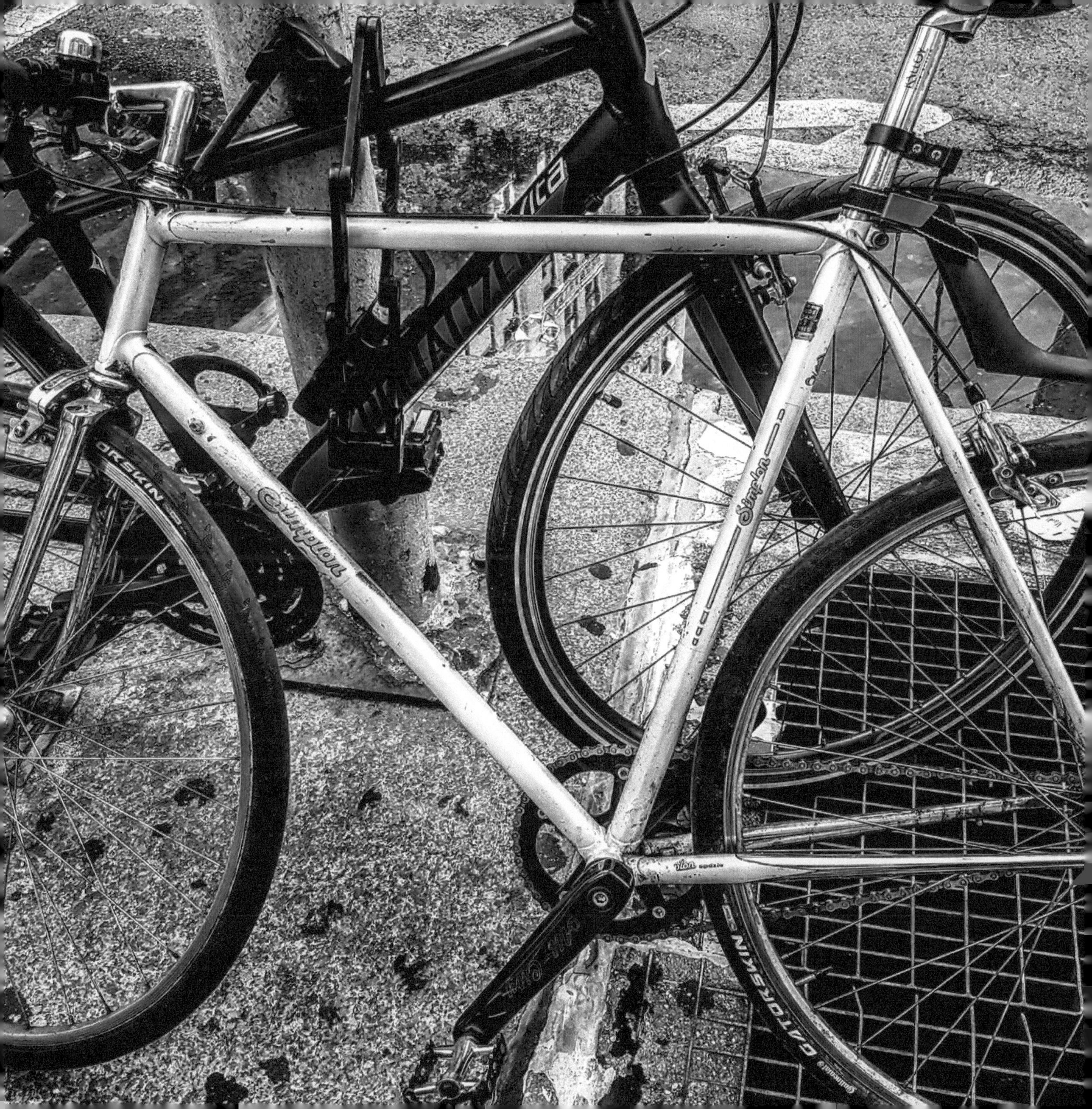
Simplon
ORSKIN

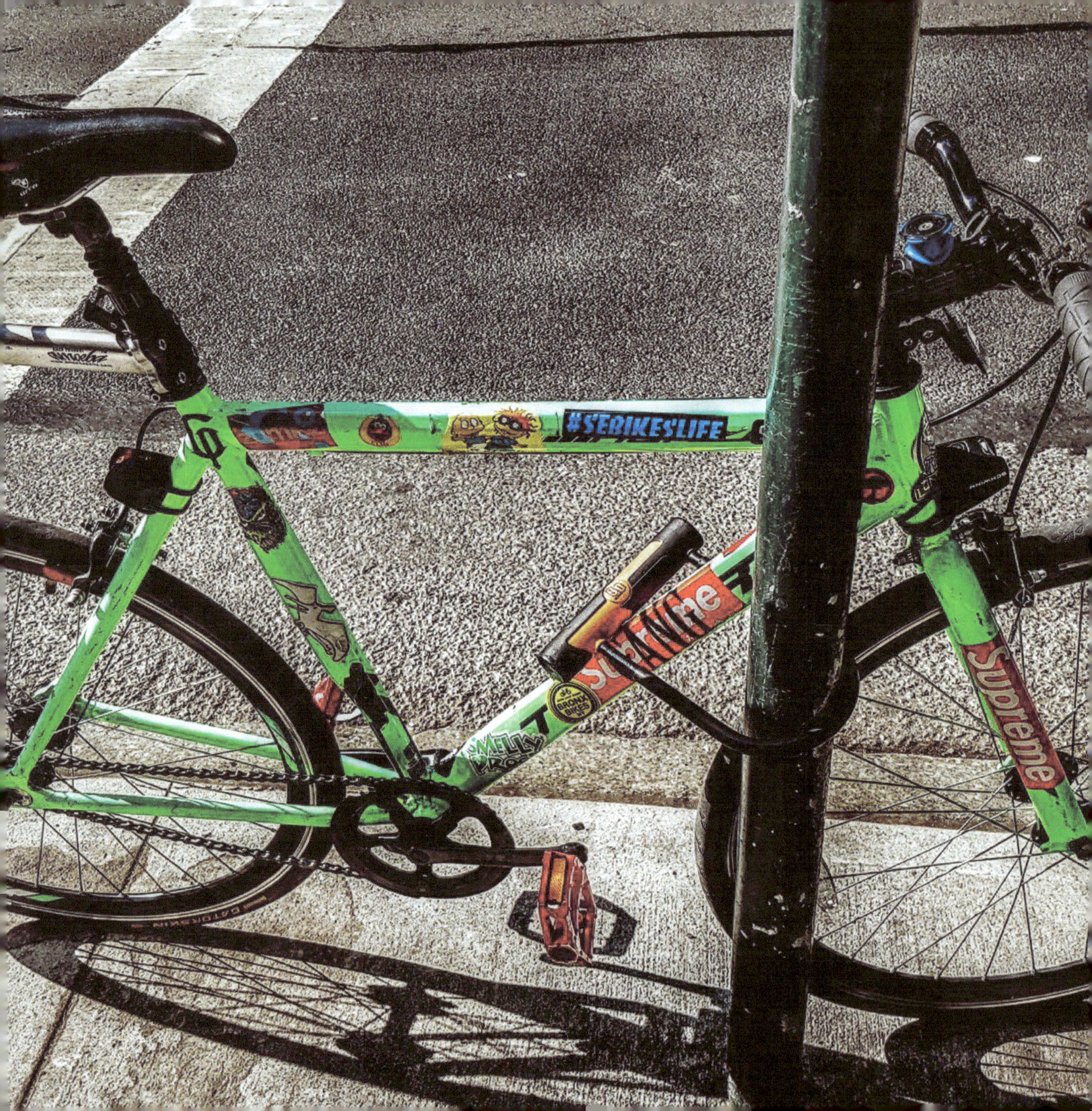
#SFBIKESLIFE
Supreme

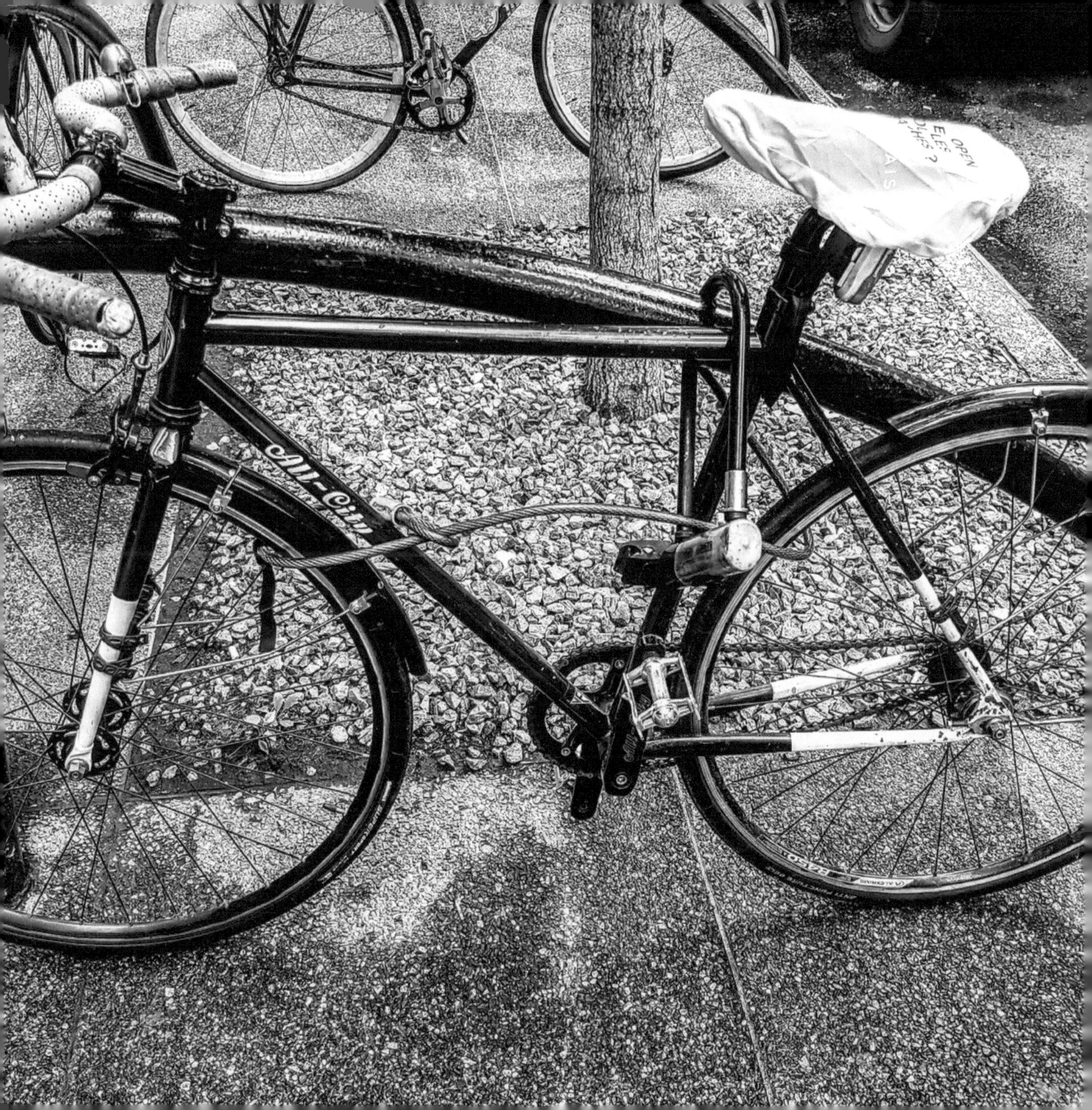
All-City

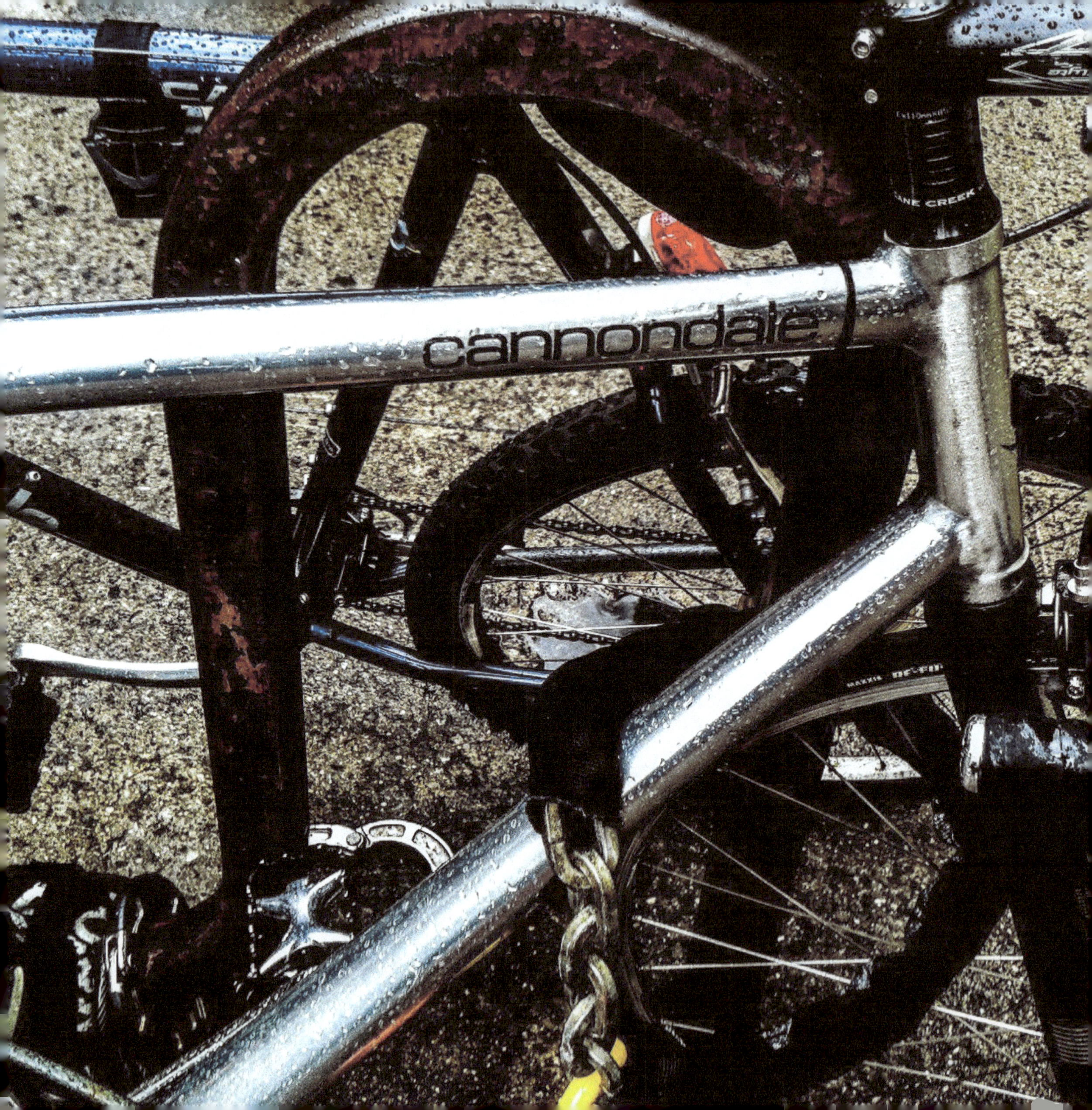
cannondale

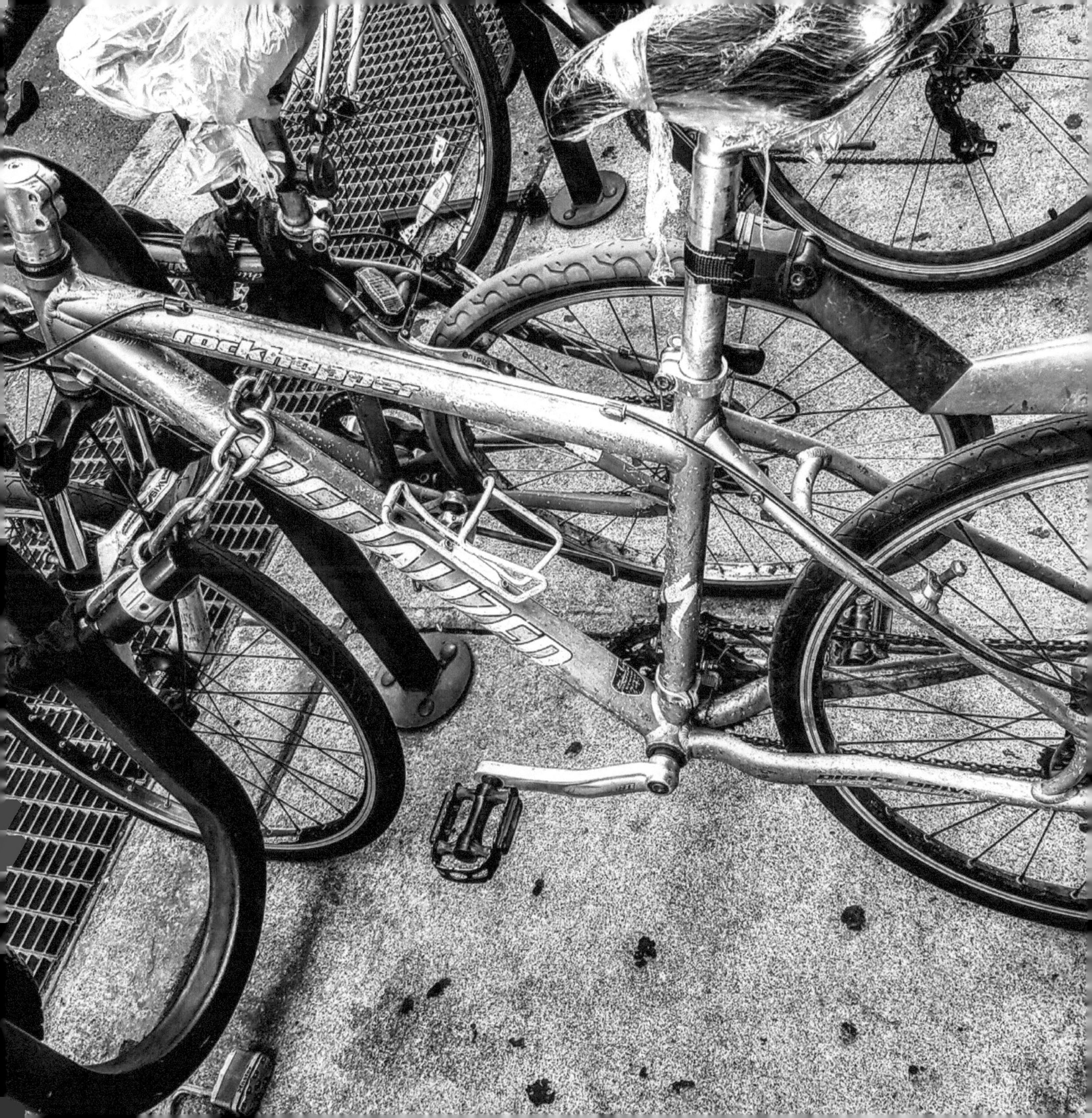
rockhopper

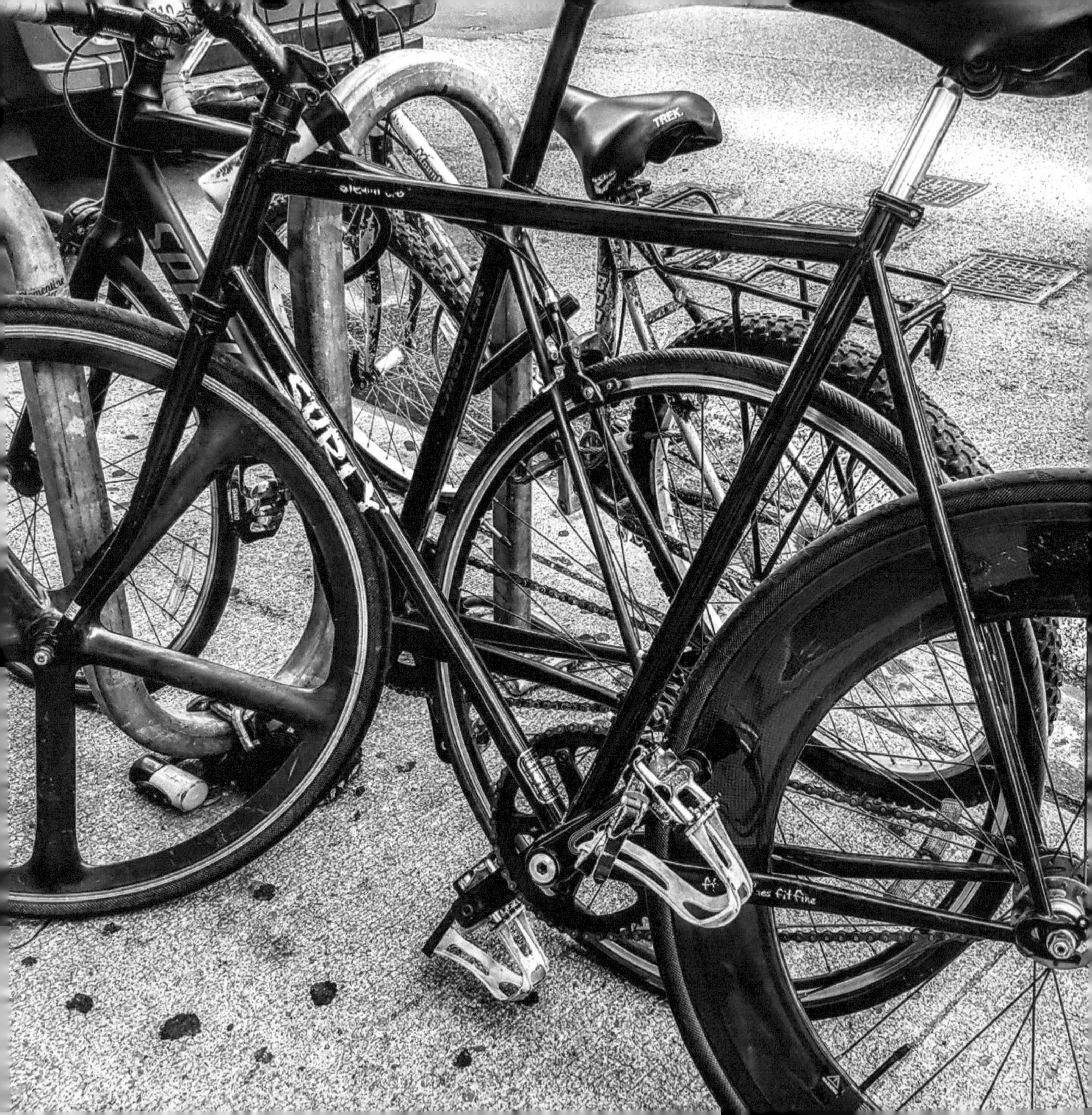
TREK

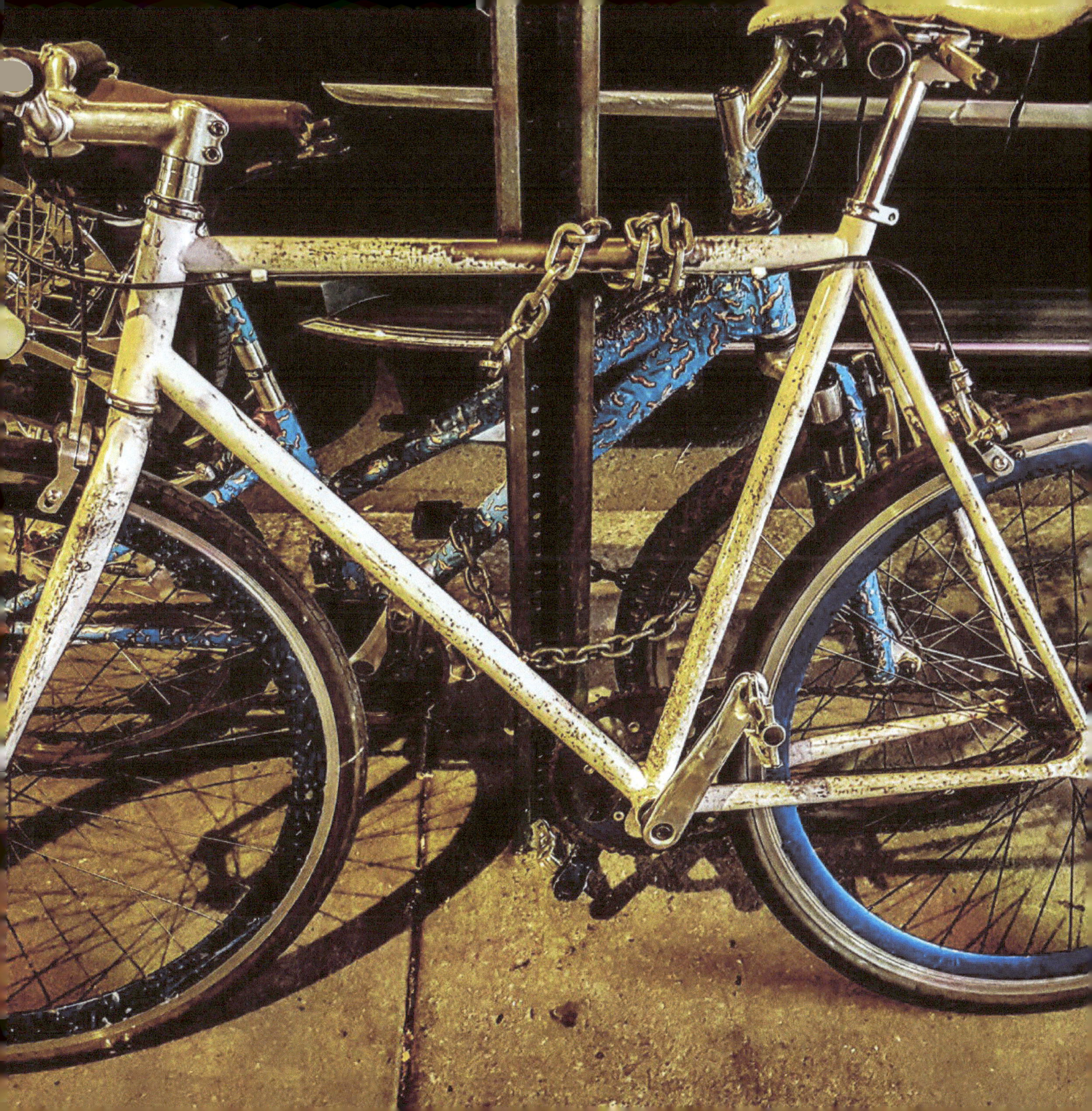

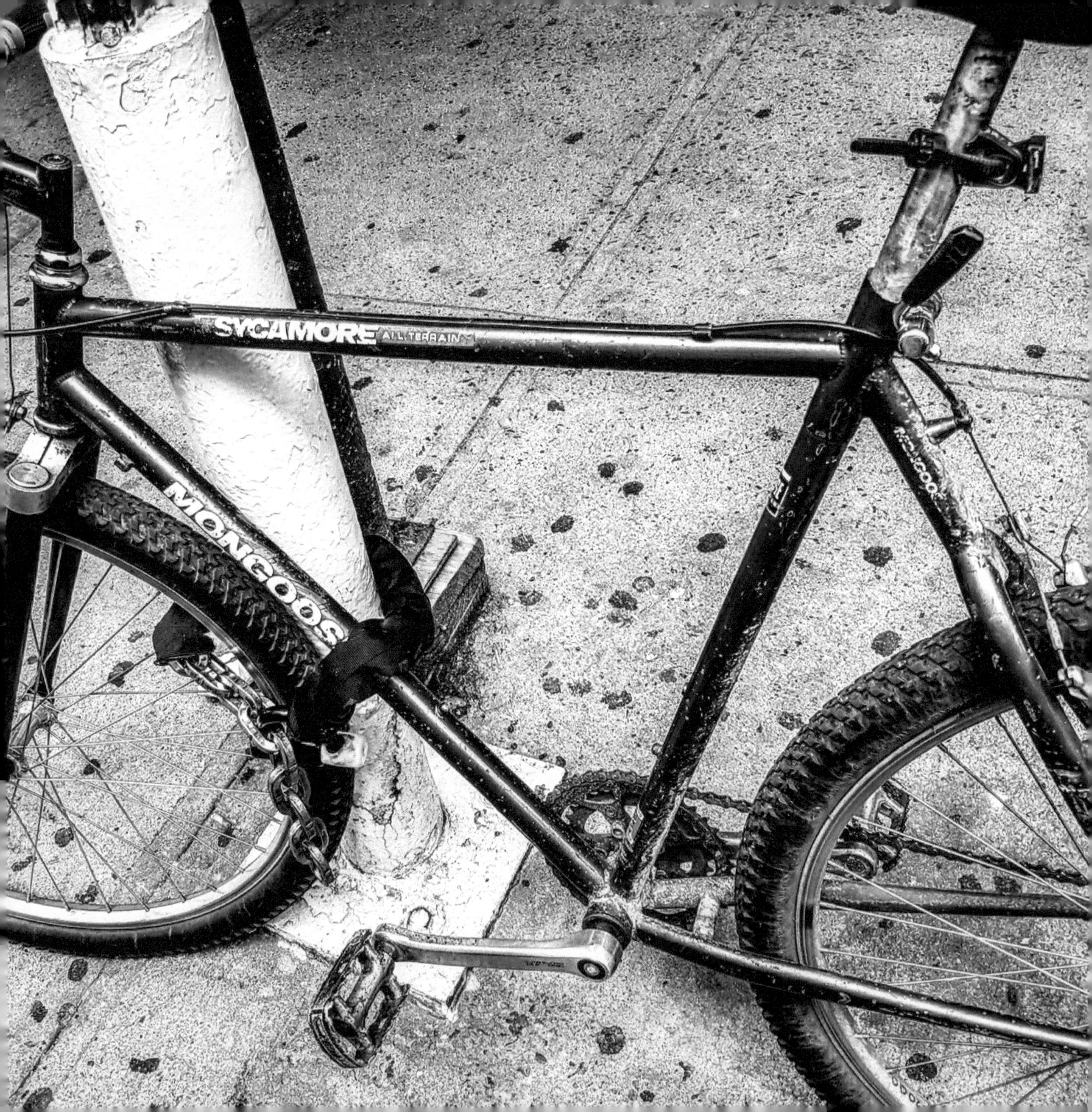
SYCAMORE
ALL TERRAIN
MONGOOS

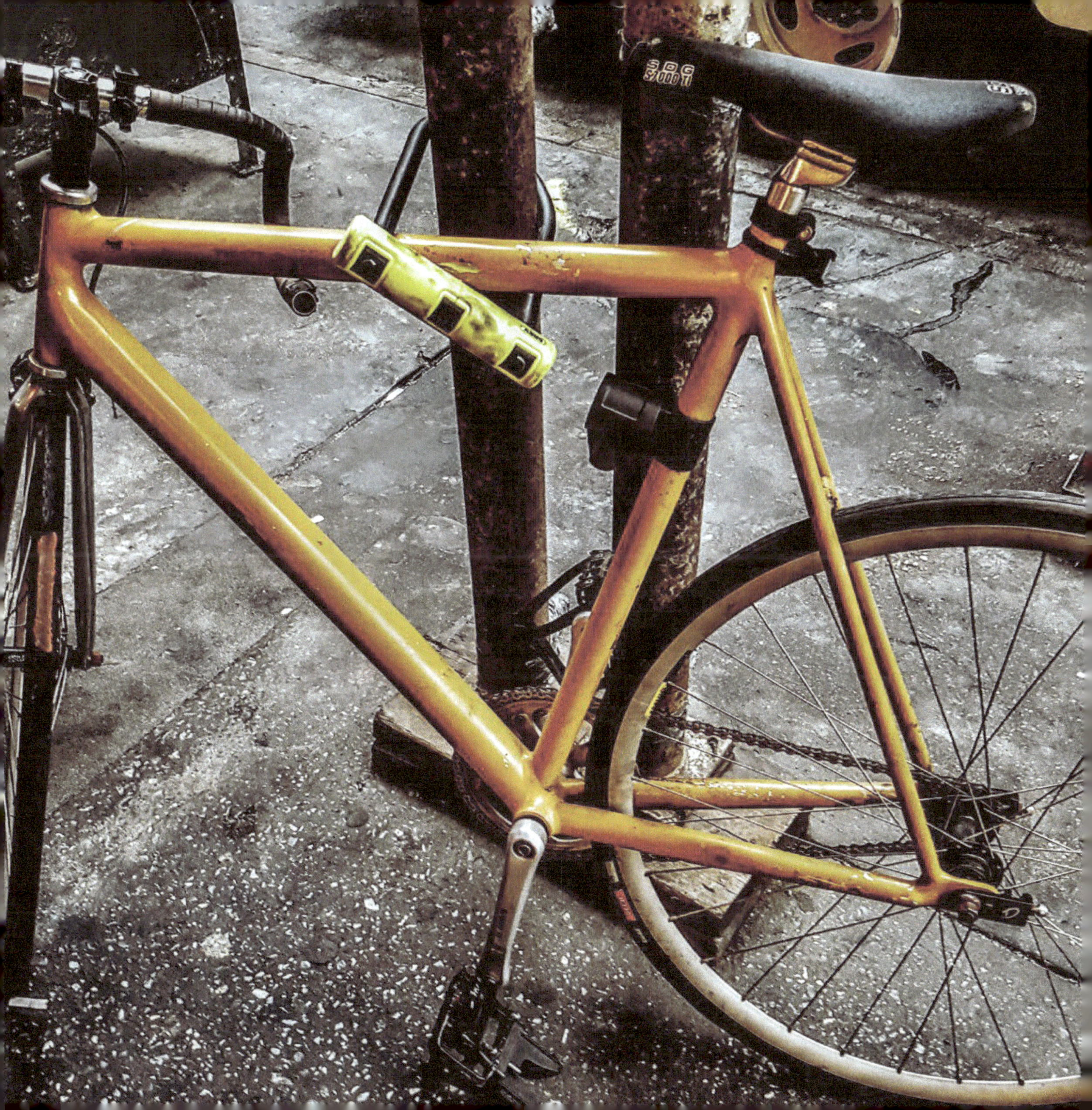
SDG

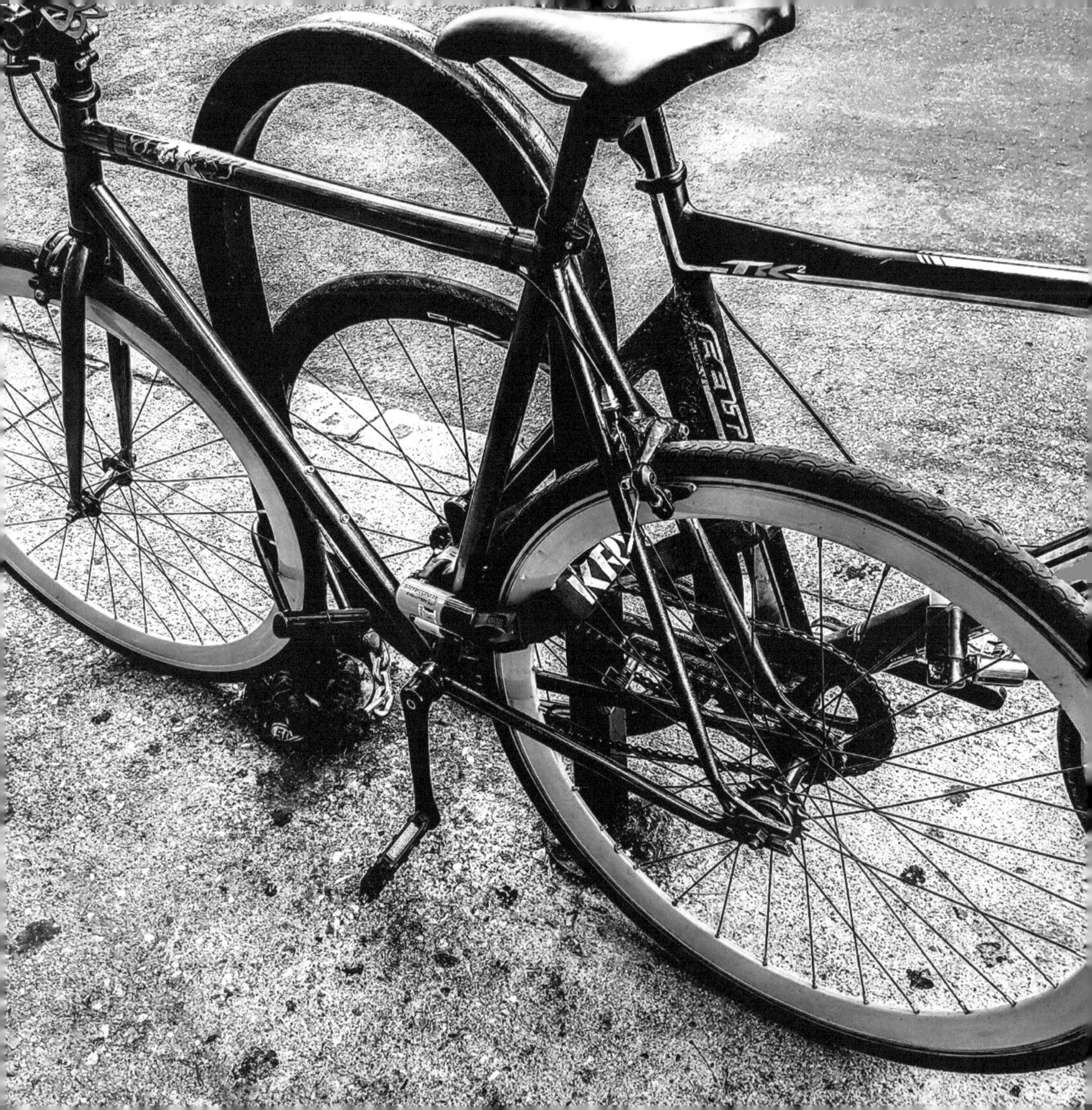

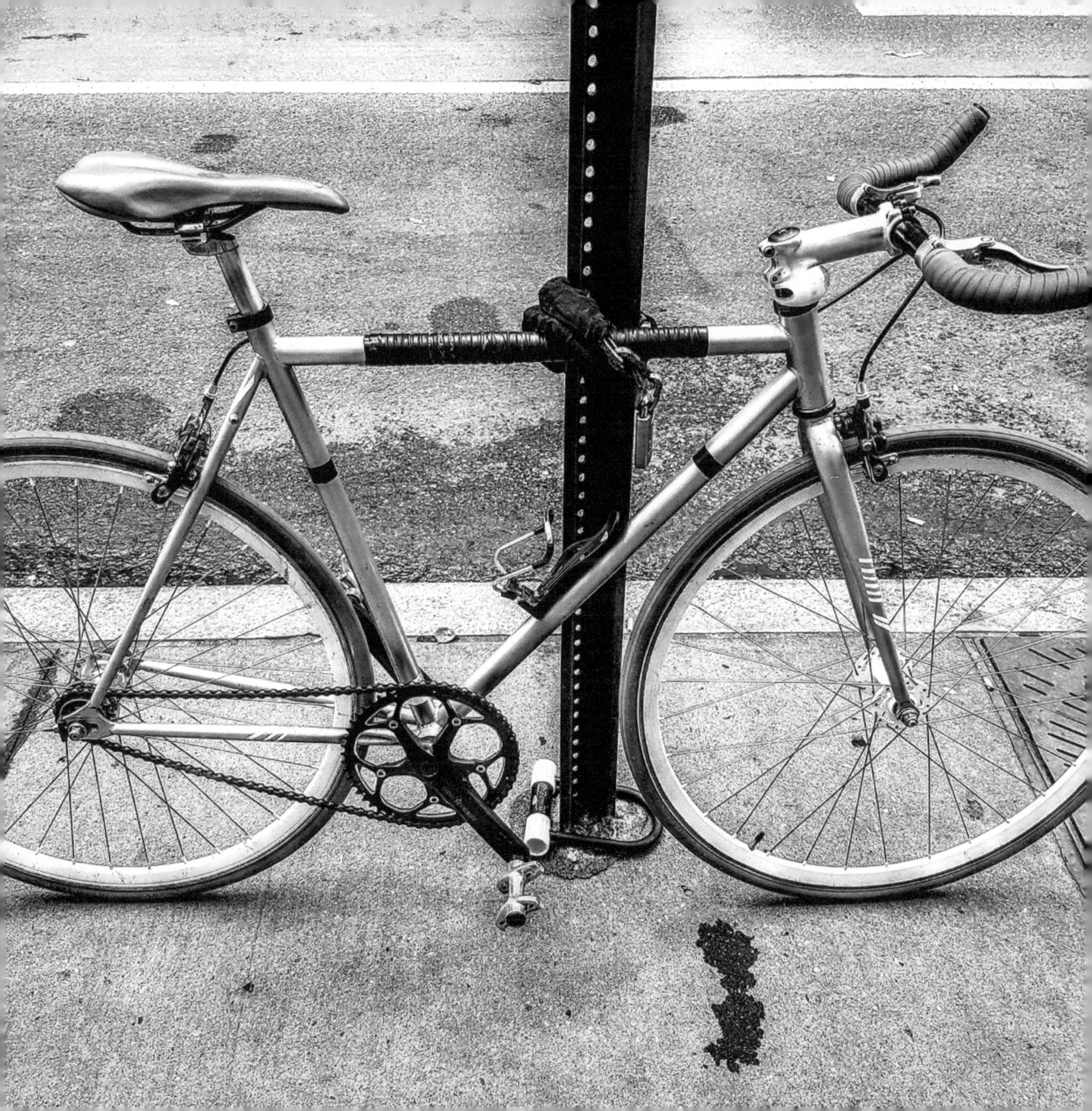

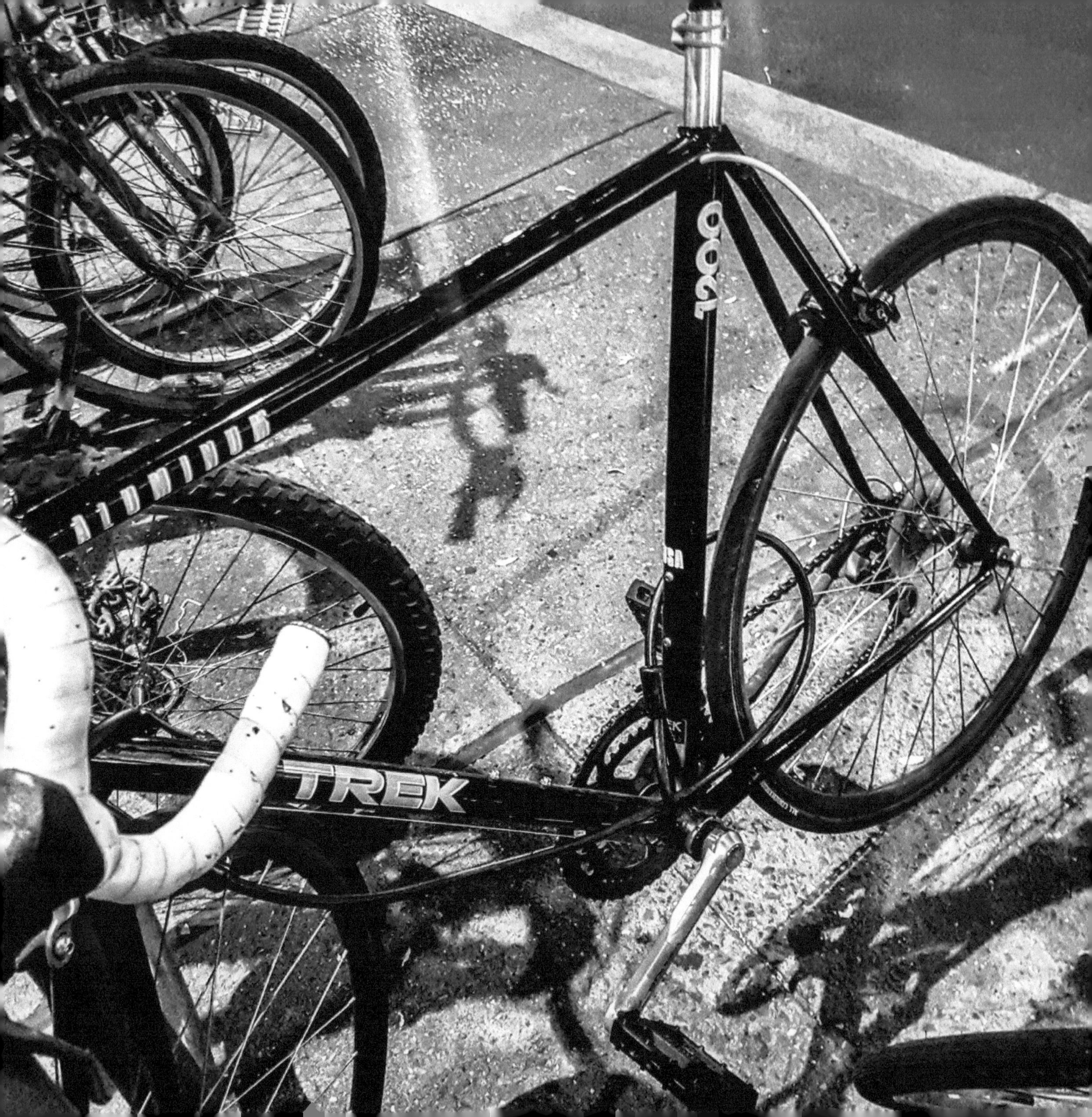
TREK

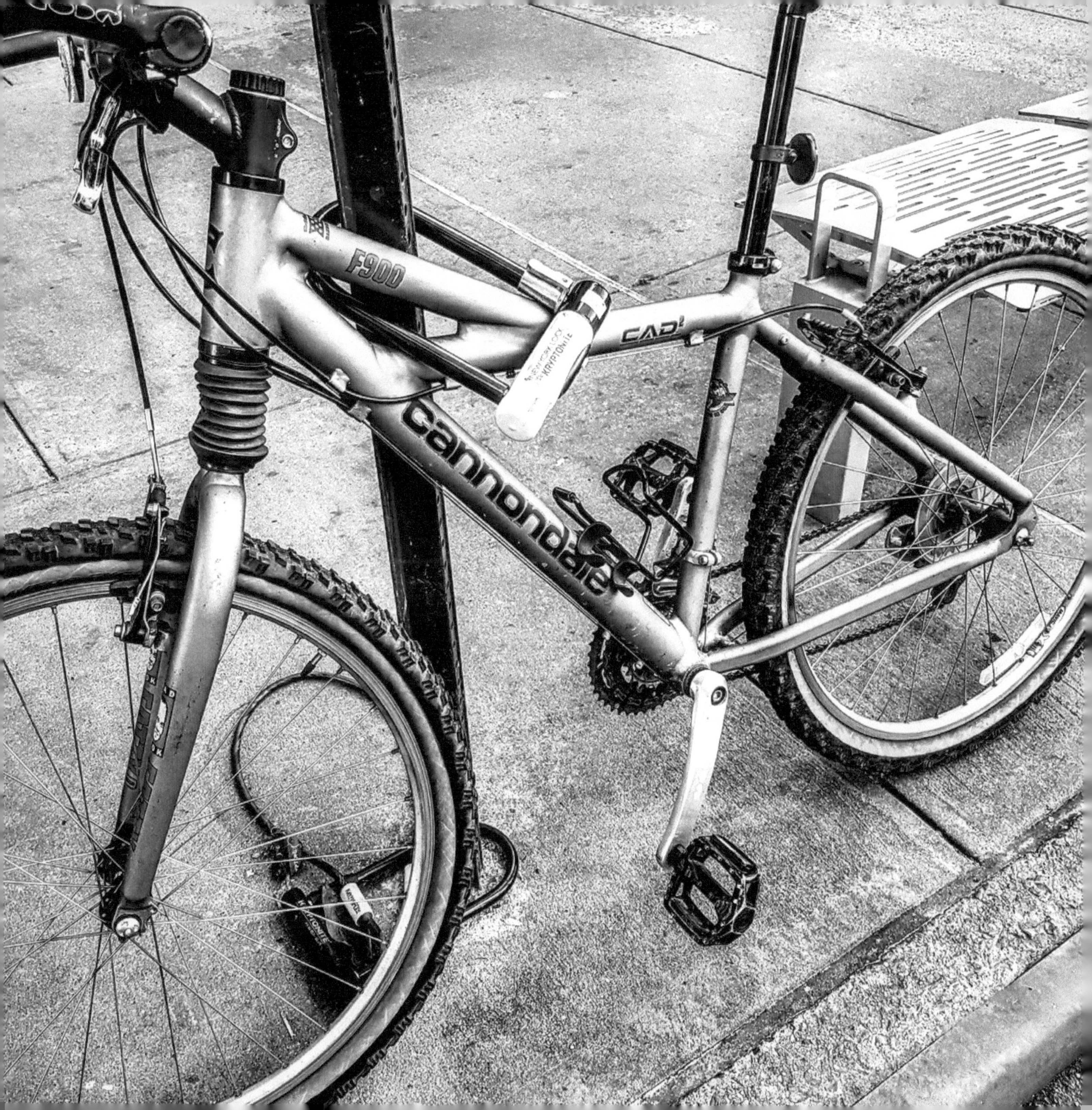
F900
cannondale

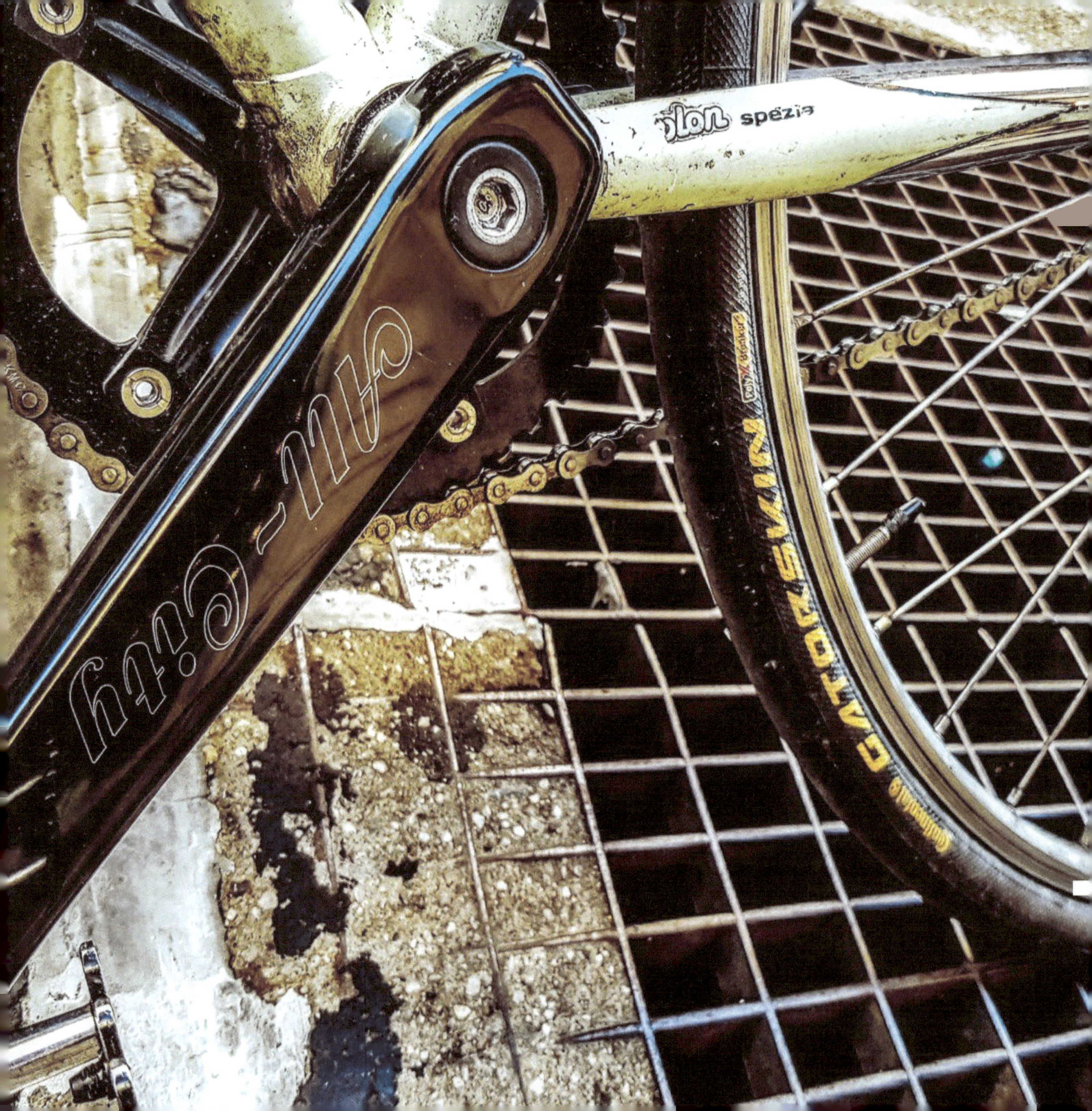
All-City
spezia
GATORSKIN

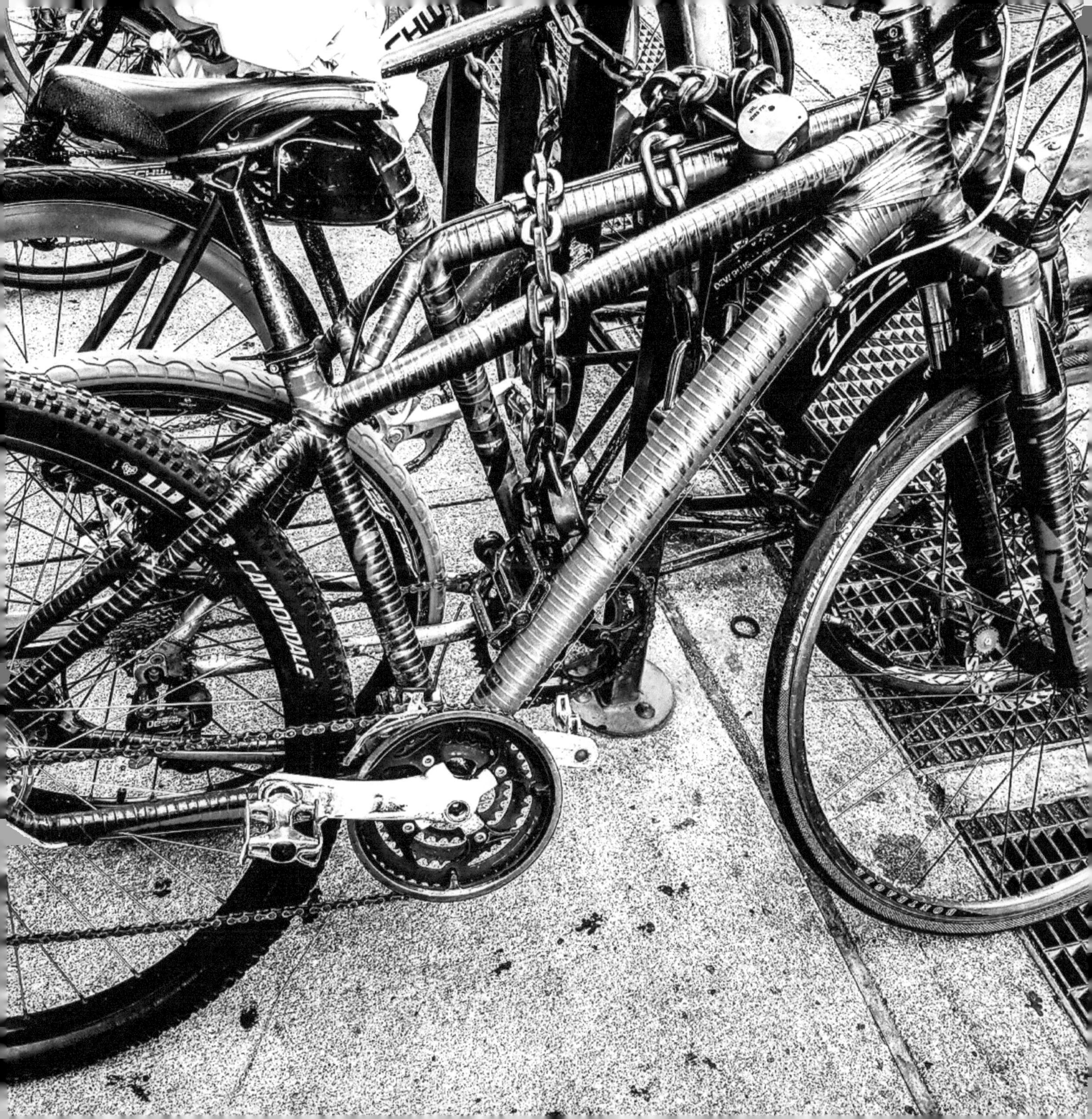
CANNONDALE

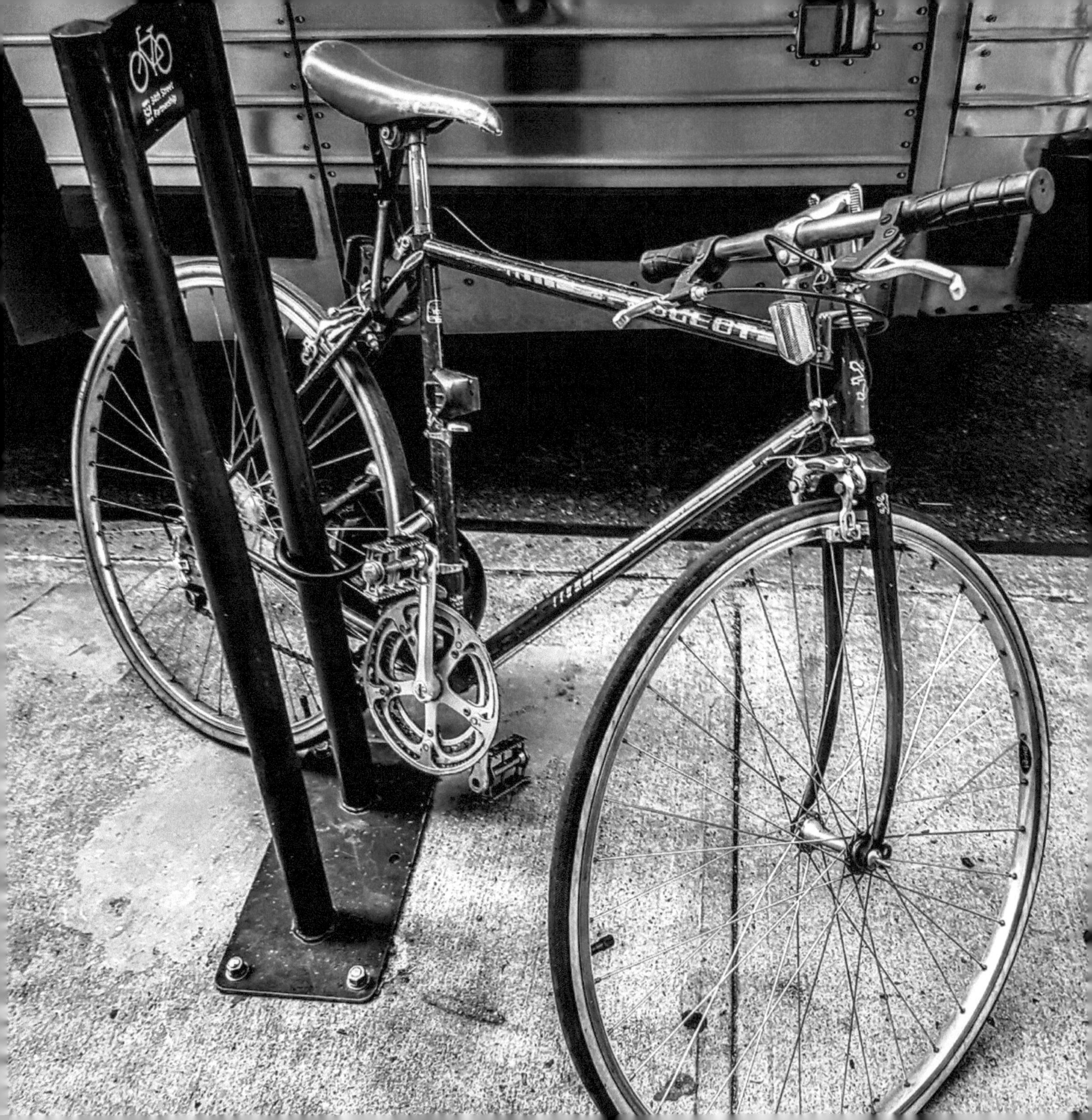

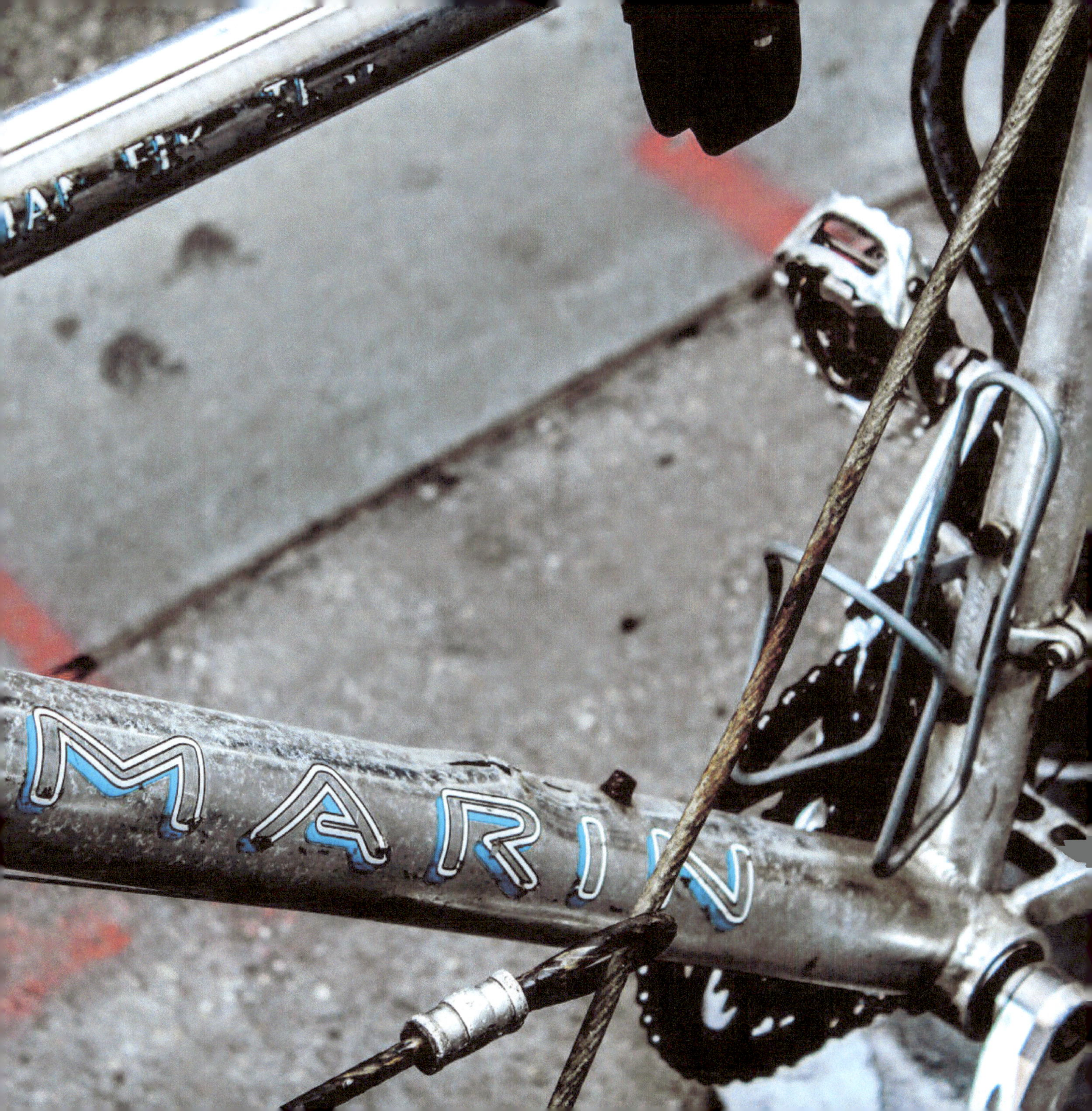
MARIN

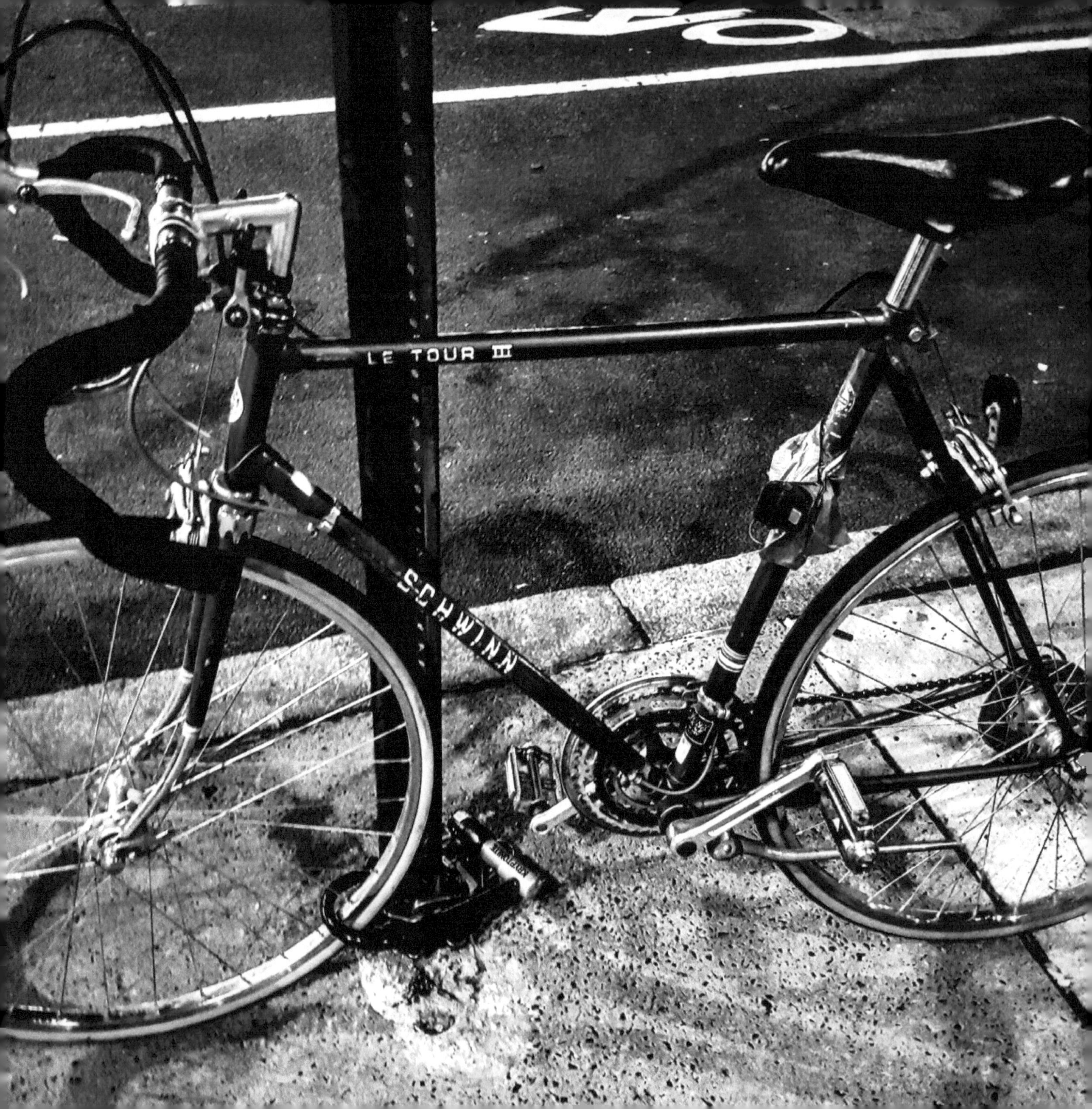
LE TOUR III
SCHWINN

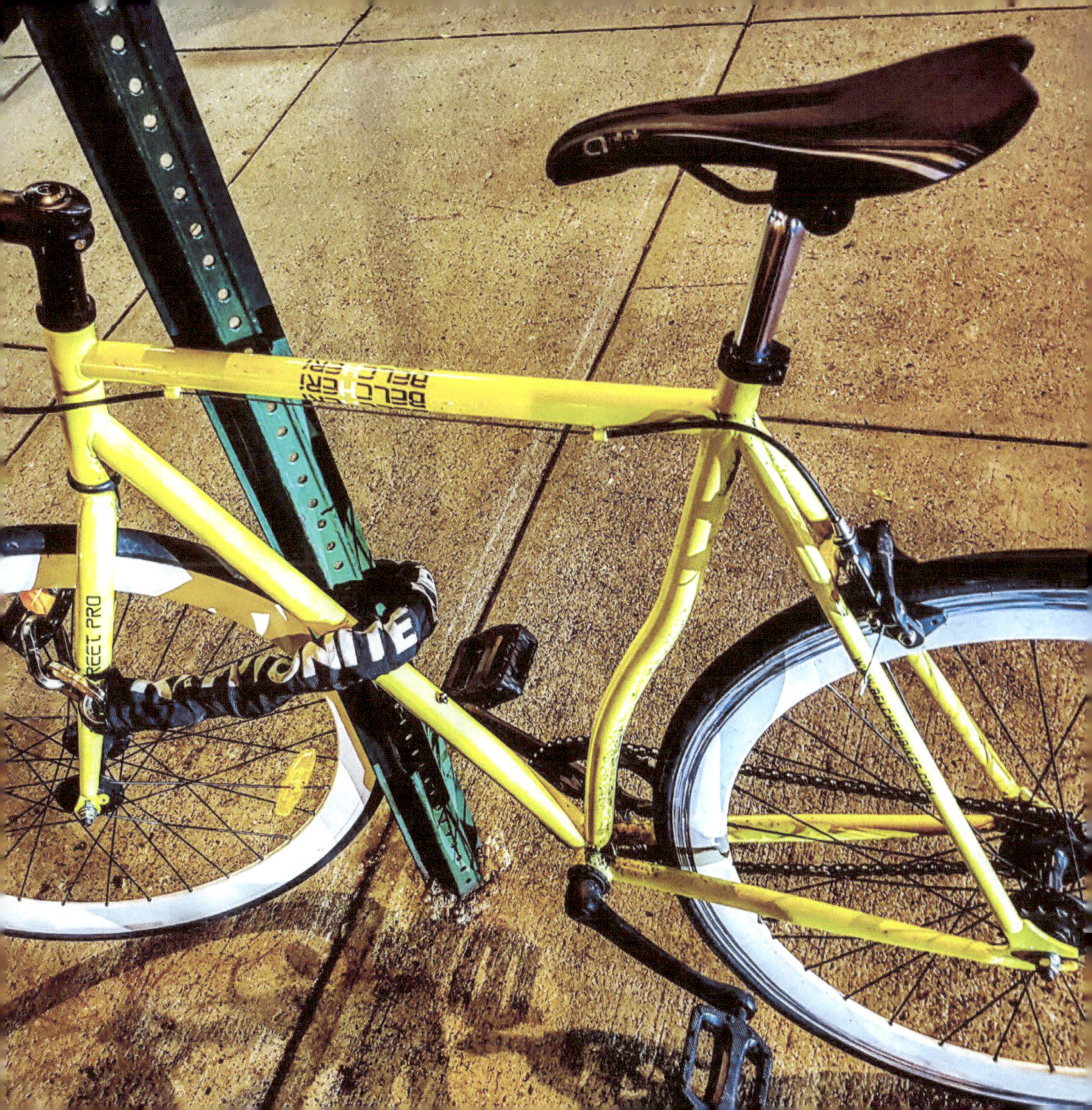
REET PRO

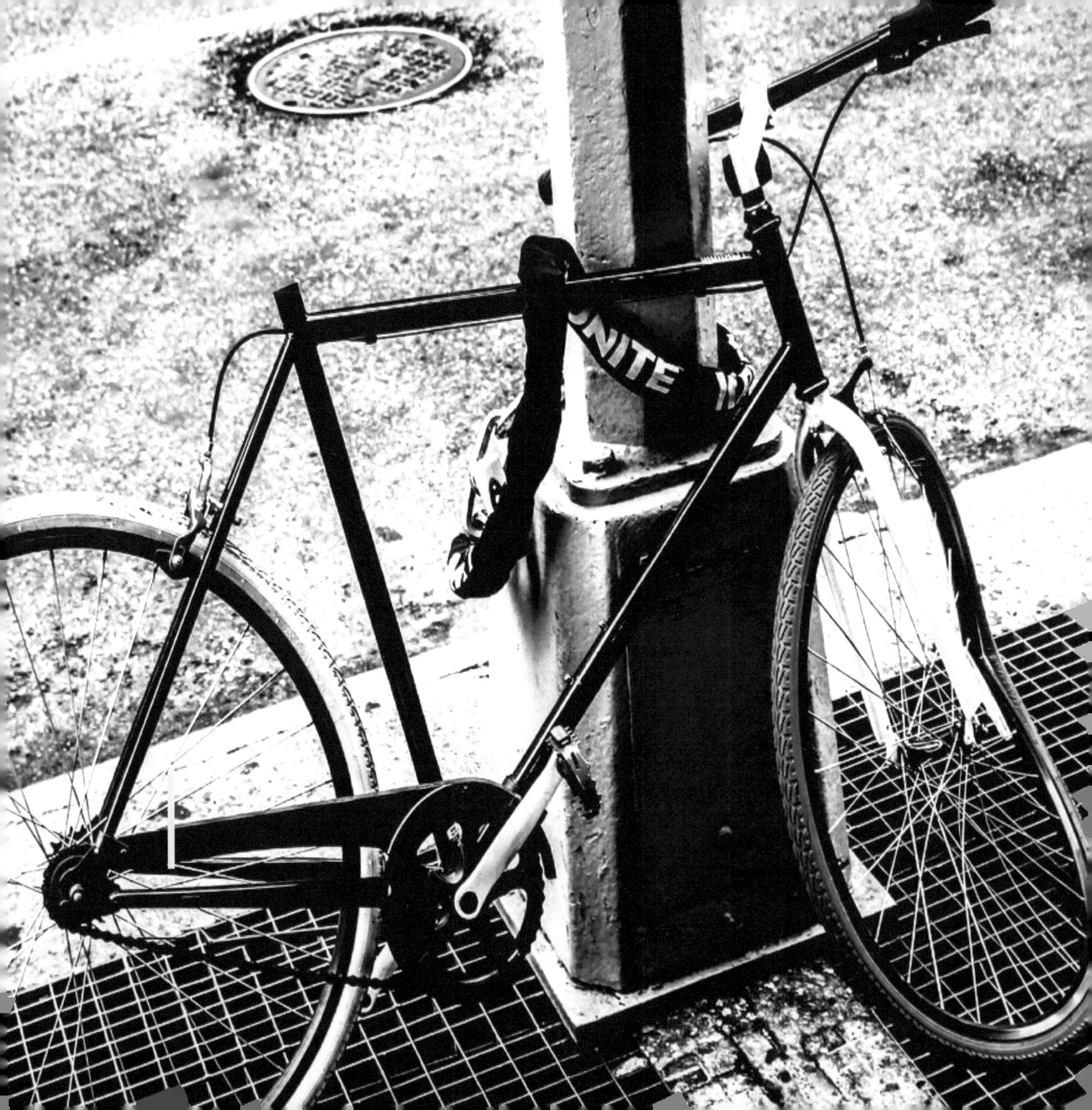

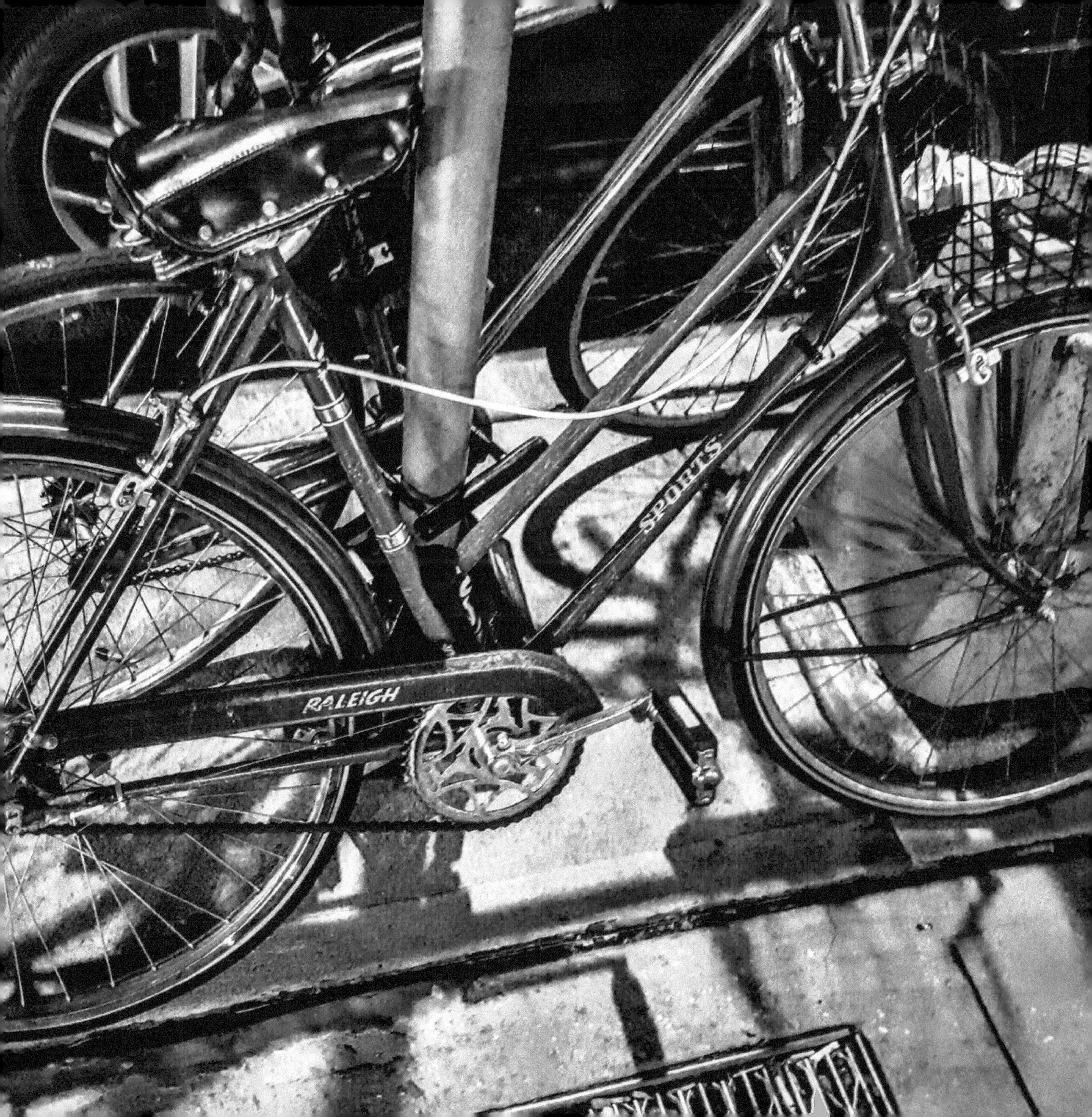
SPORTS
RALEIGH

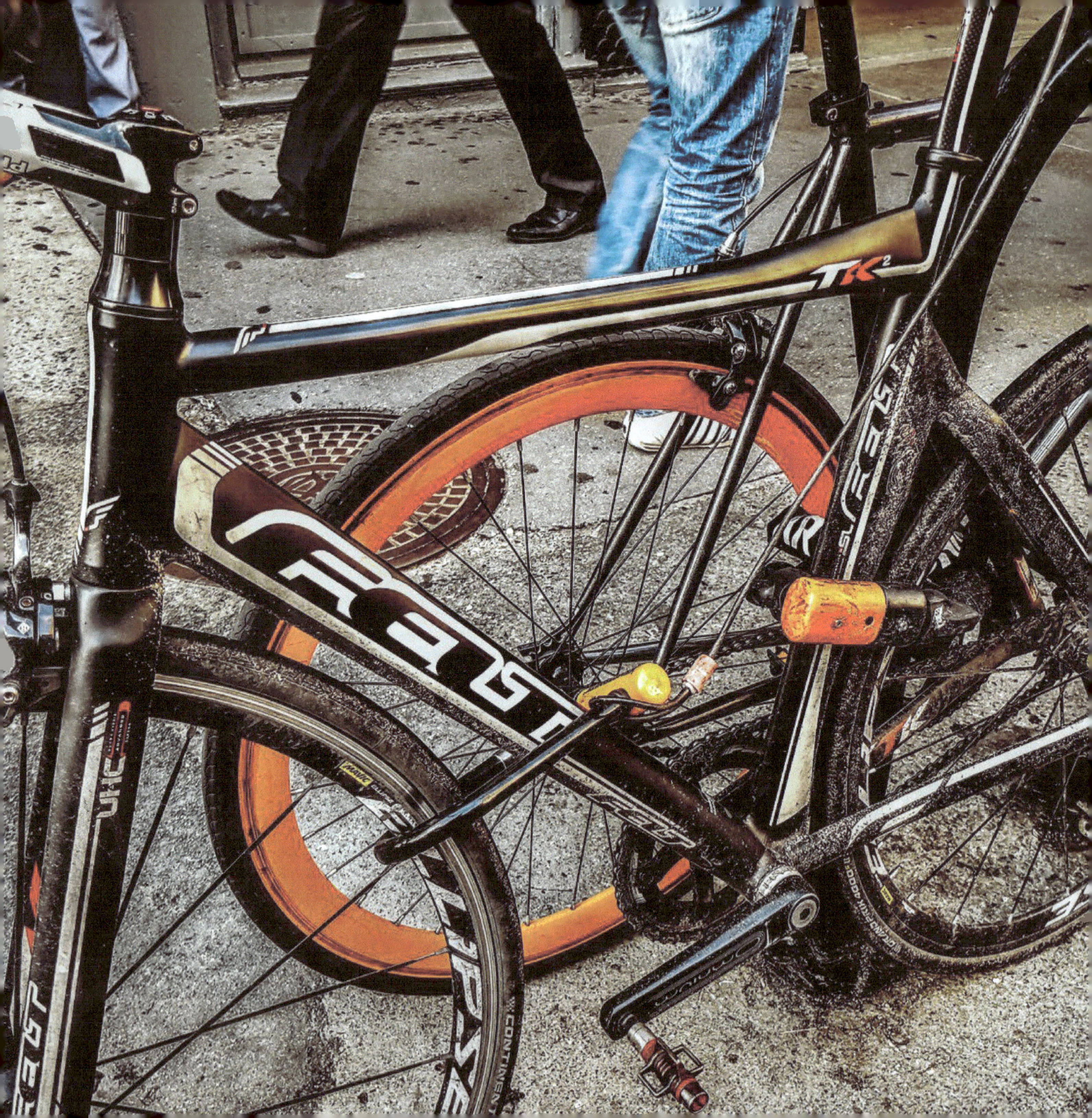

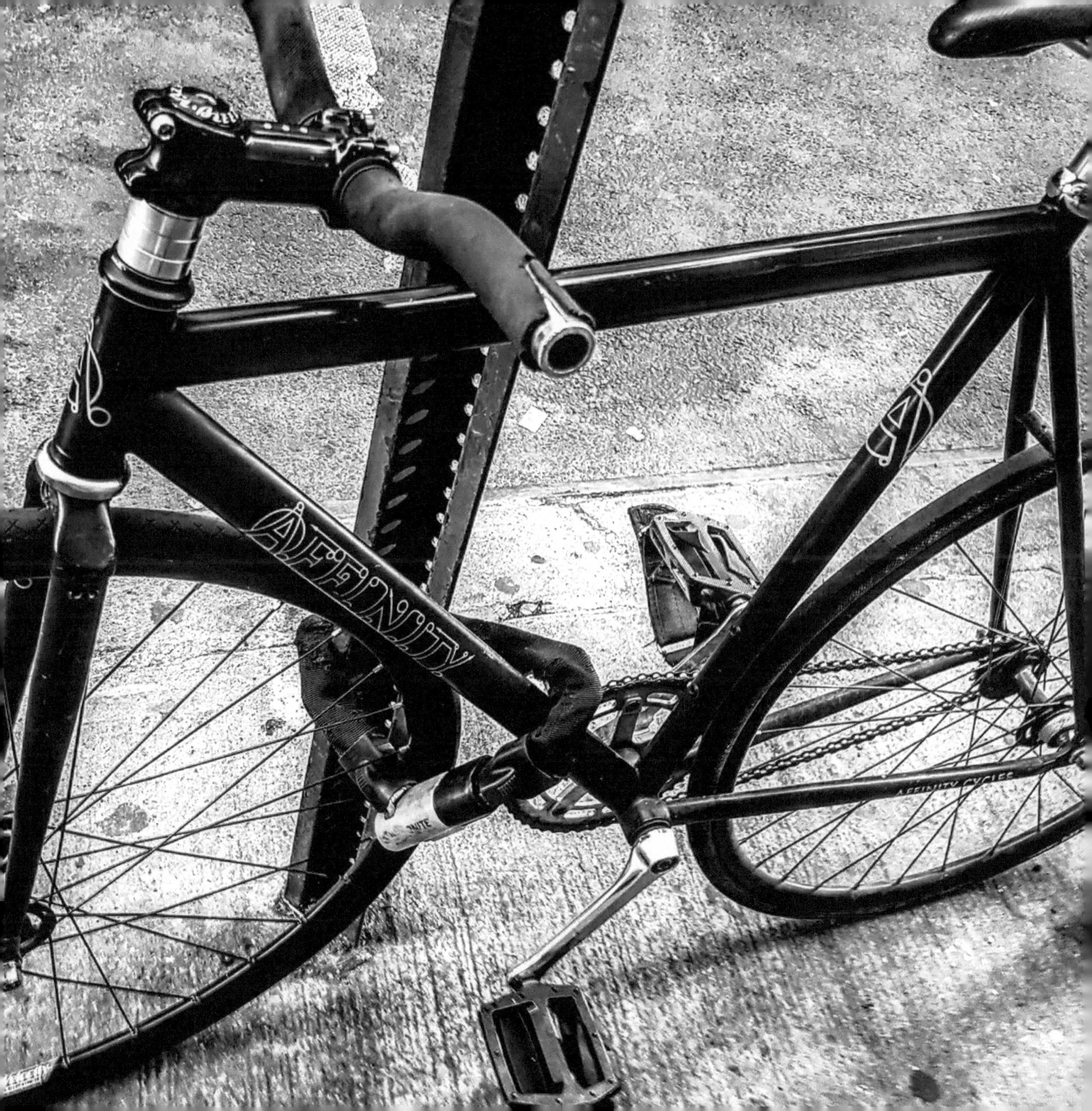
AFFINITY
AFFINITY CYCLES

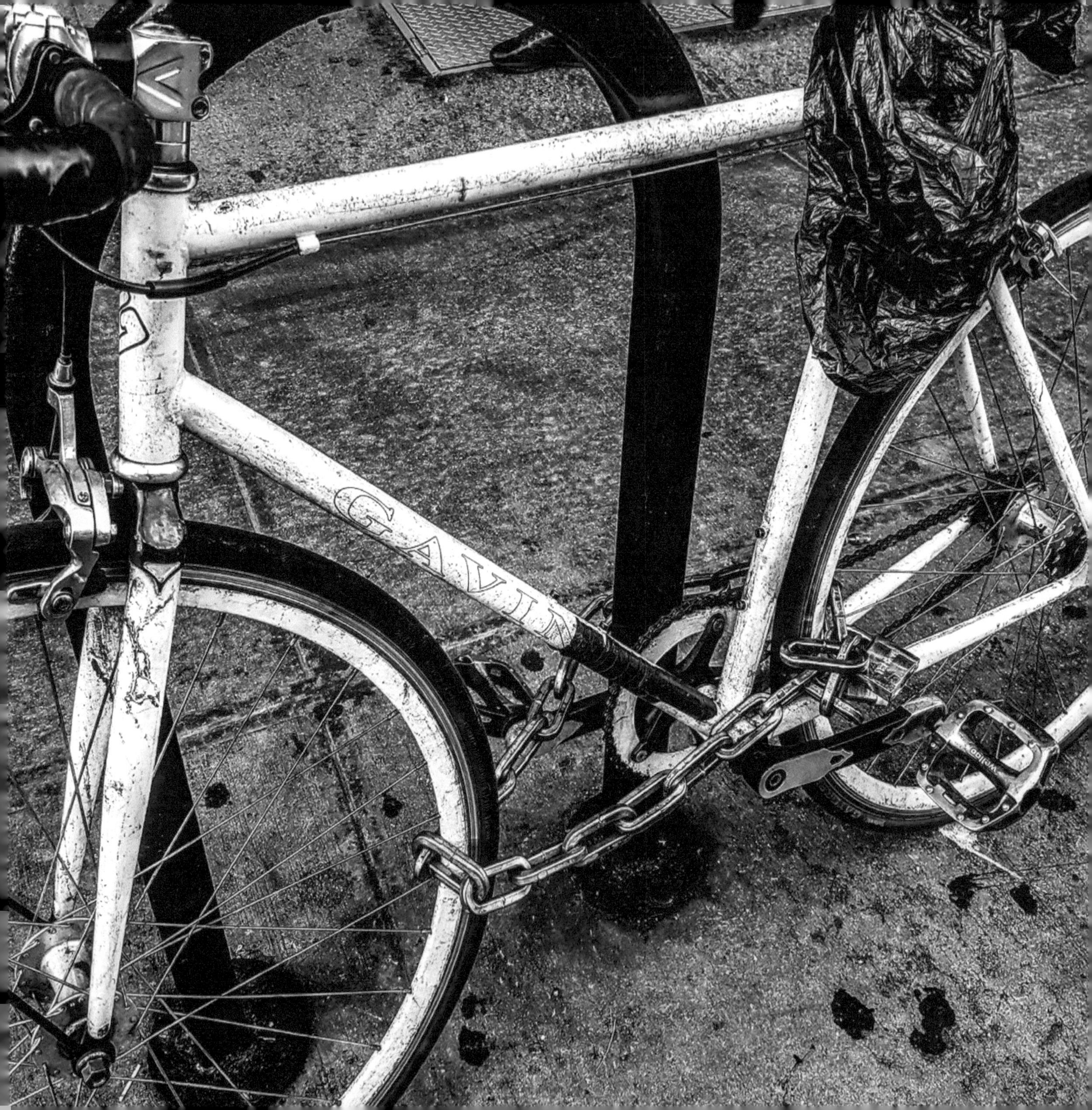
GAVI

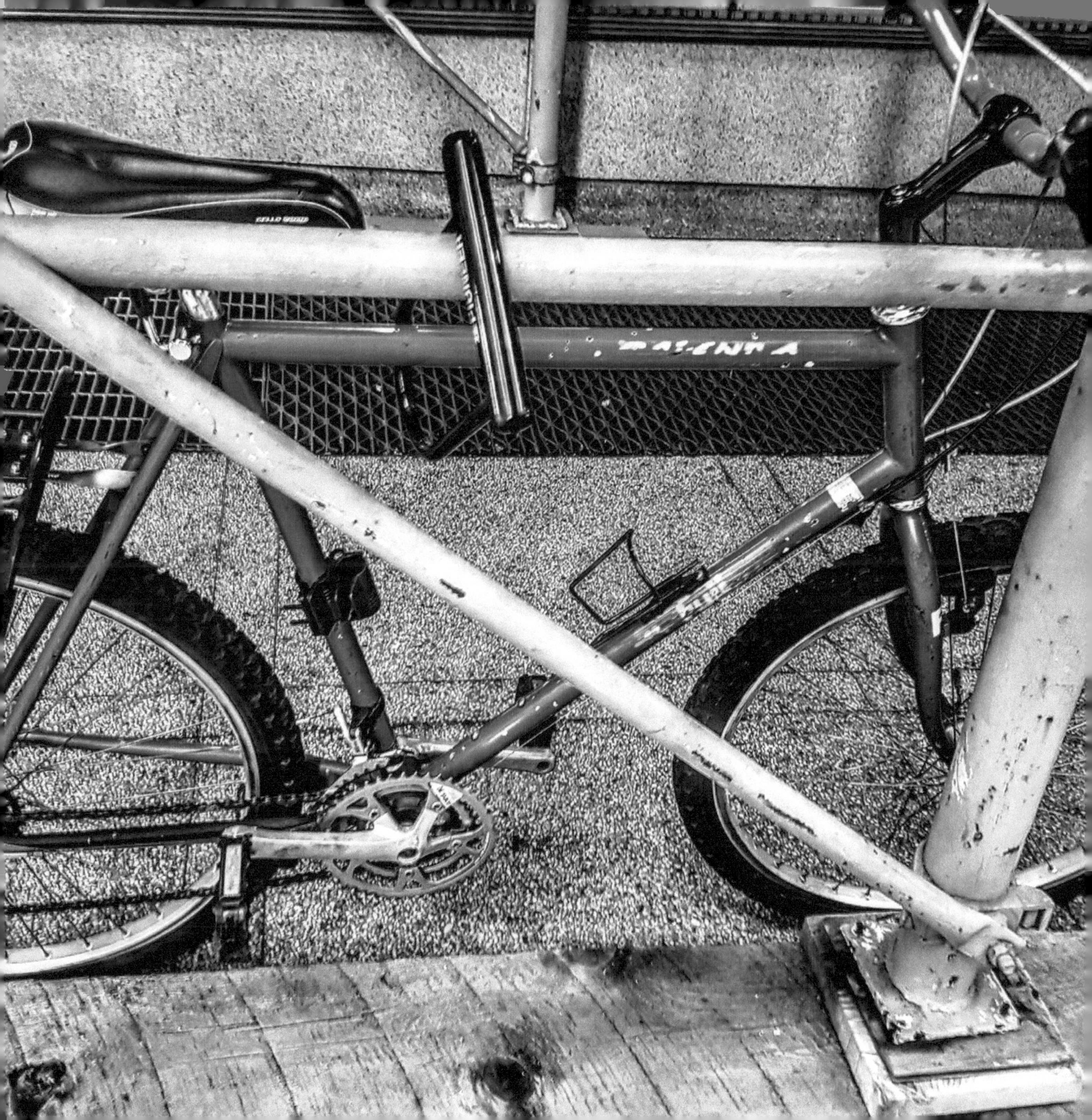

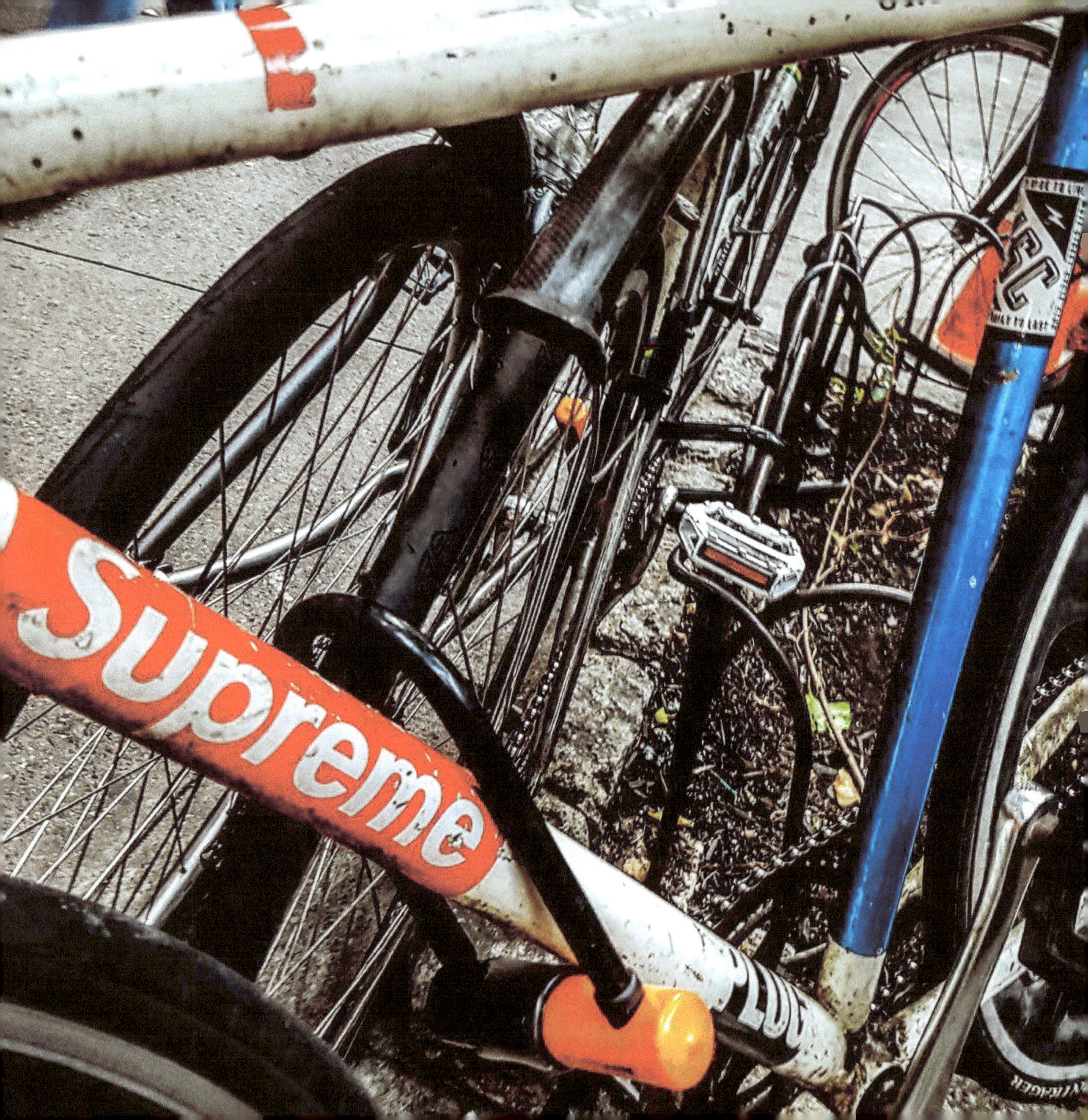
Supreme

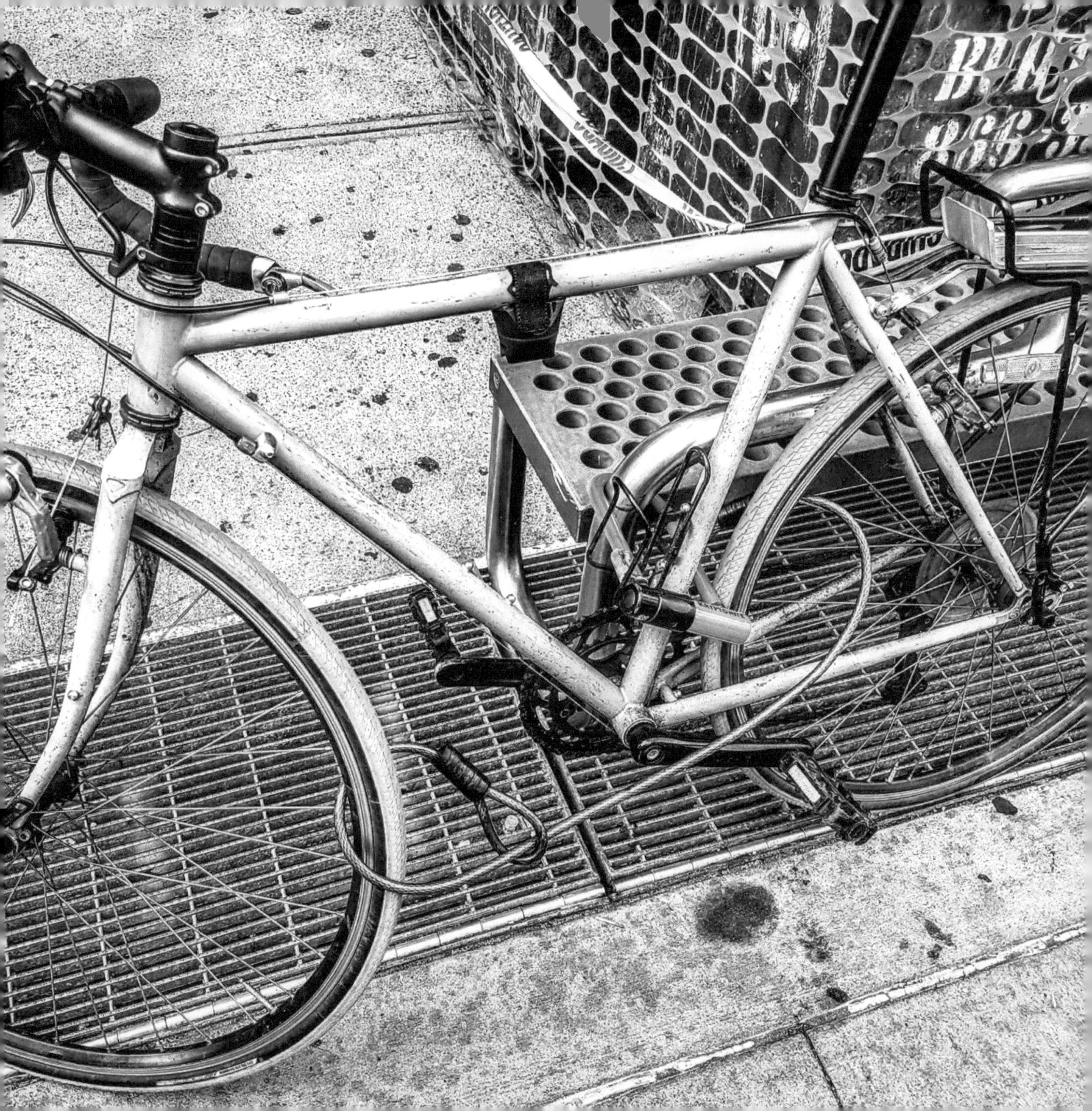

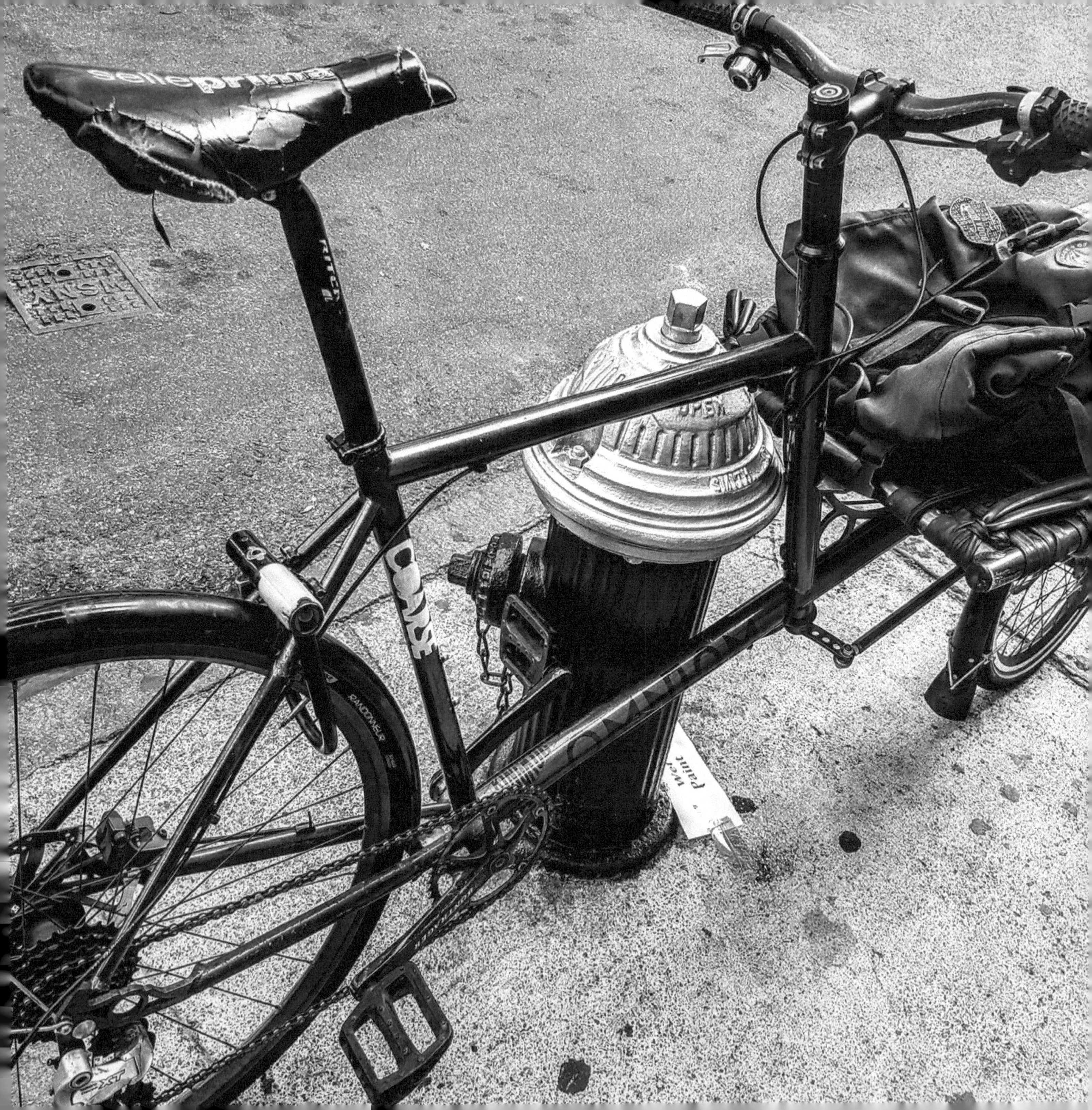
OPEN
OMNIUM
wet paint

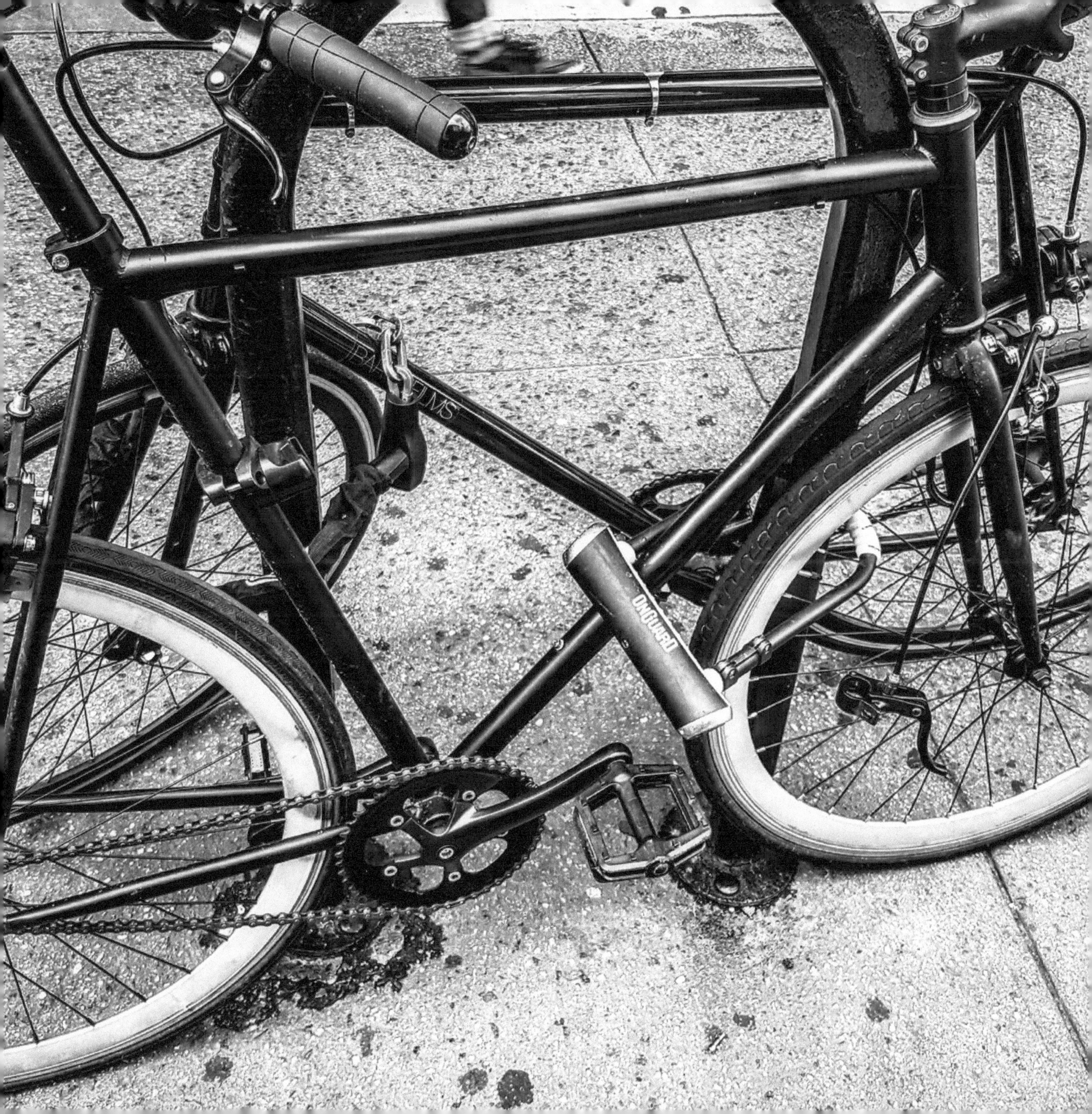
ONGUARD

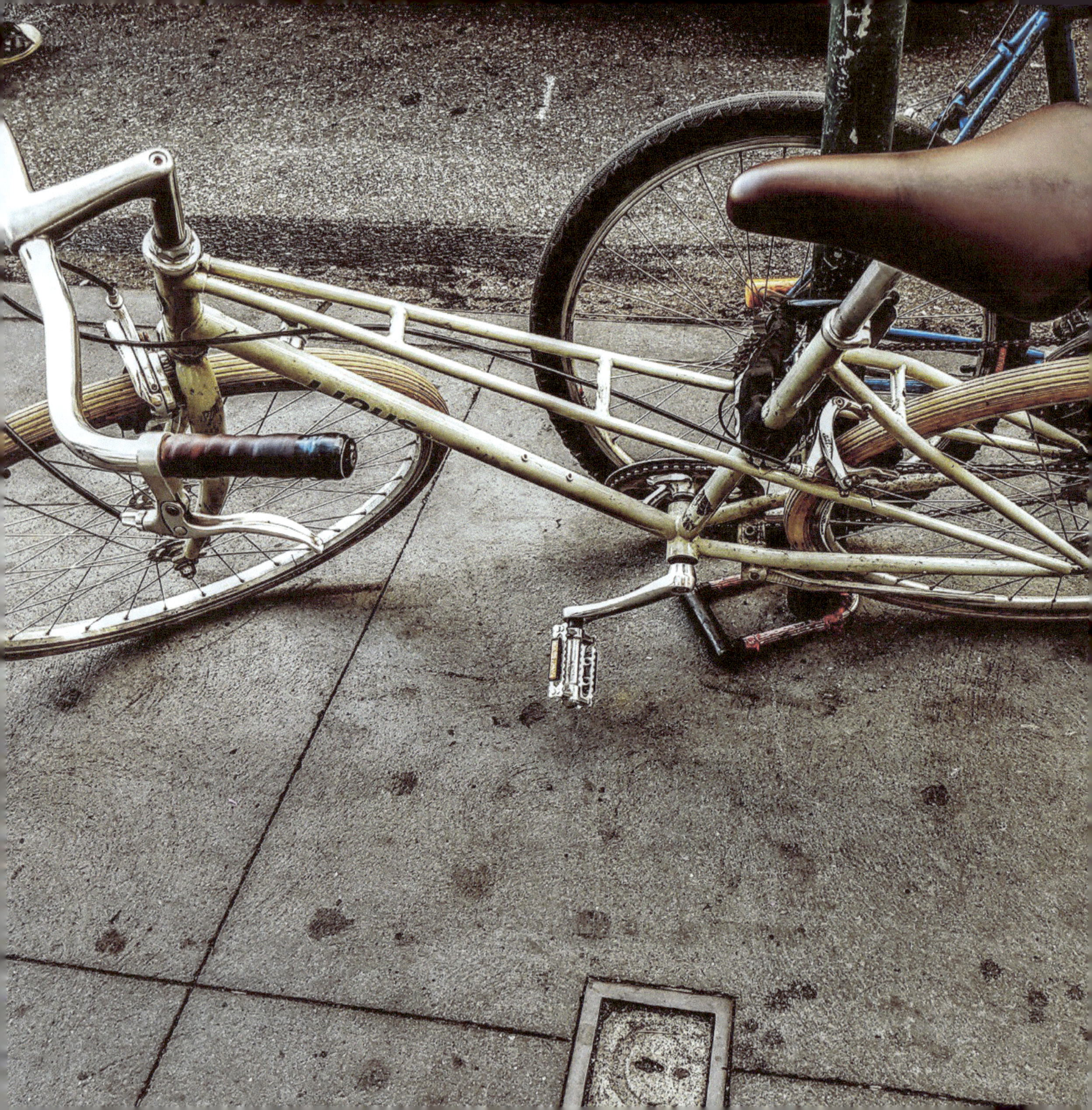

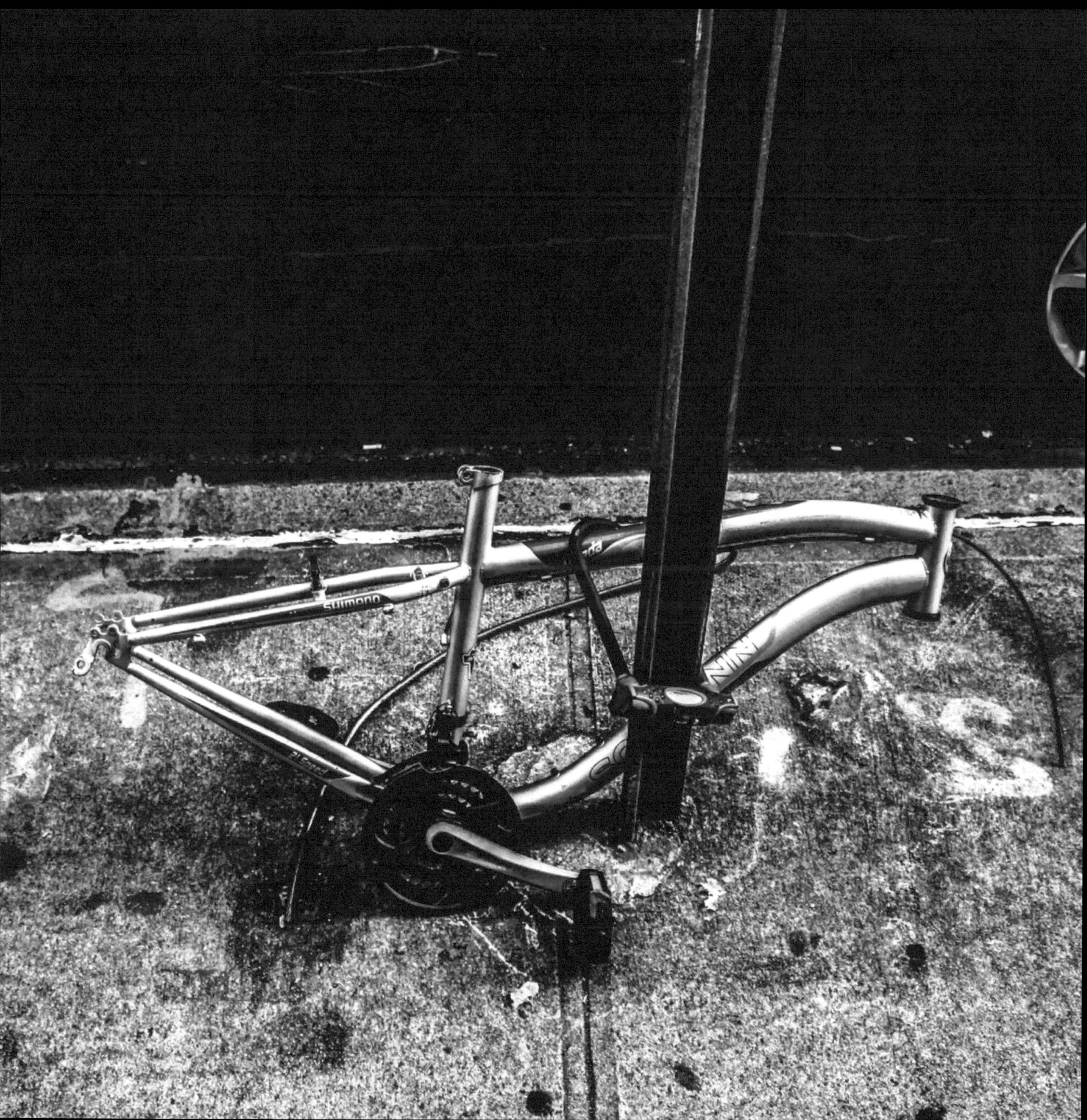
SHIMANO
21 Speed

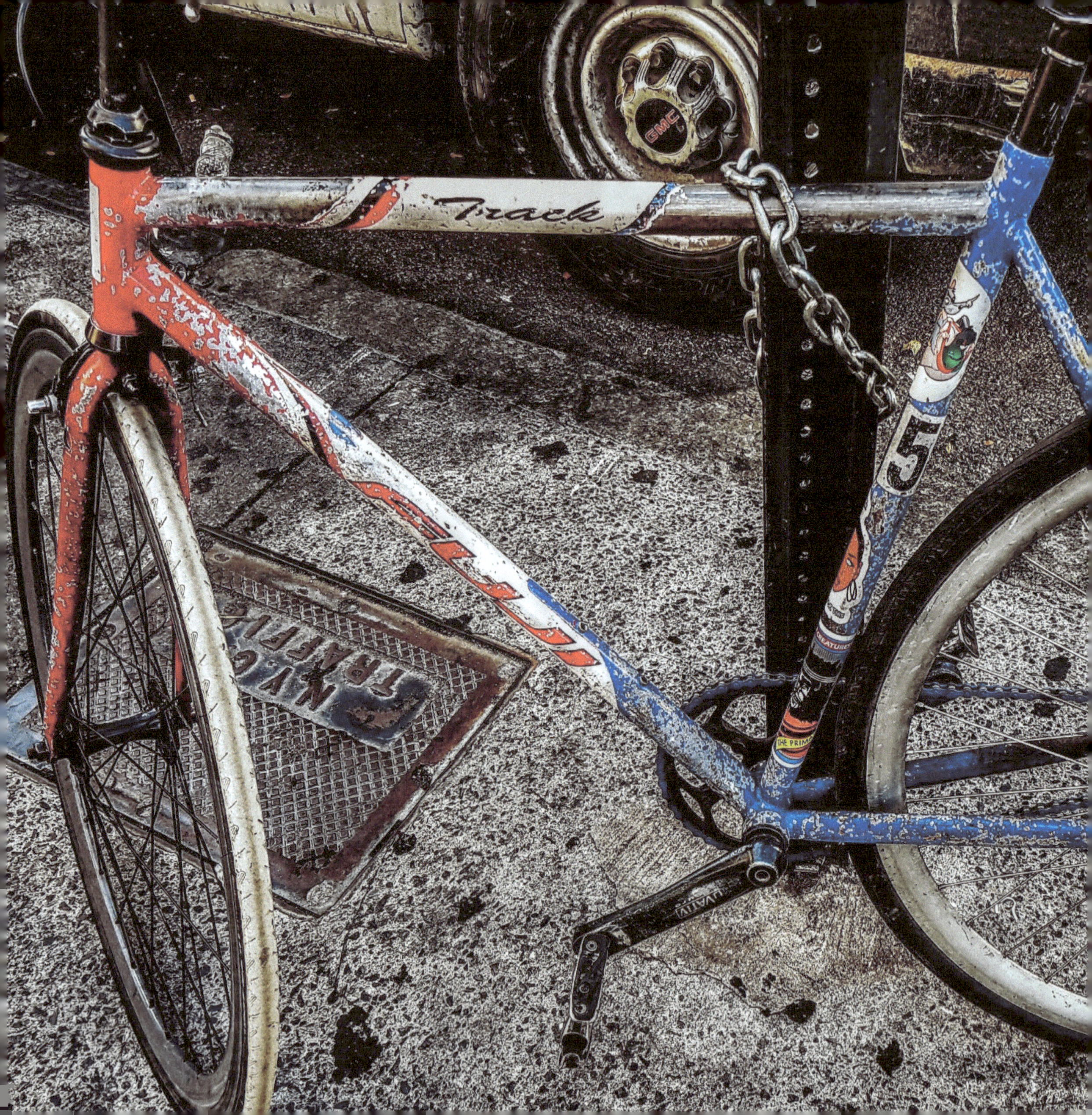
GMC
Track

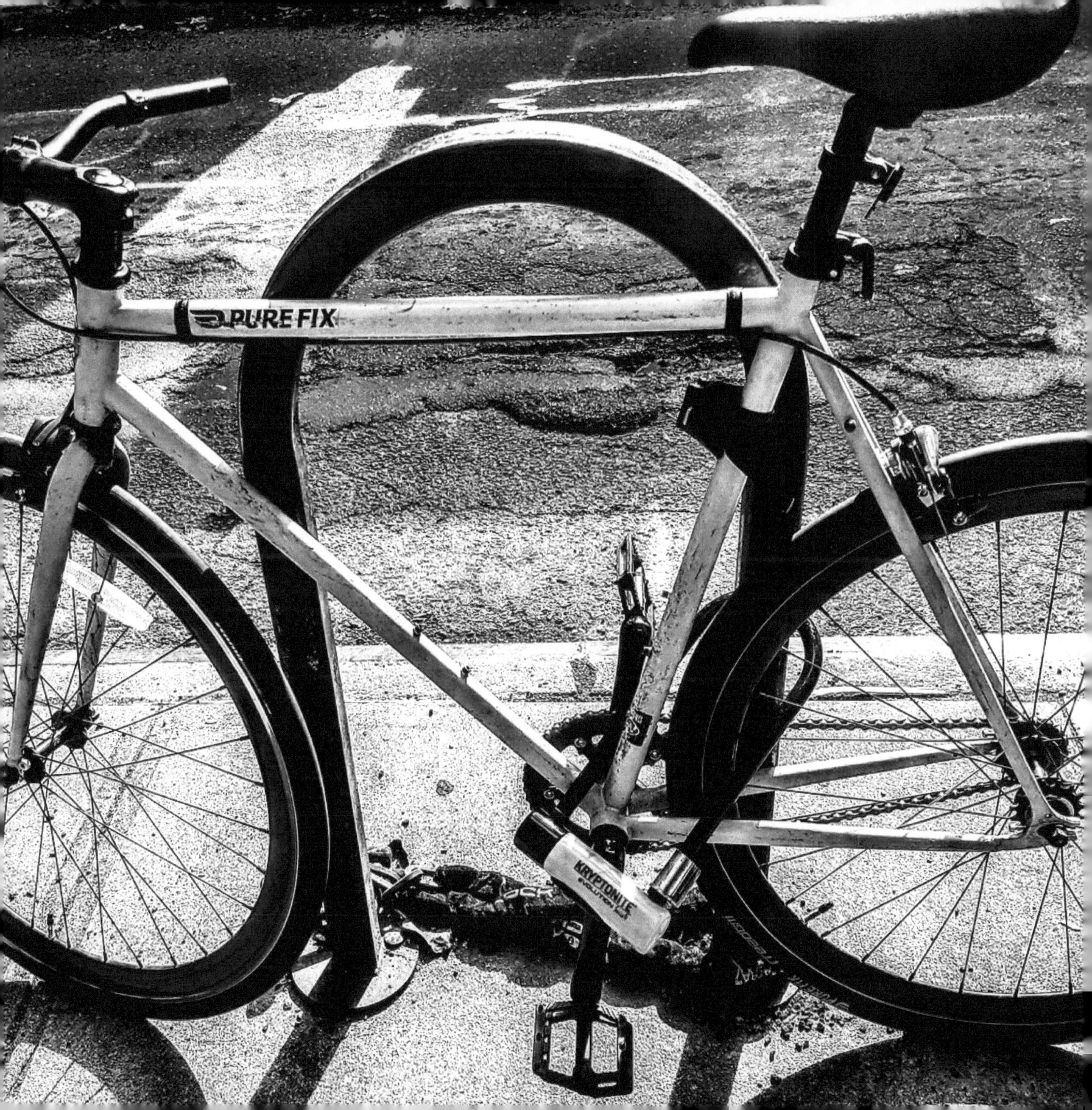
PURE FIX
KRYPTONITE

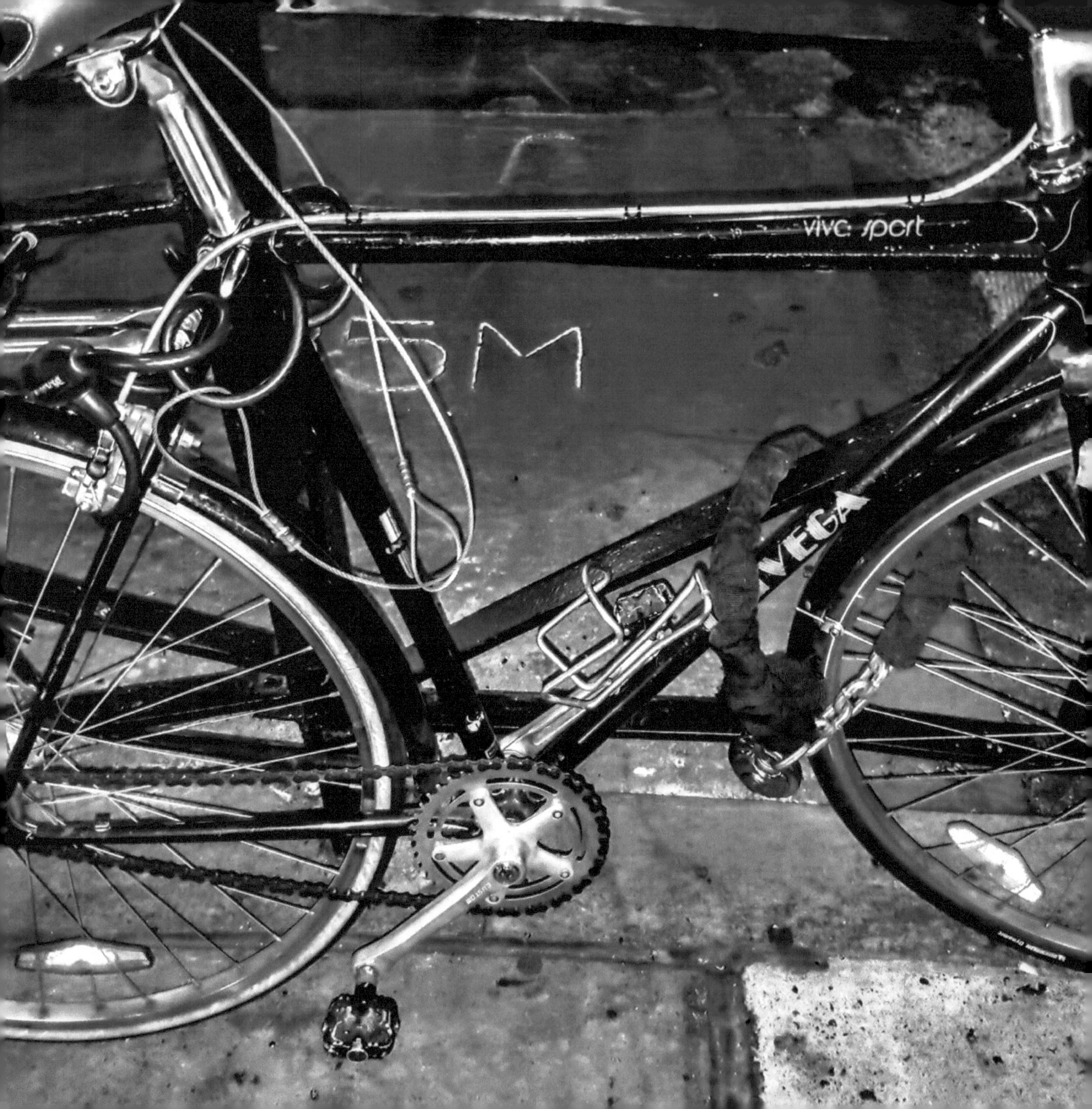
viva sport
VEGA

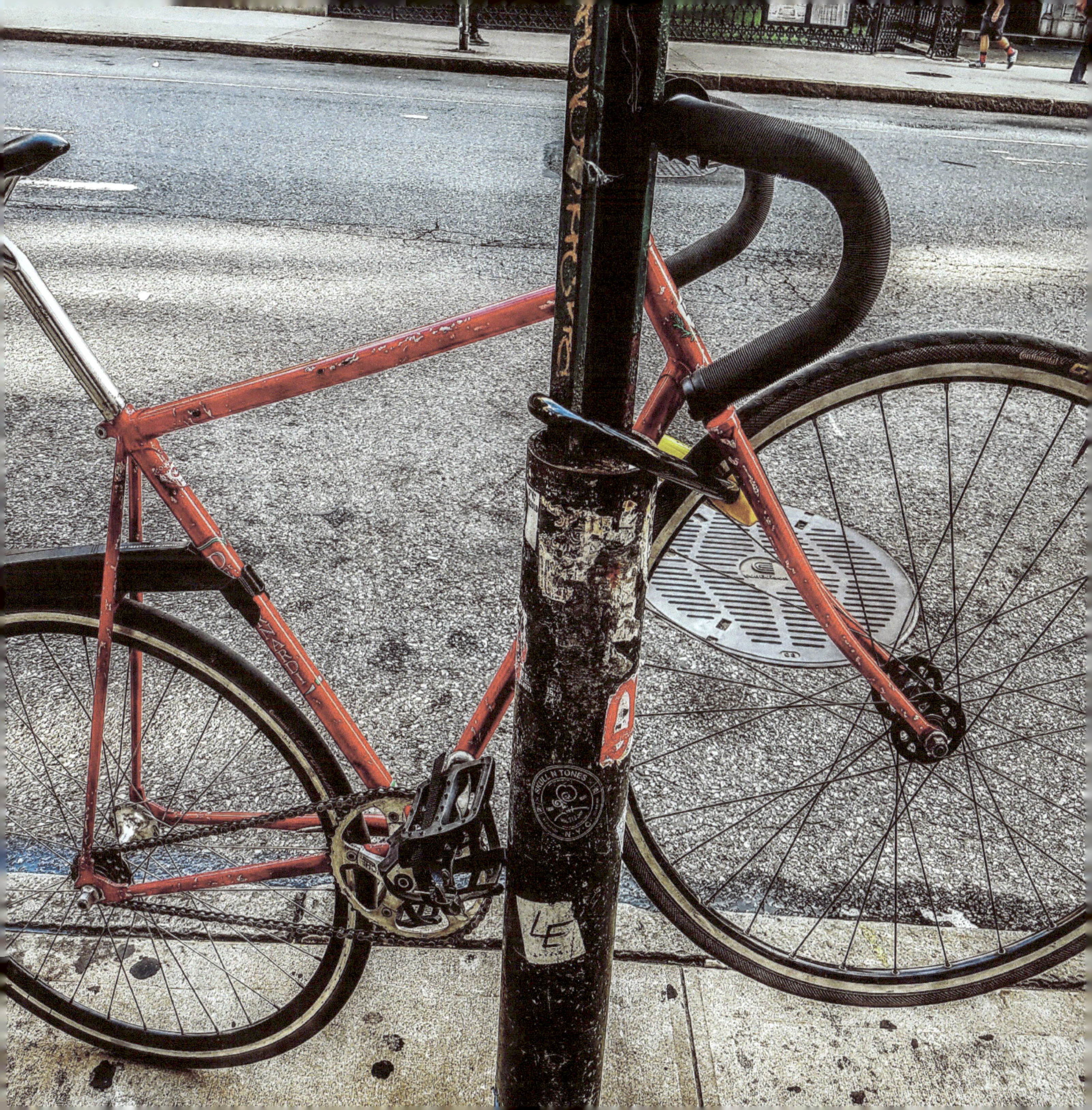
SKULL N TONES
N.Y.C.
LE

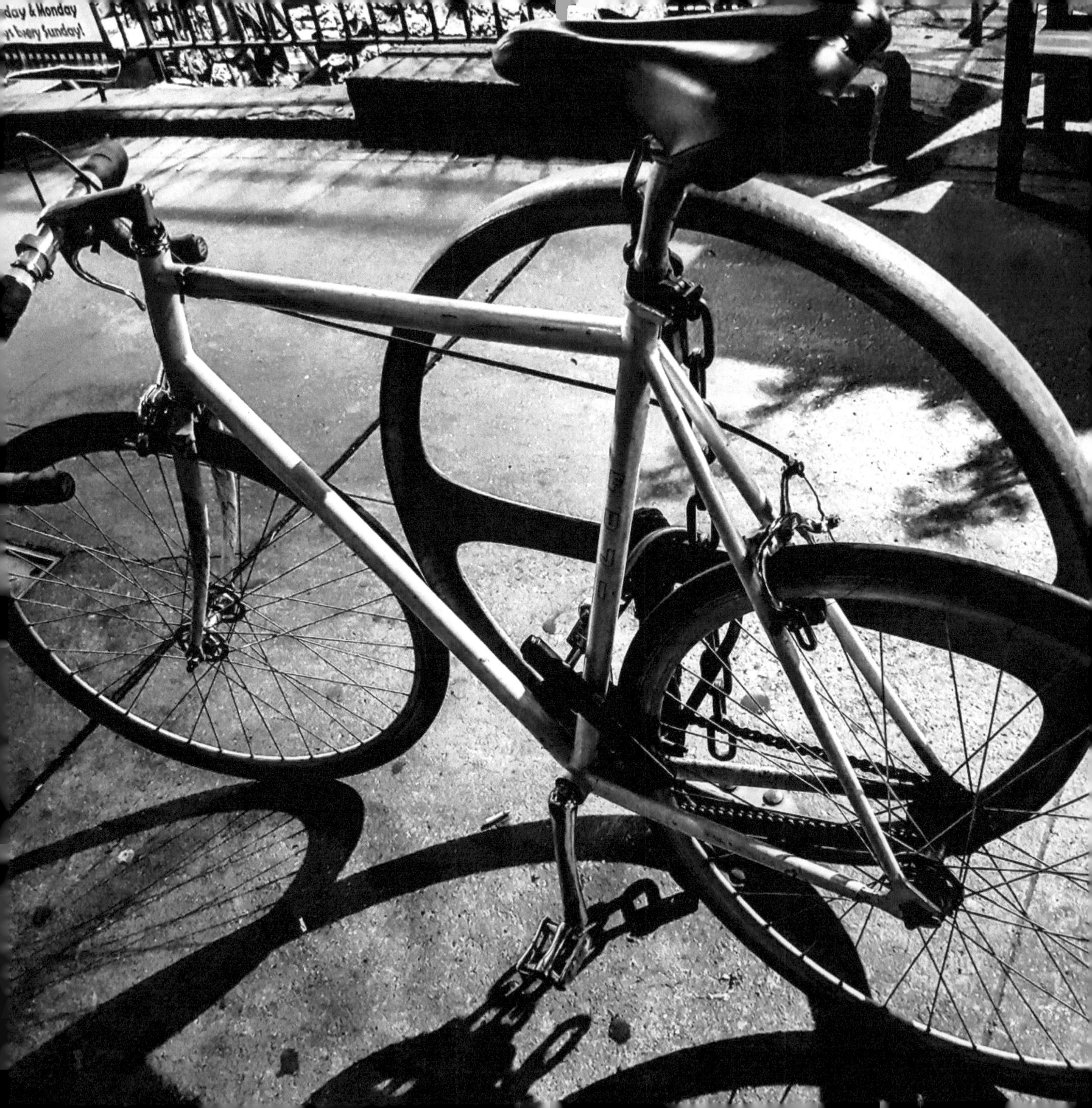
day & Monday
Every Sunday!

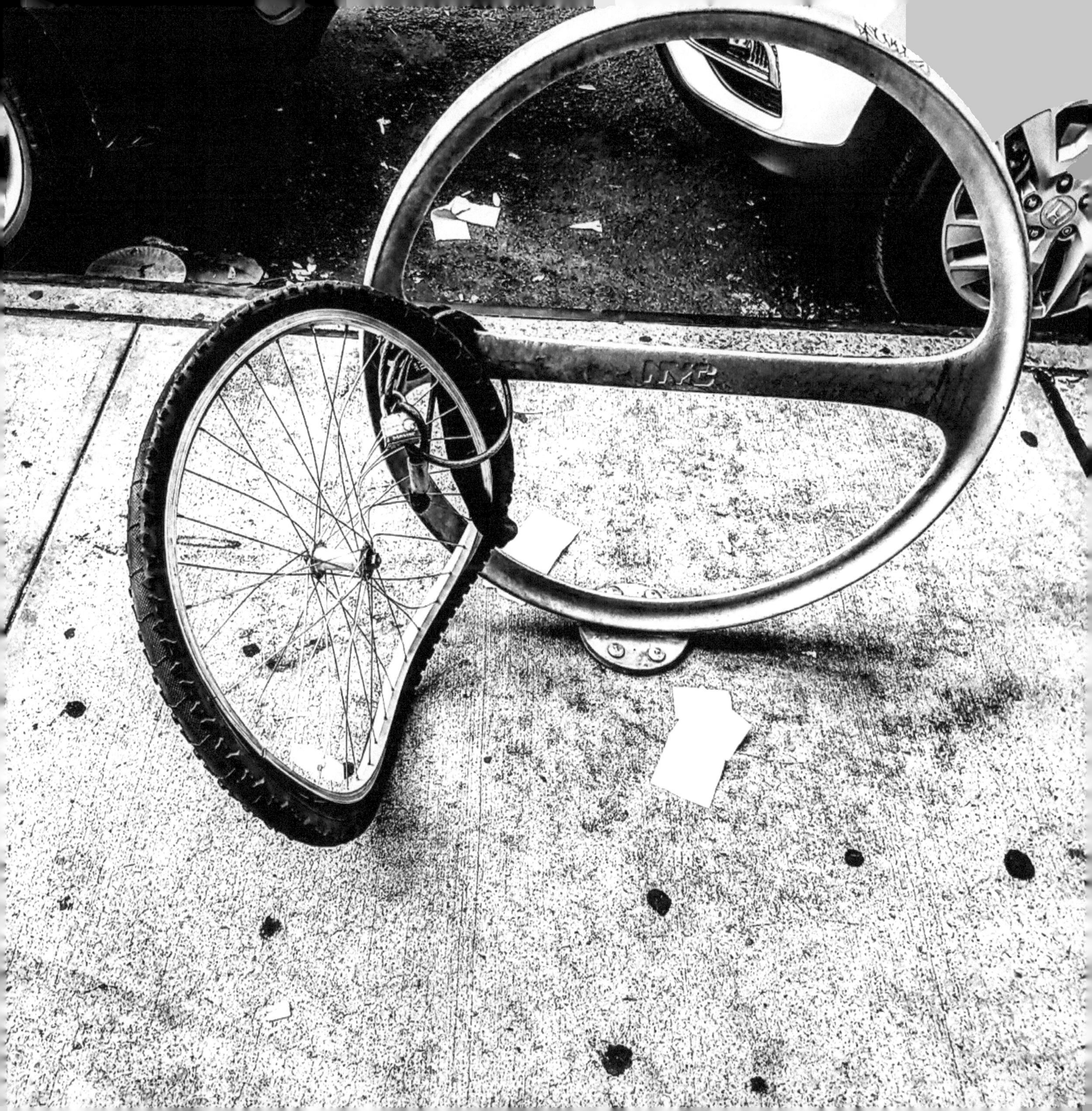
NYC

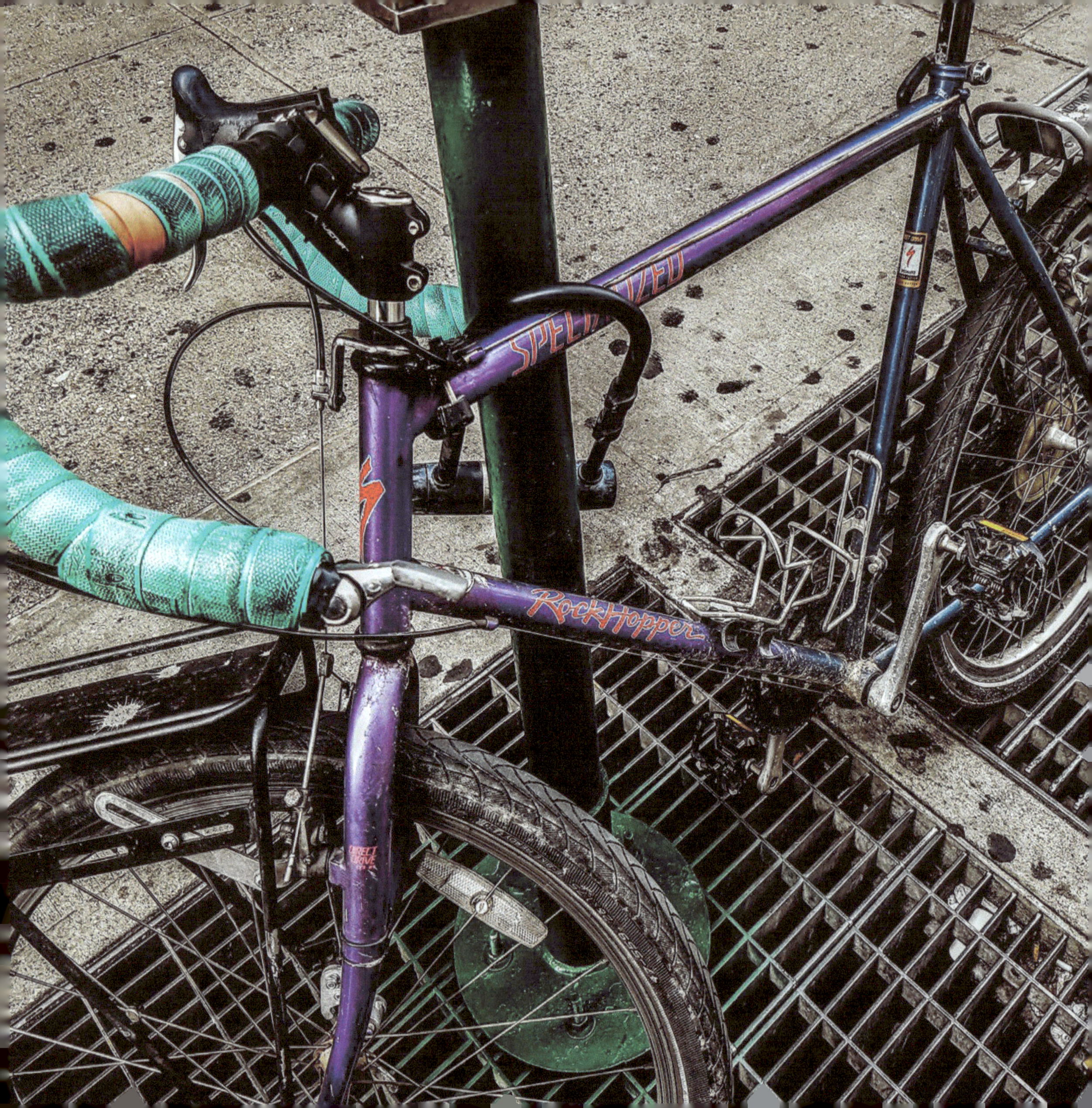
RockHopper

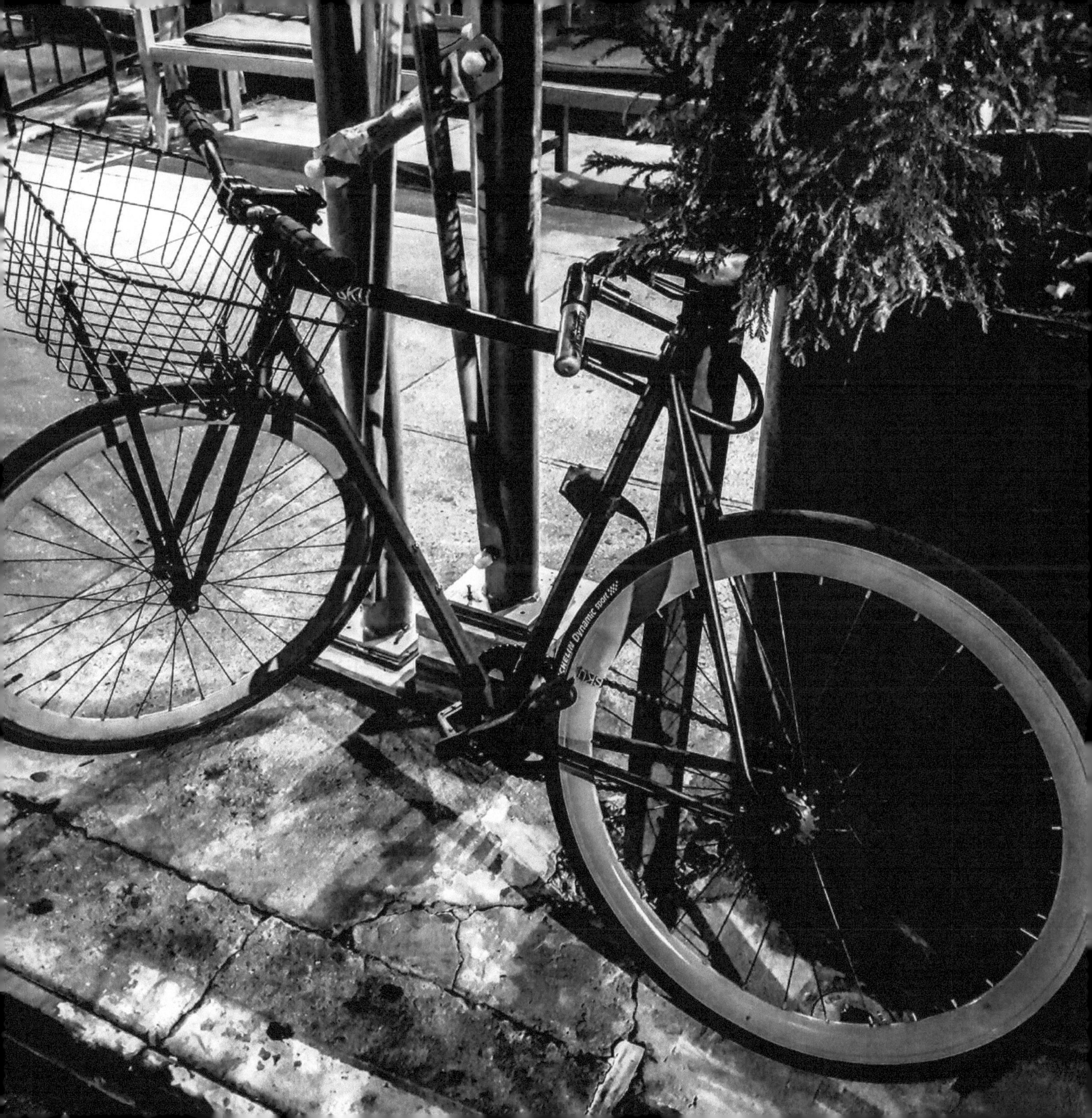
Dynamic sport

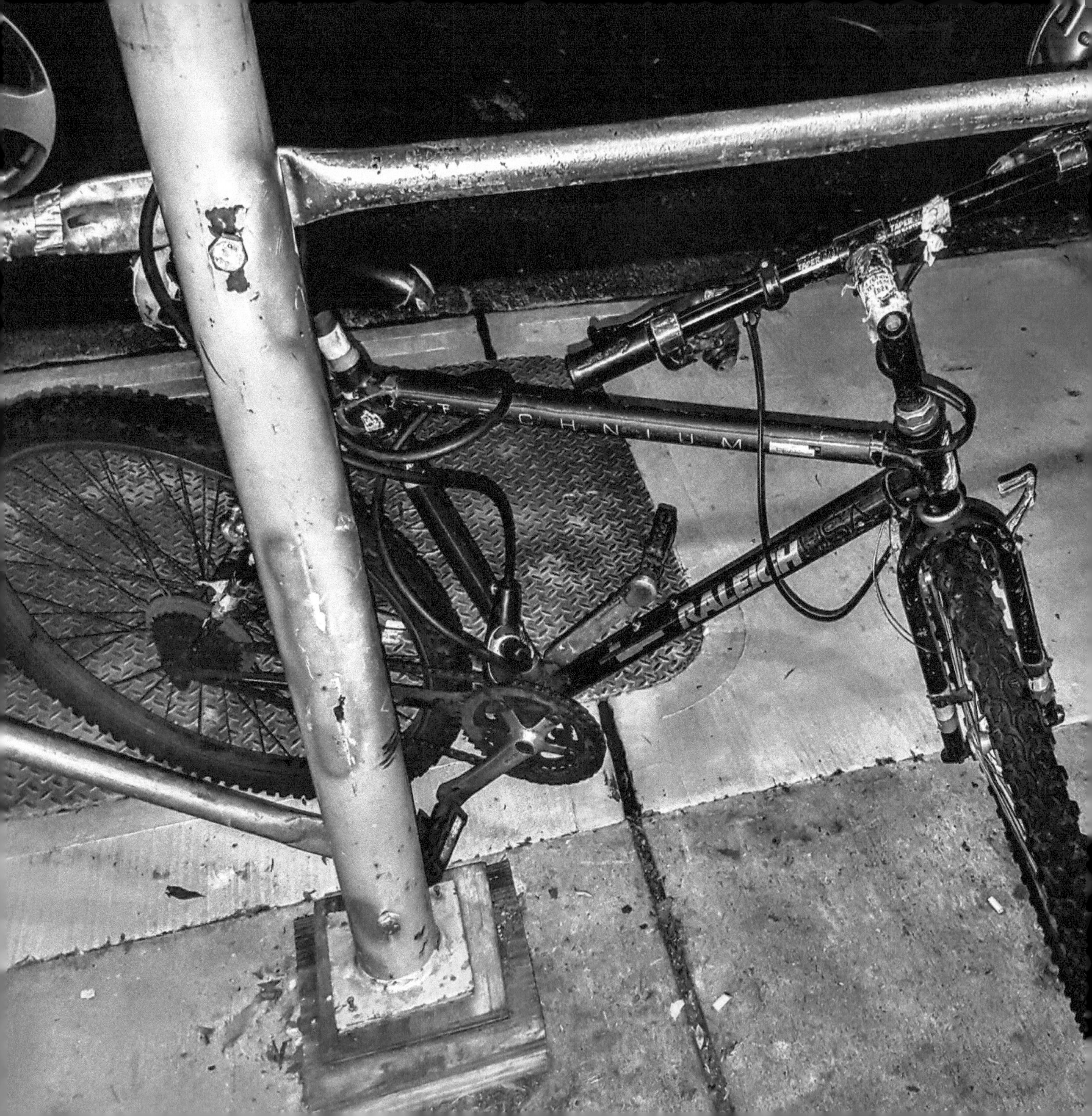
TECHNIUM
RALEIGH USA

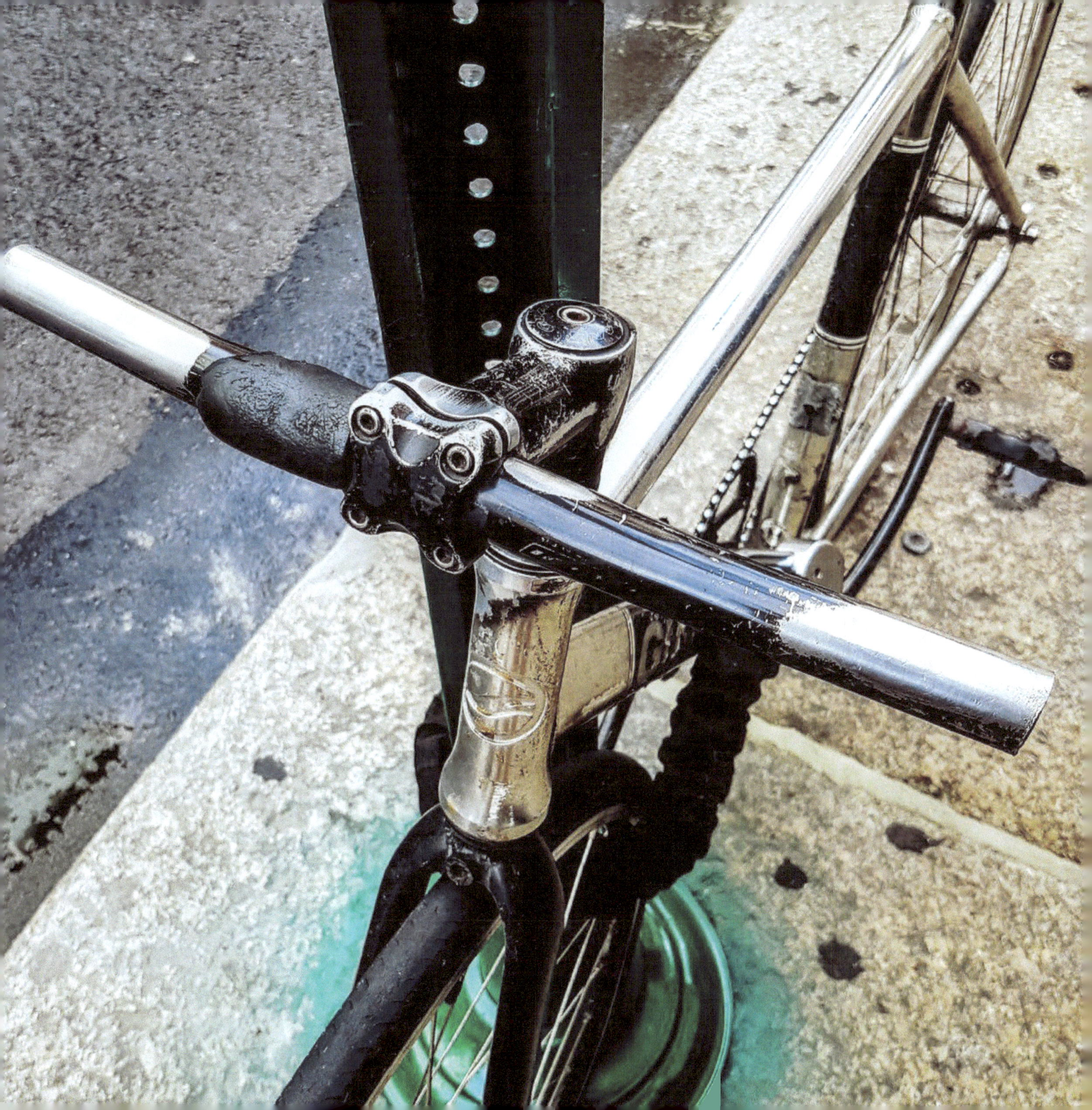

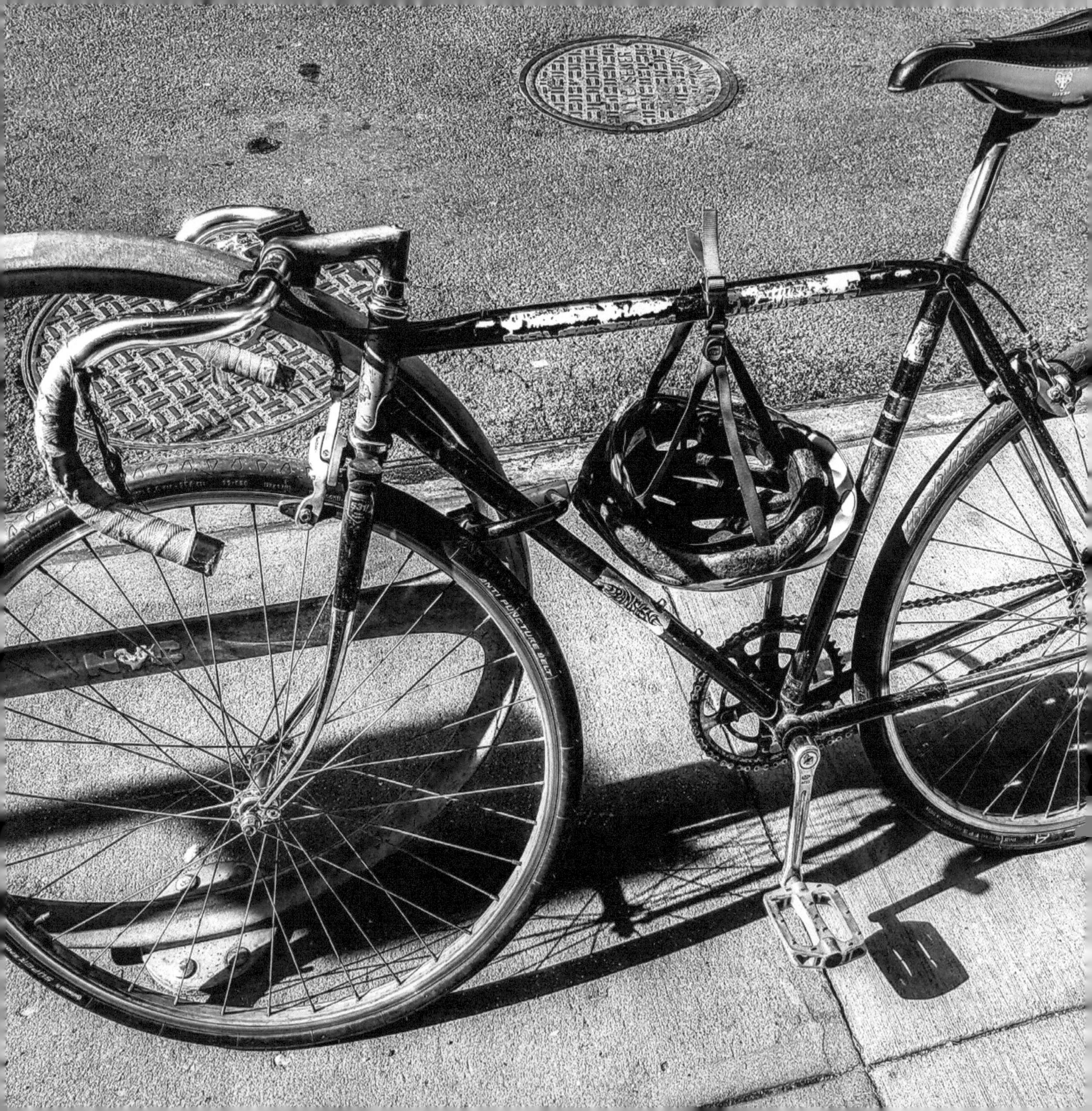
ANTI PUNCTURE BELT

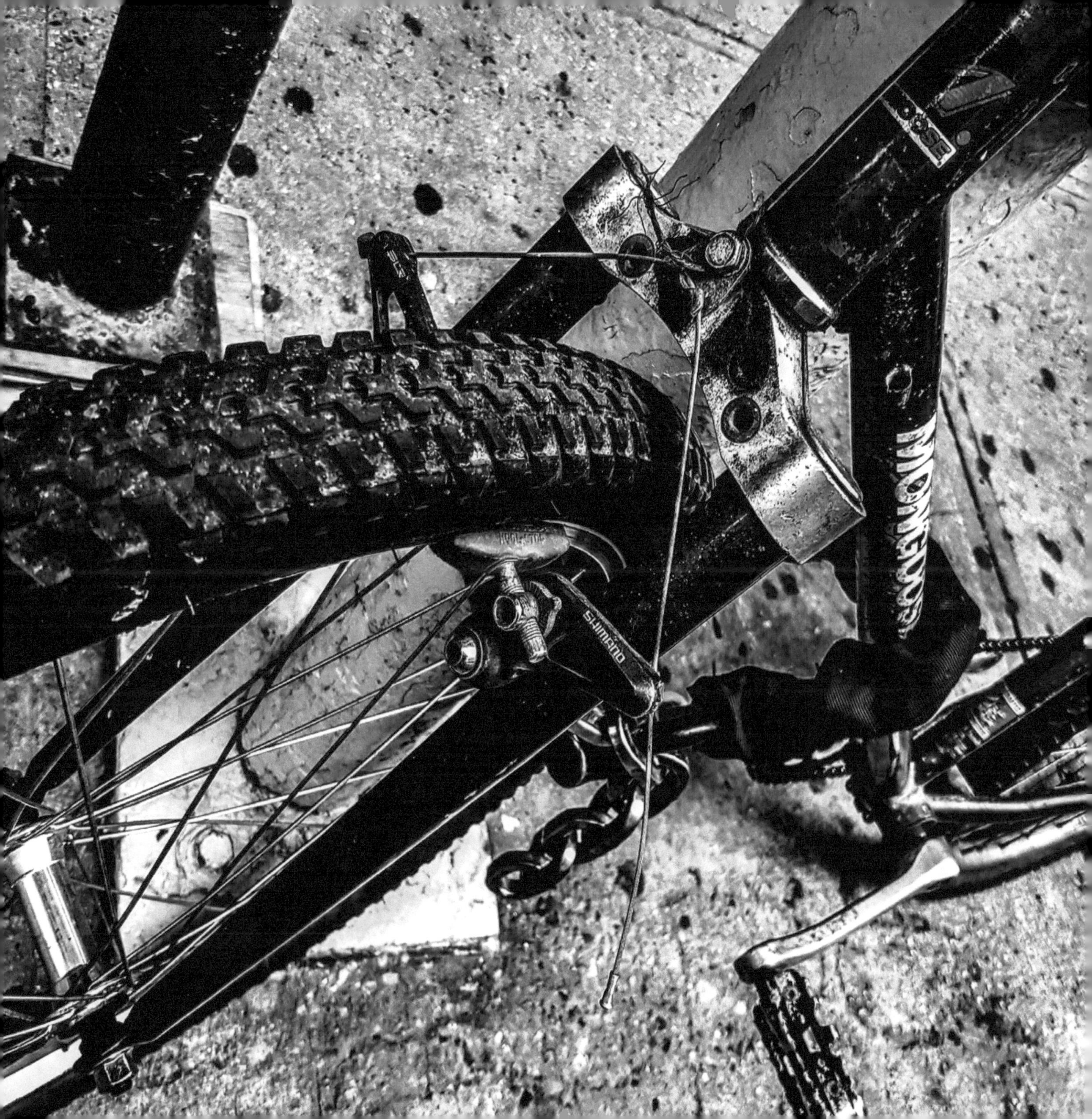
DOSE
SHIMANO

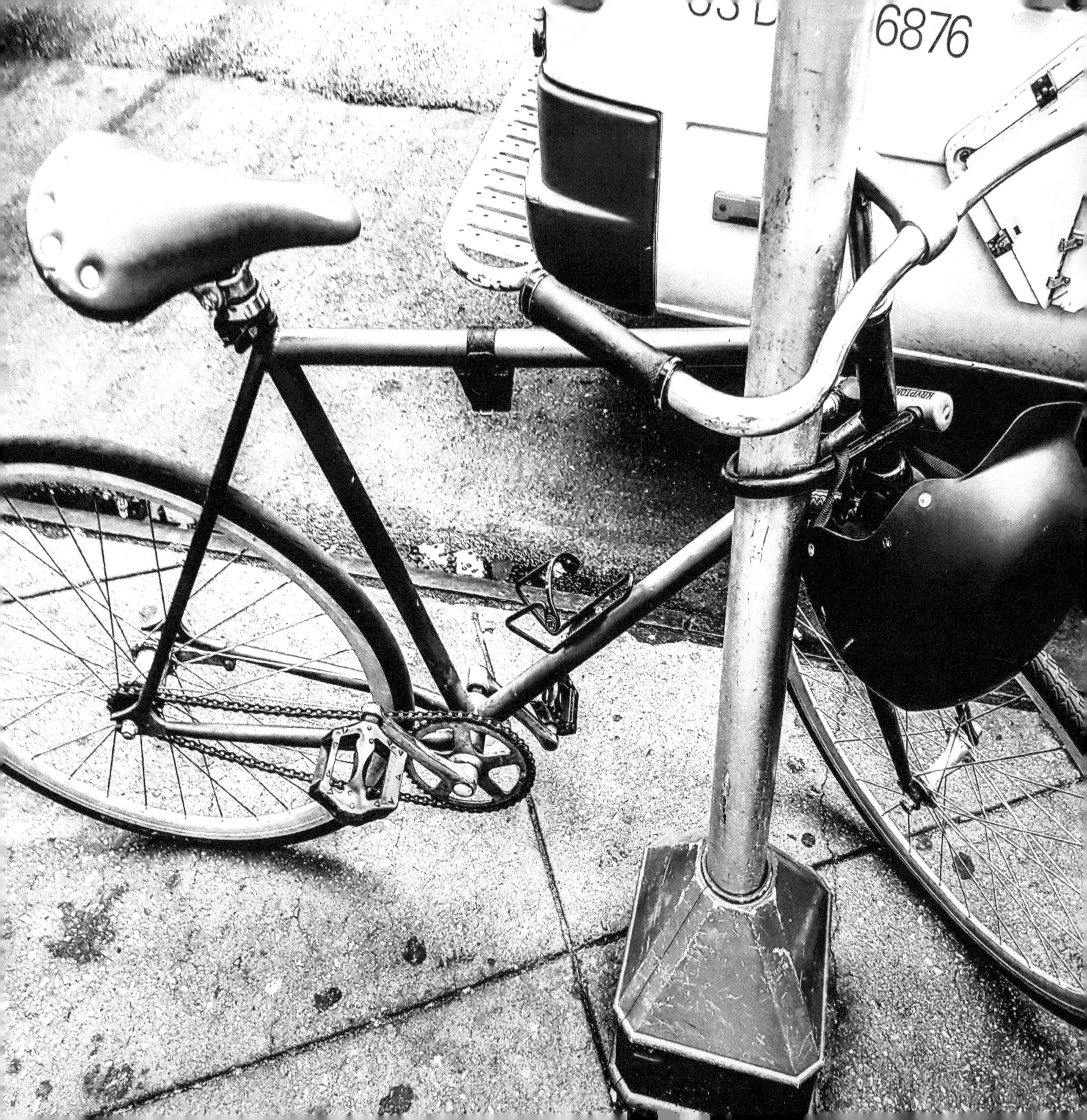
6876

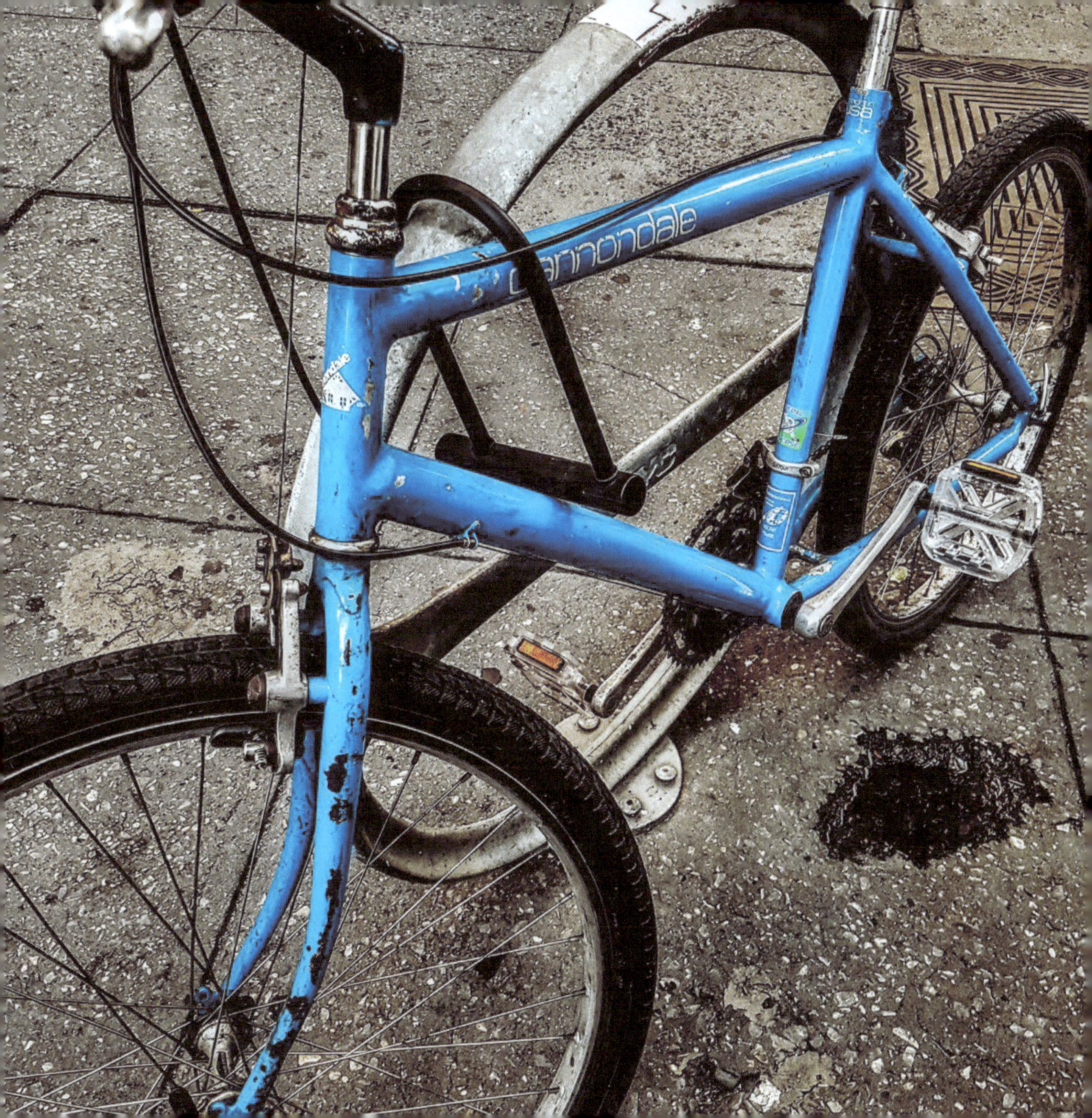
cannondale

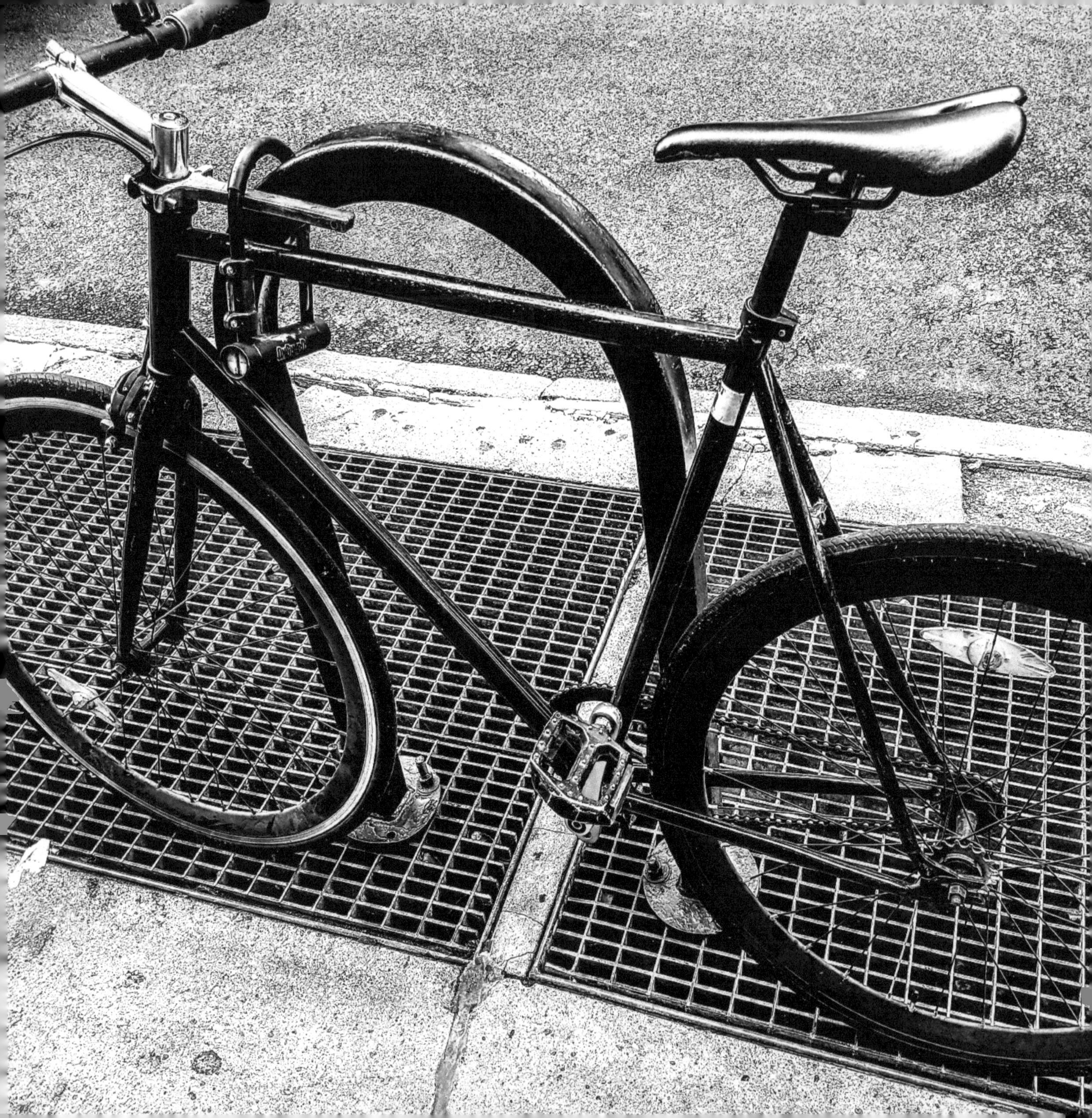

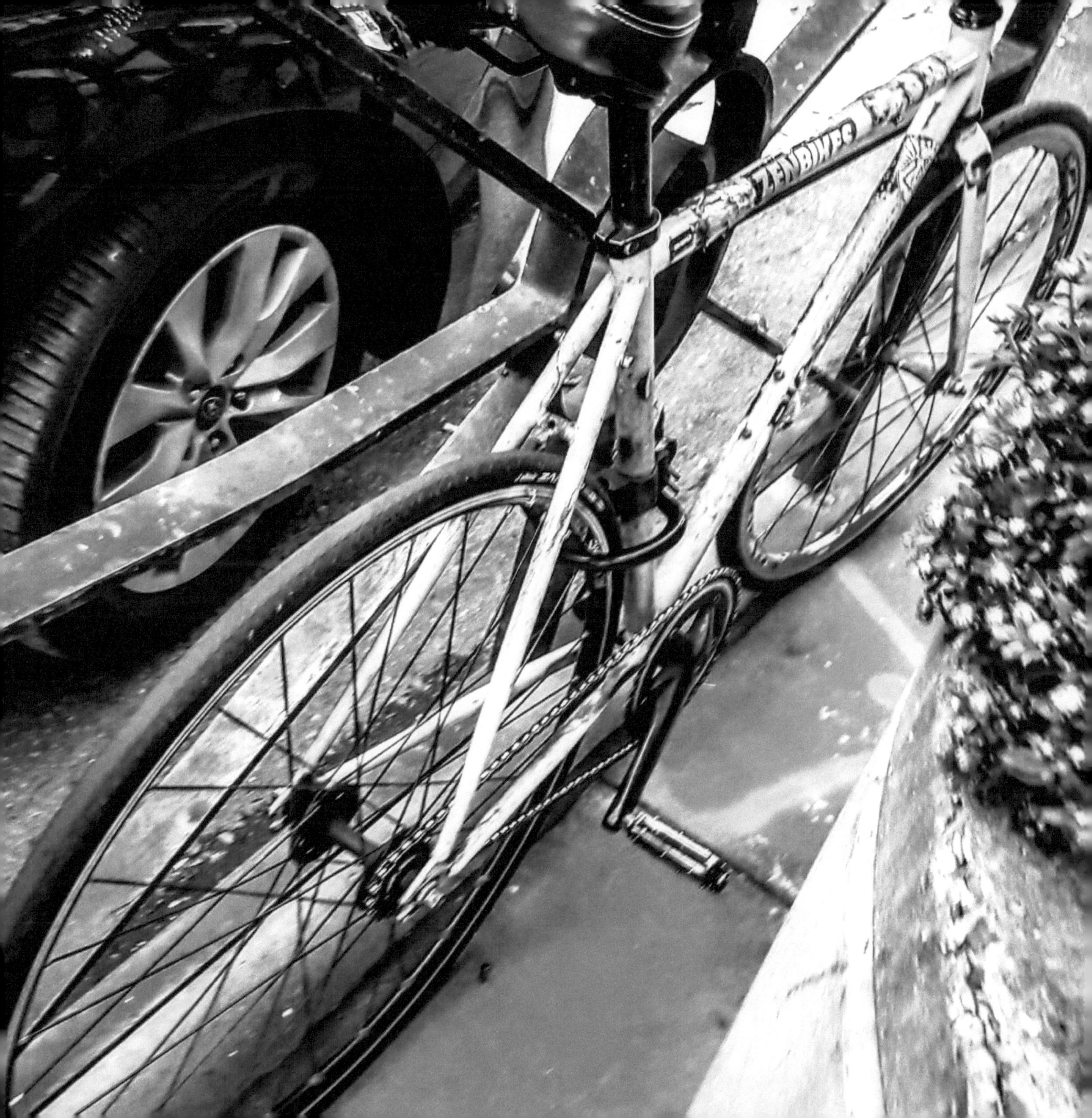
ZENBIKES

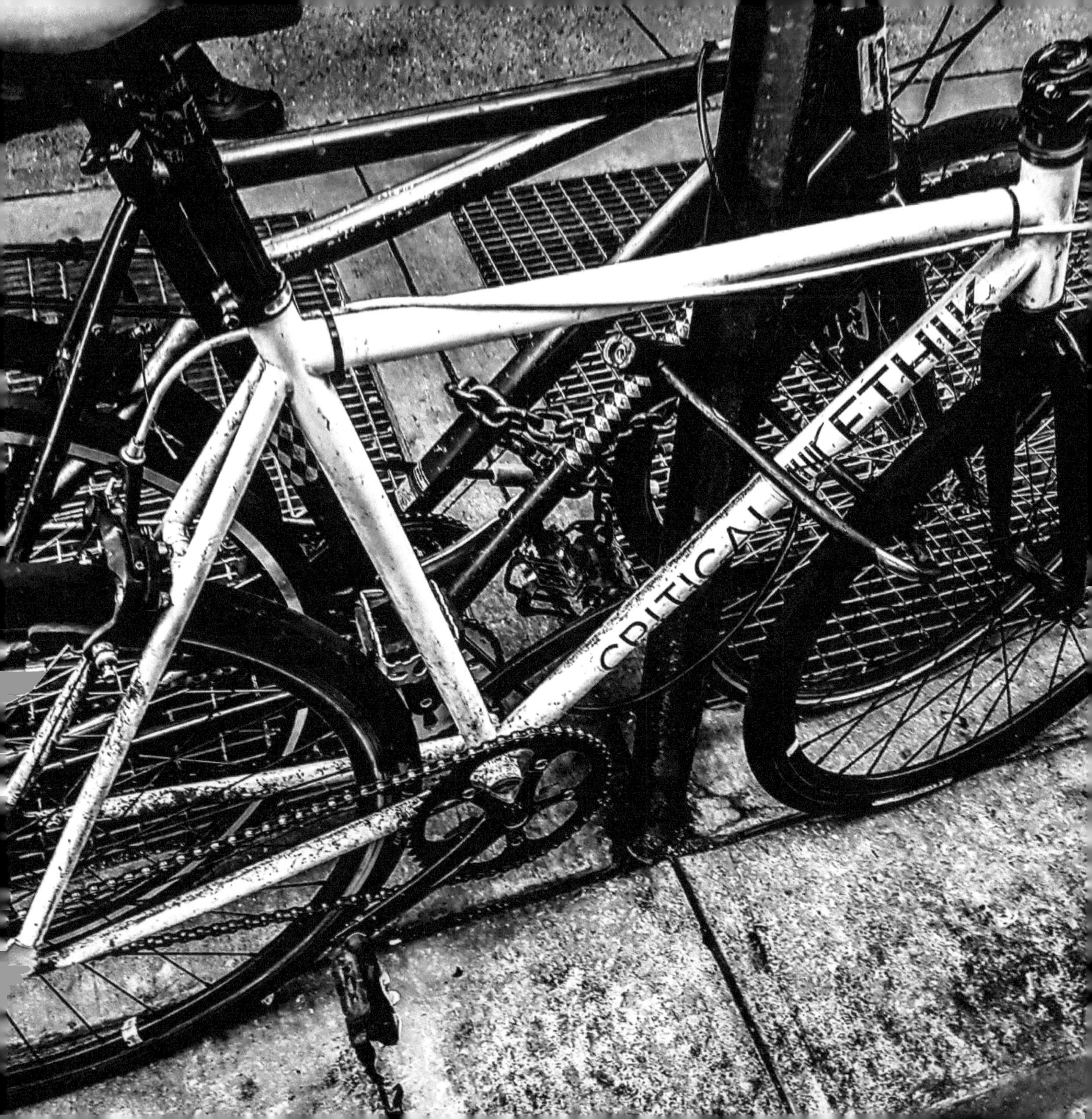
CRITICAL

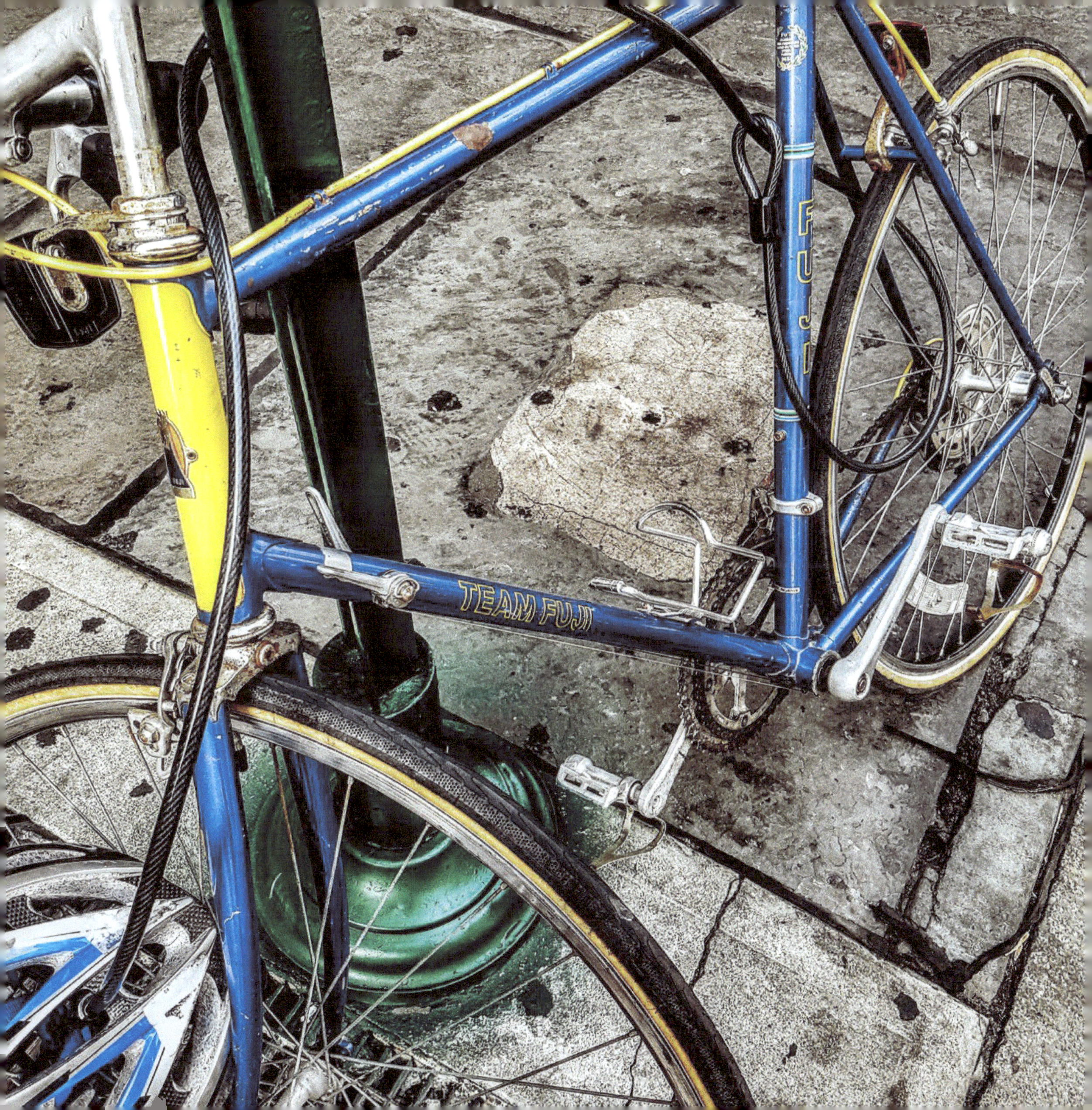
TEAM FUJI

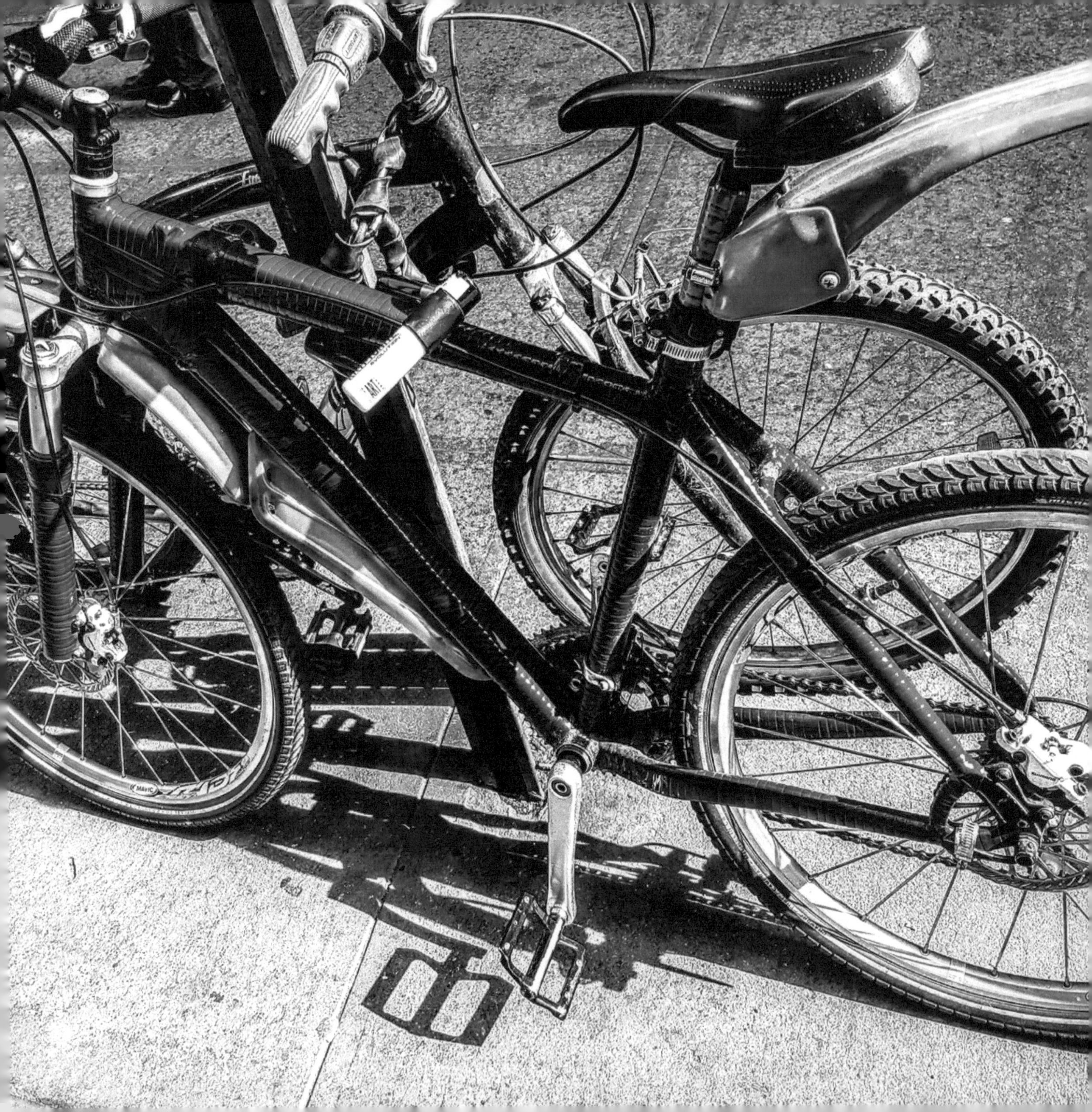

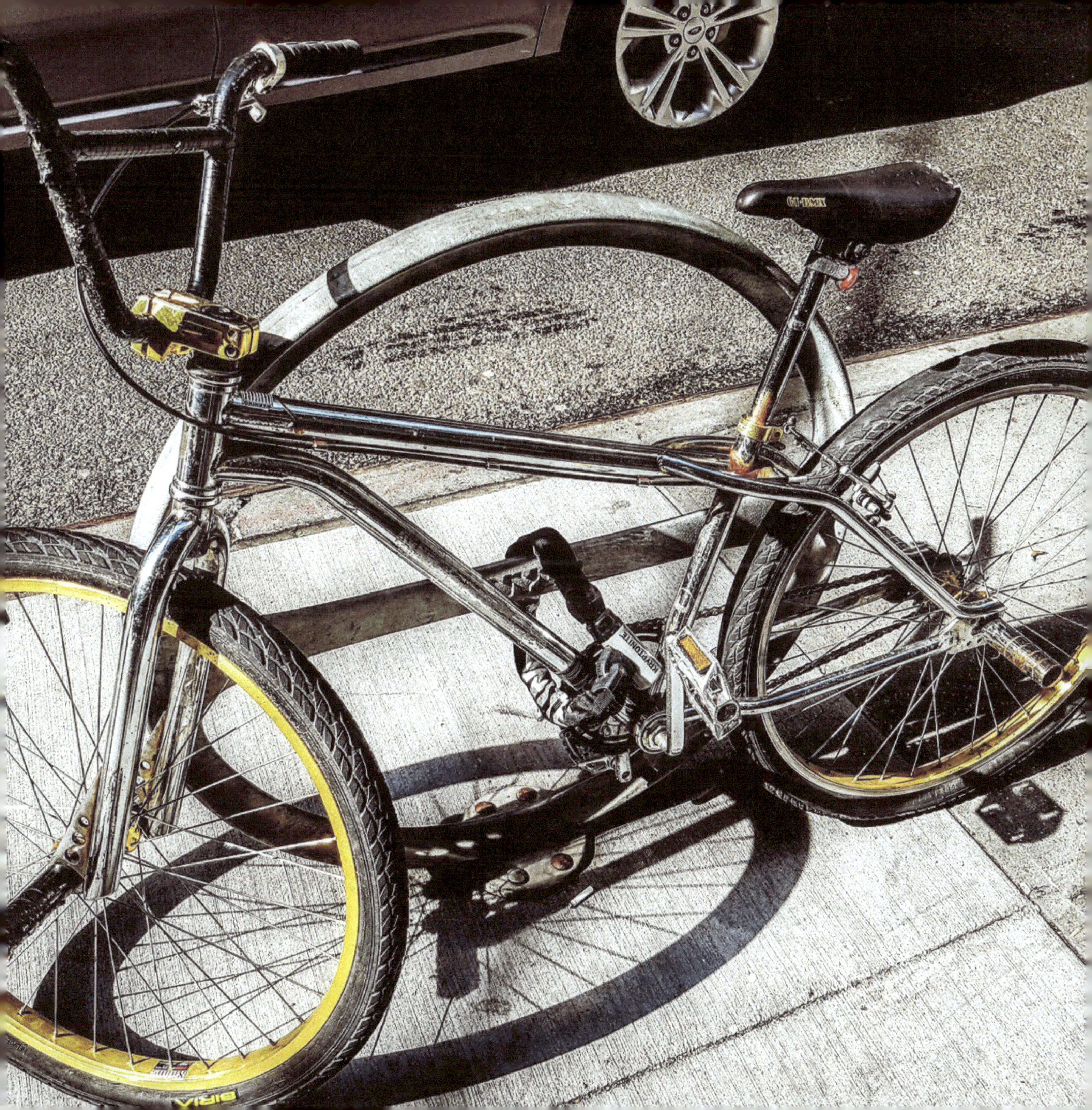
GT-BMX
KRYPTONITE

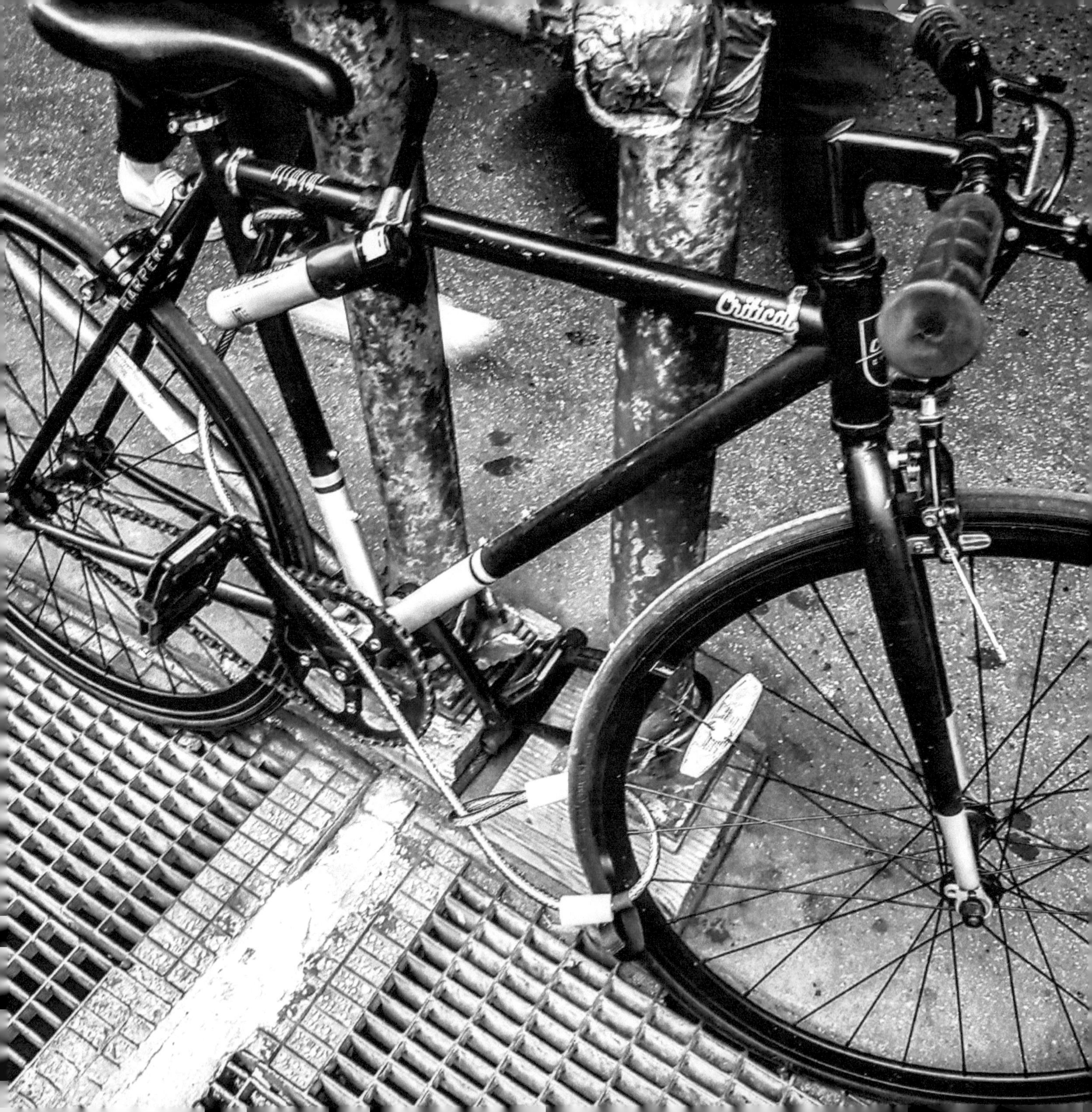
HARPER
Critical

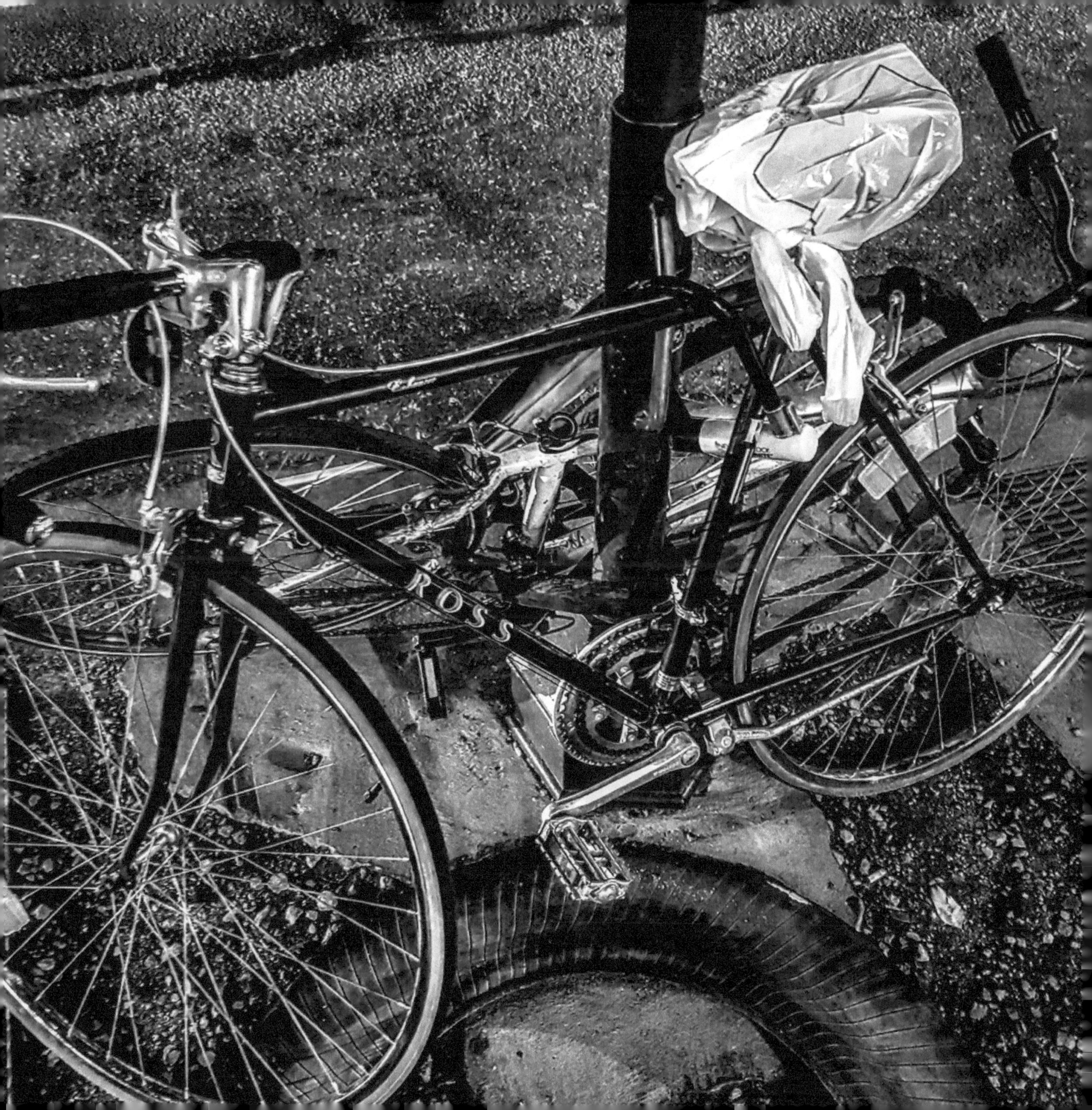
ROSS

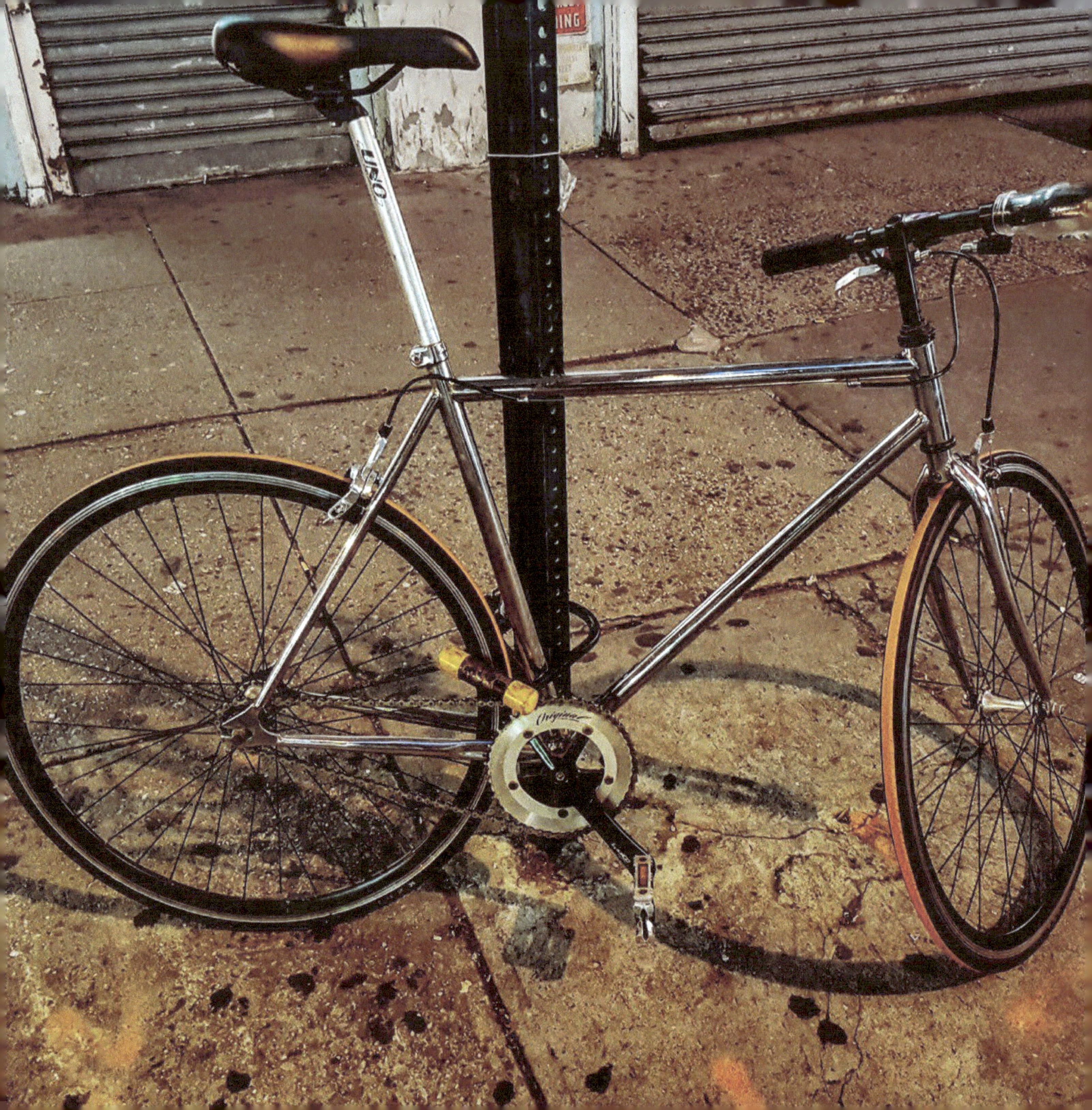
UNO

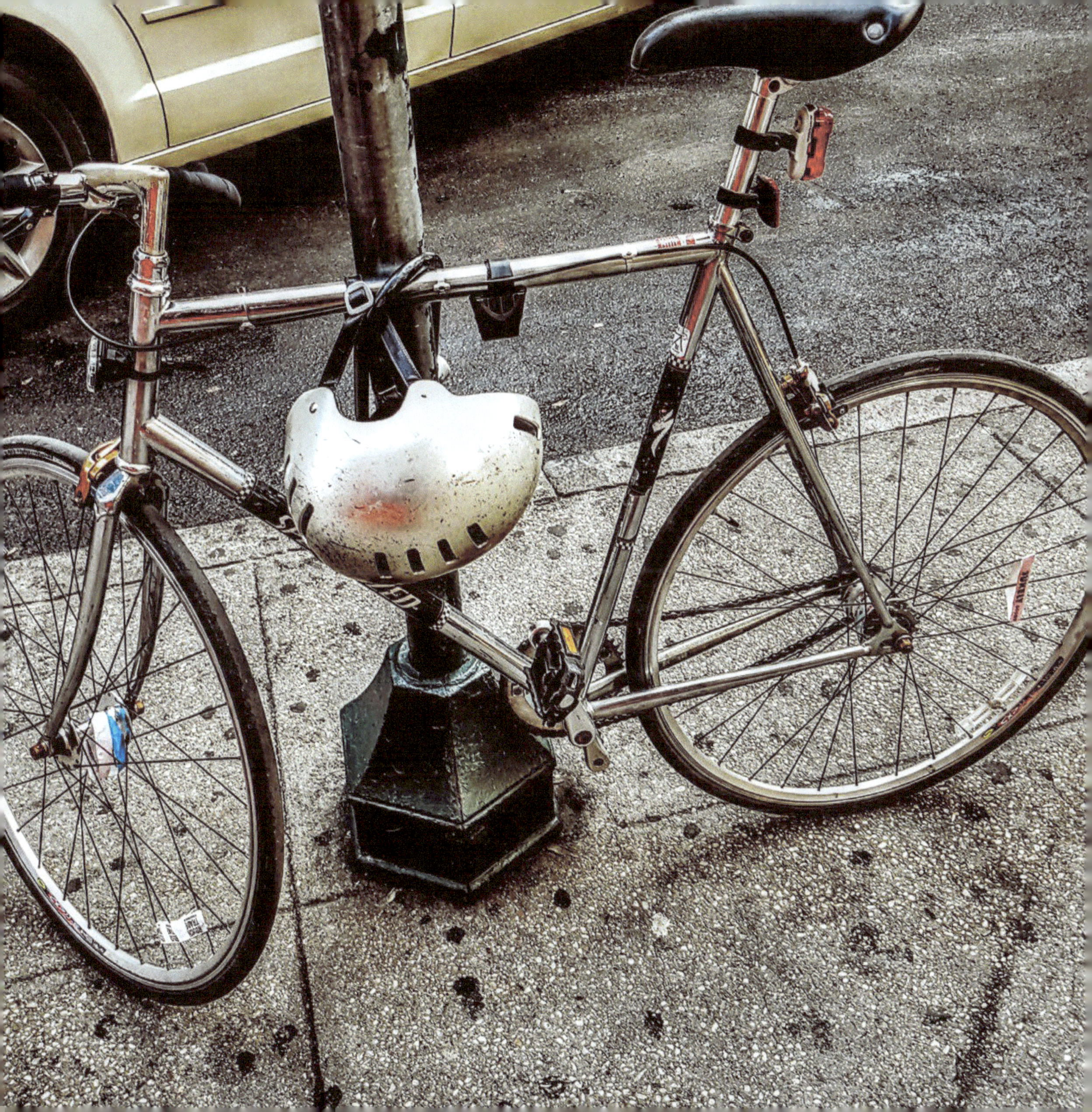

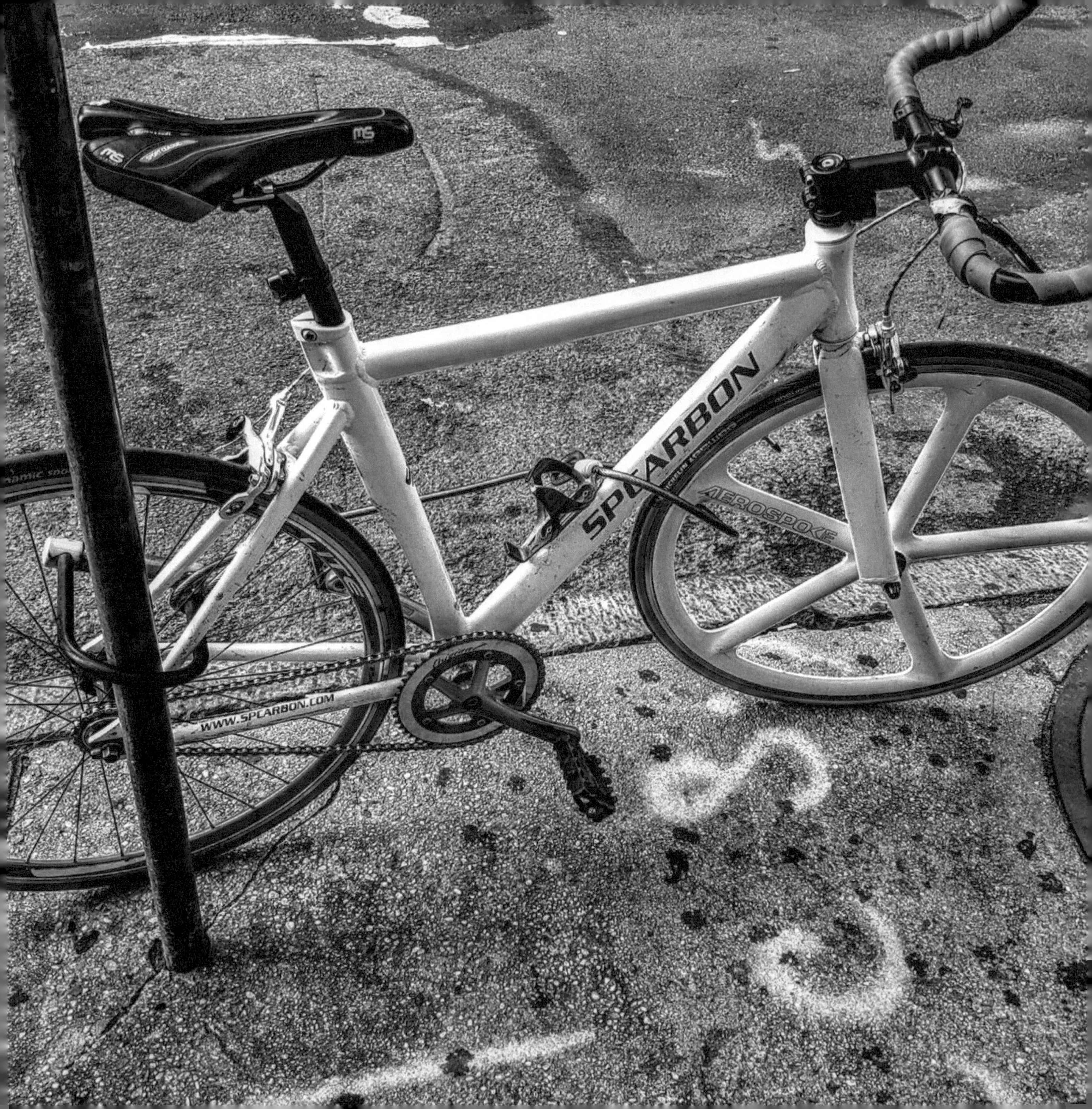
SPCARBON
AEROSPOKE
WWW.SPCARBON.COM

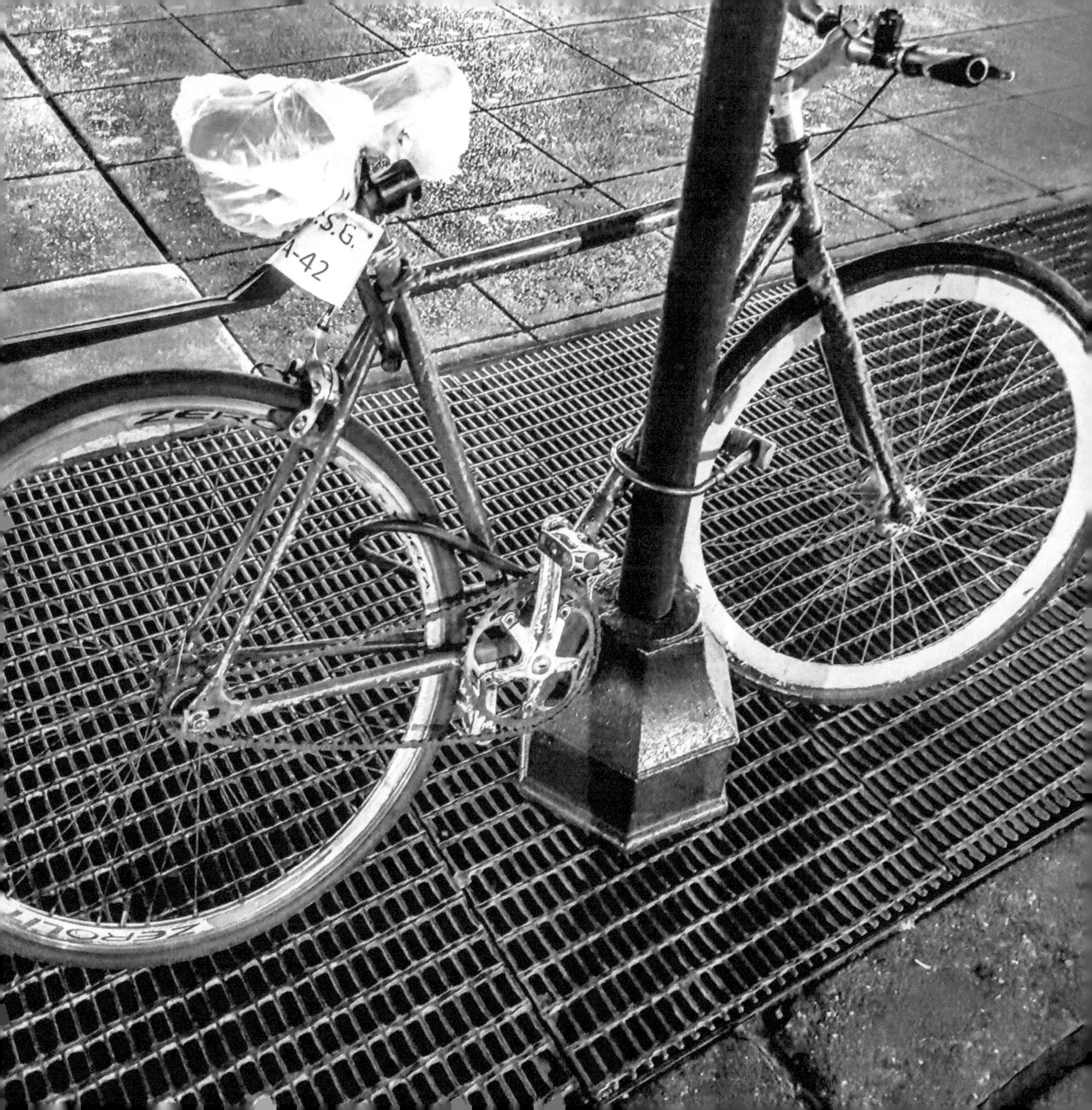
S.G.
A-42
ZERO

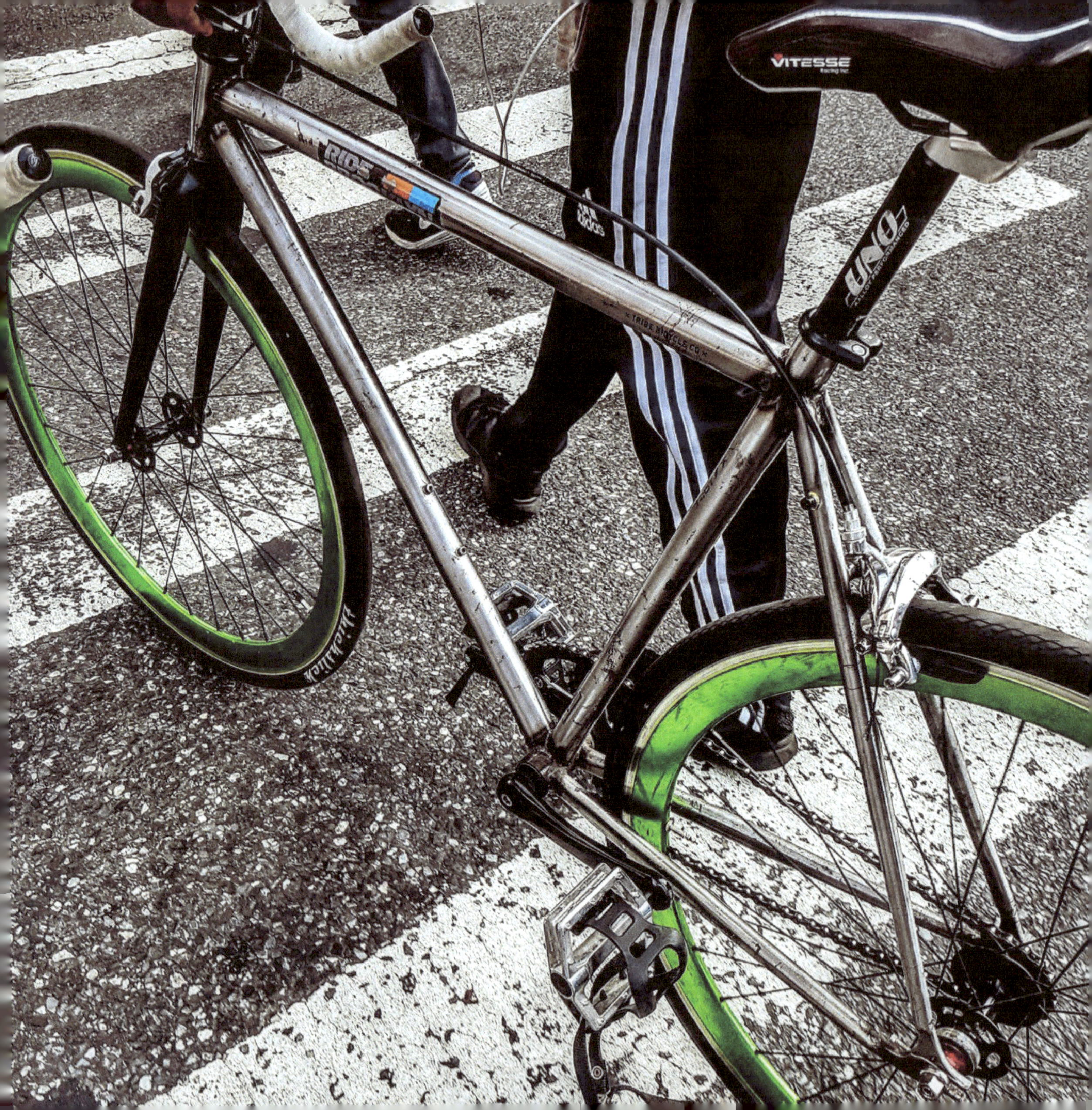
VITESSE
RIDE
UNO

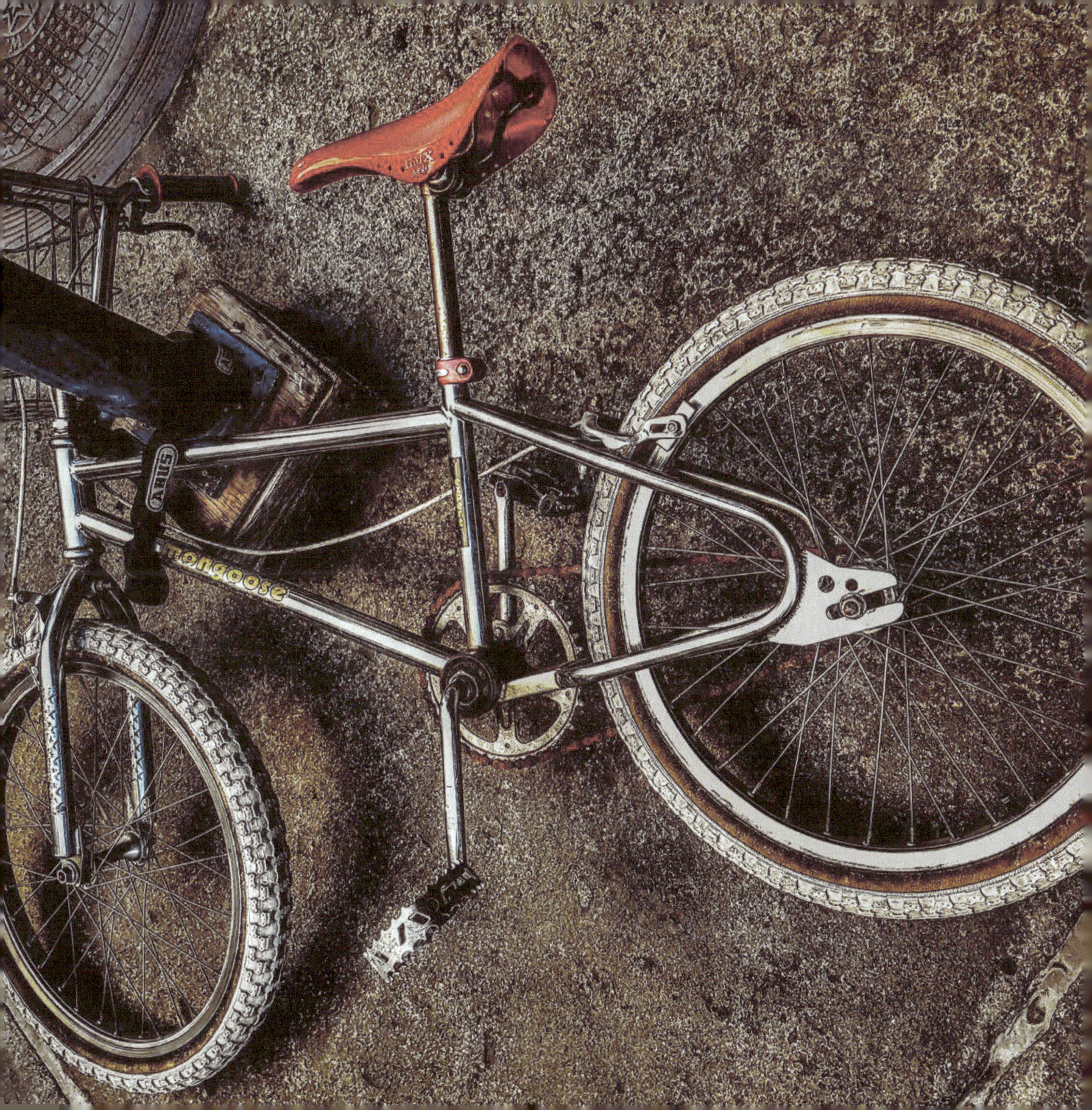
mongoose

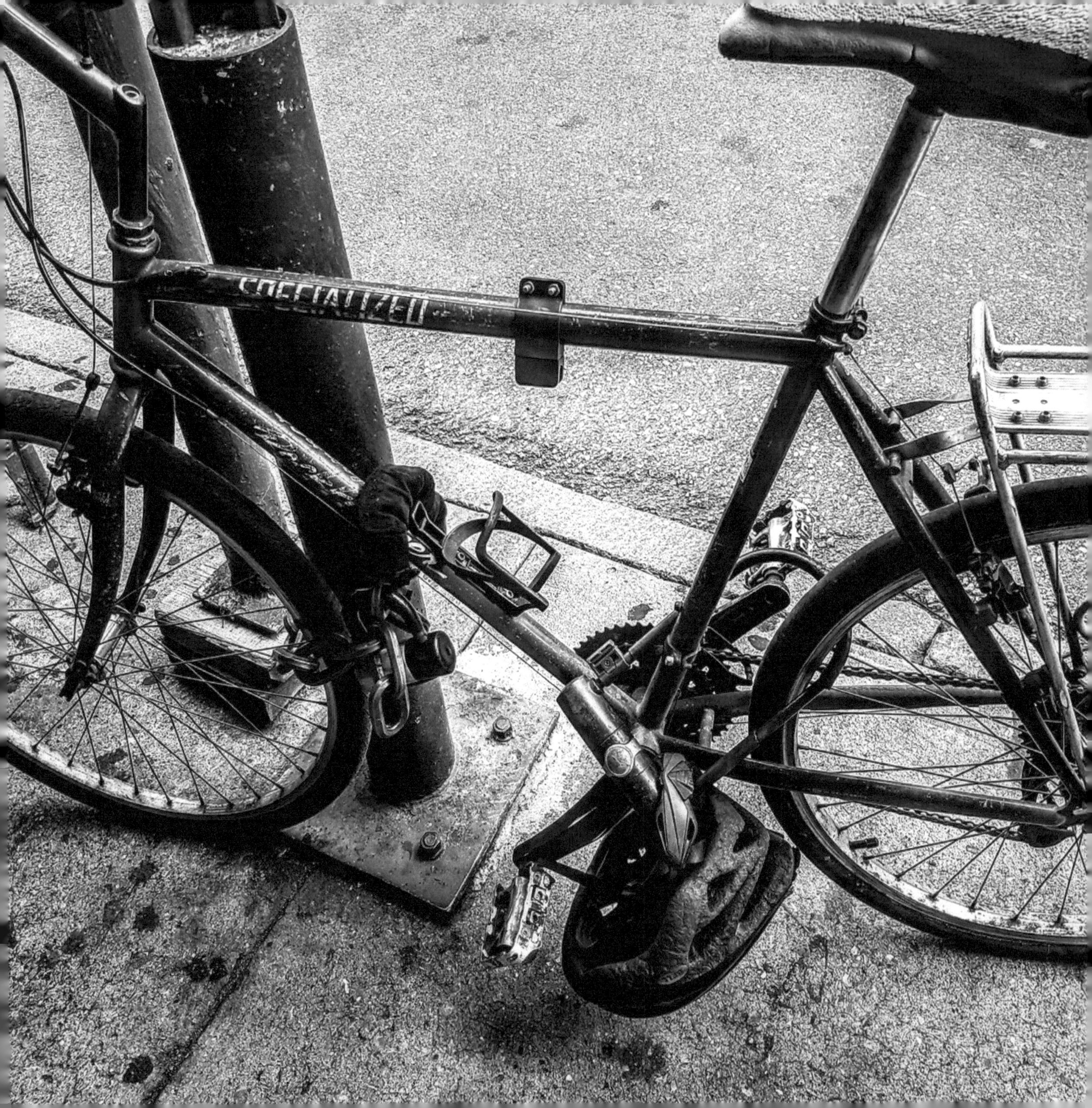

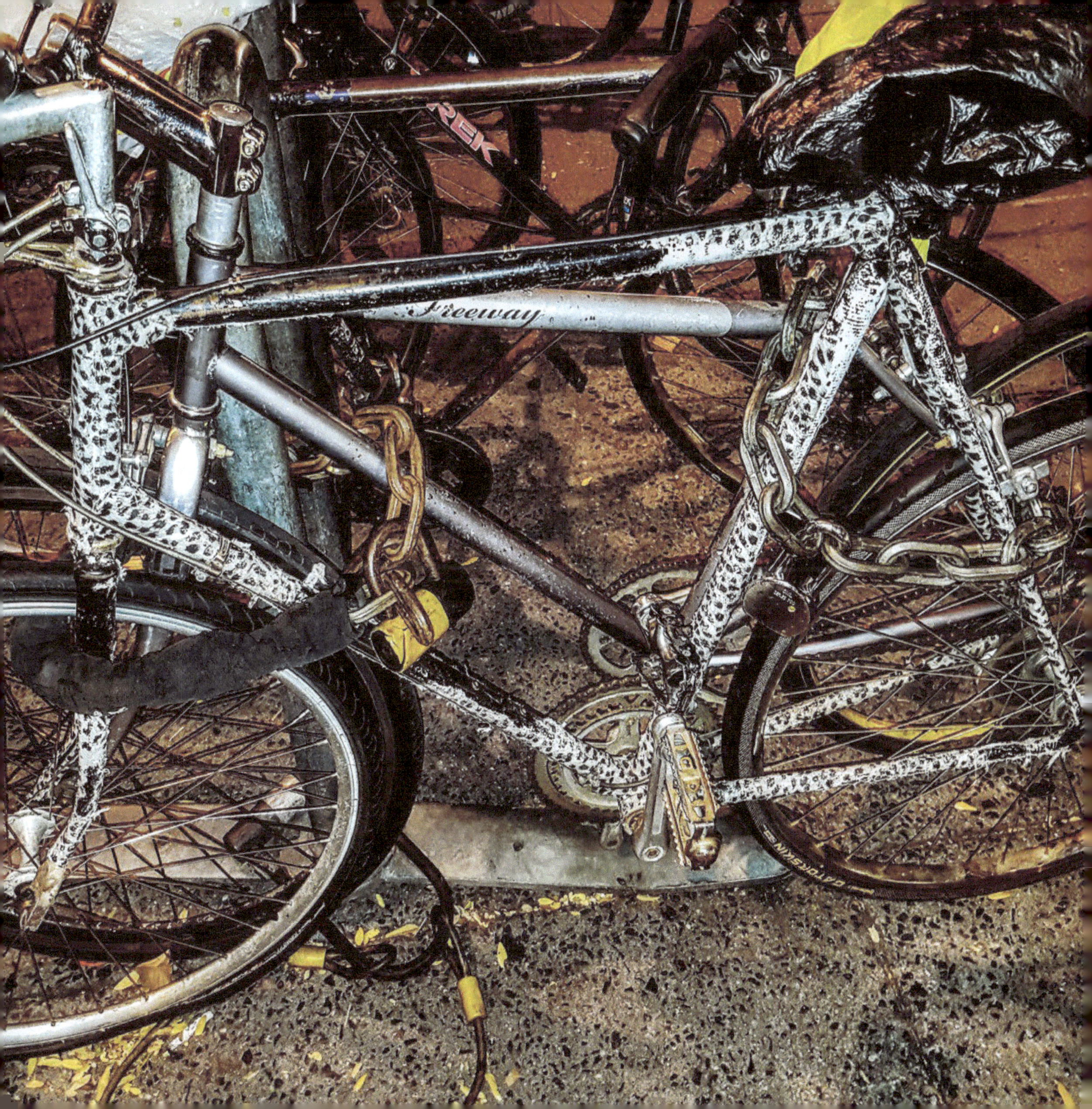
Freeway

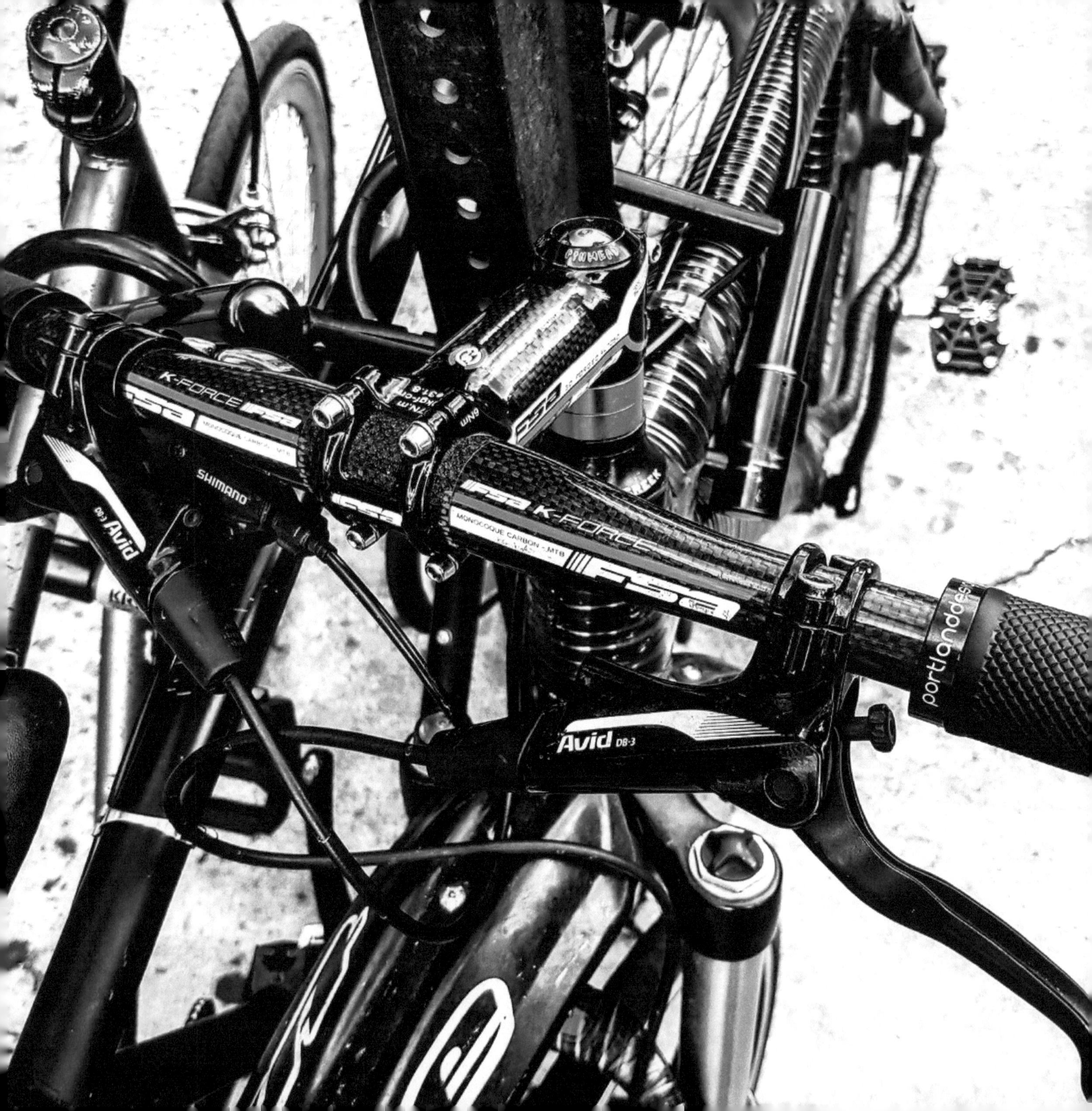
K-FORCE
FSA
SHIMANO
Avid DB-3
K-FORCE
MONOCOQUE CARBON - MTB
FSA
Avid DB-3

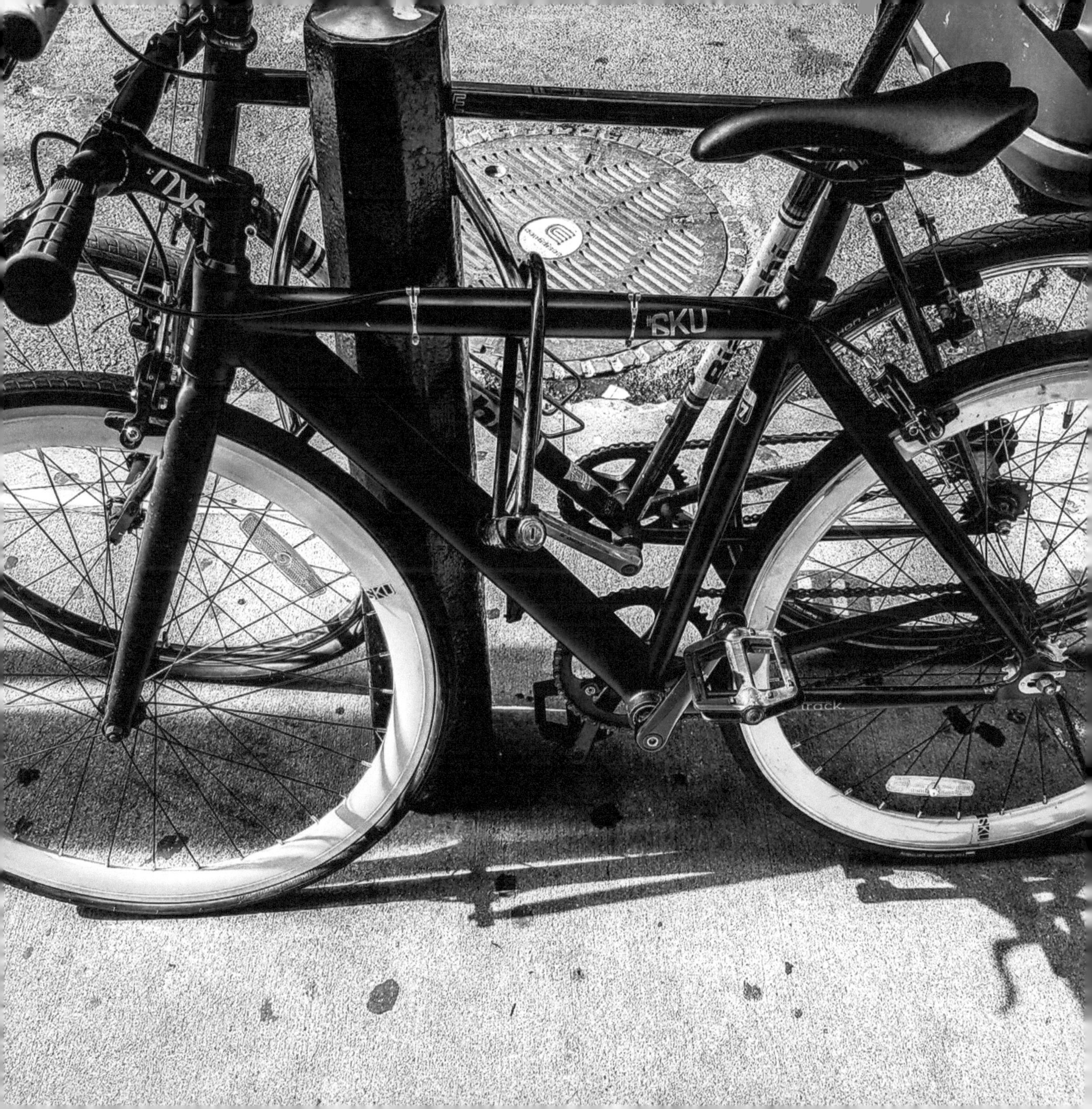
SKU
track.
SKU

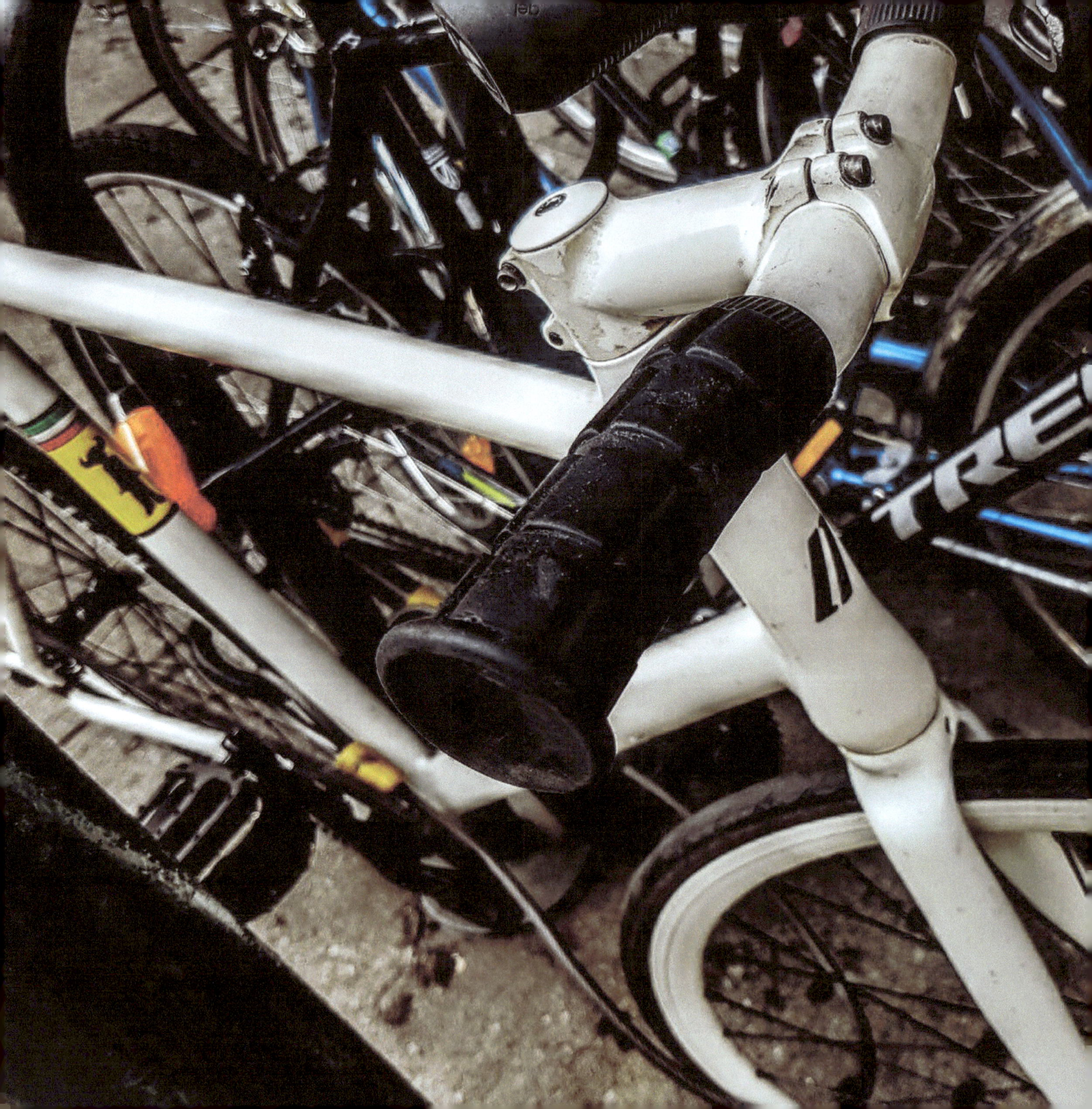

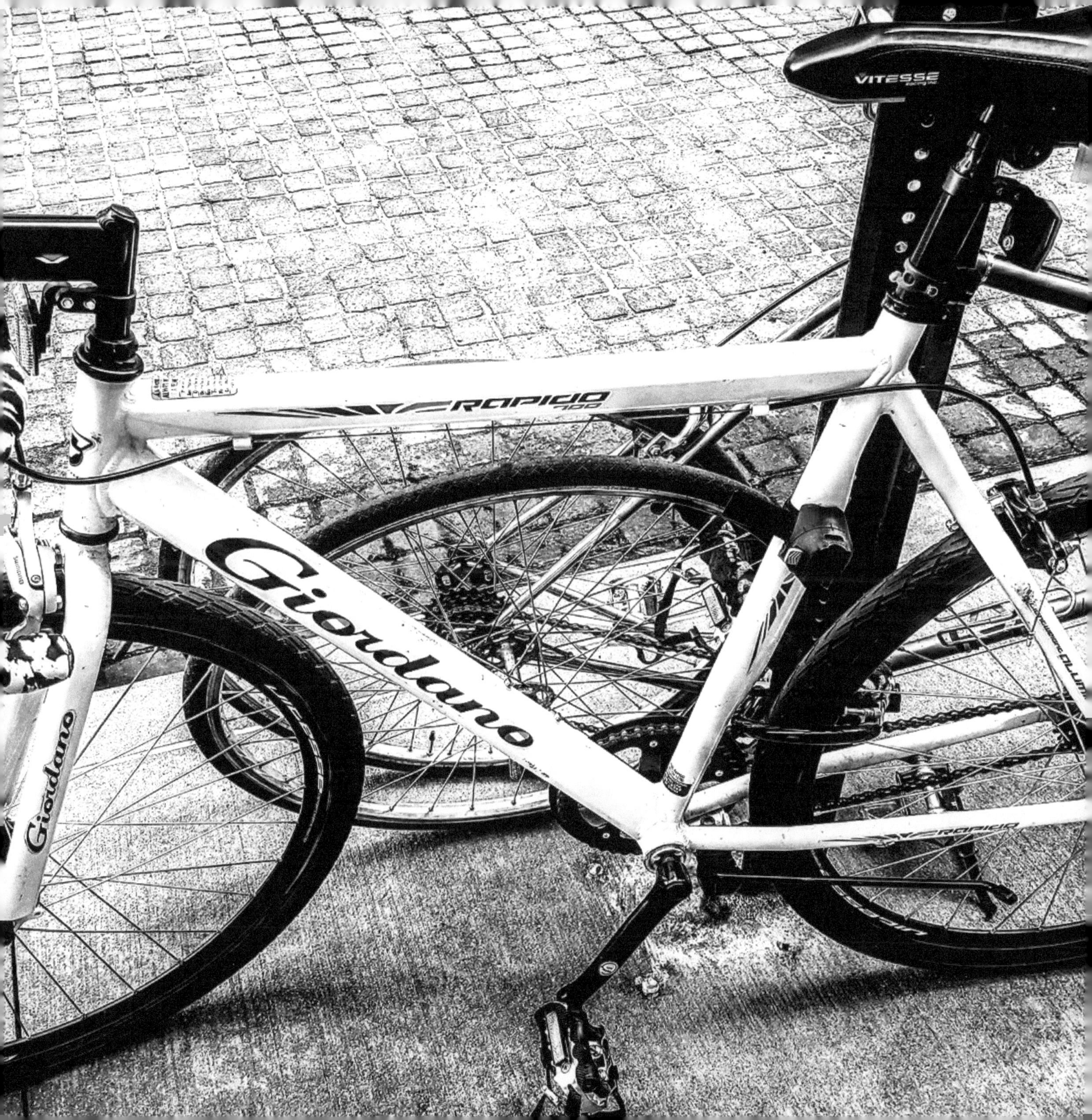
VITESSE
RAPIDO
Giordano
Giordano

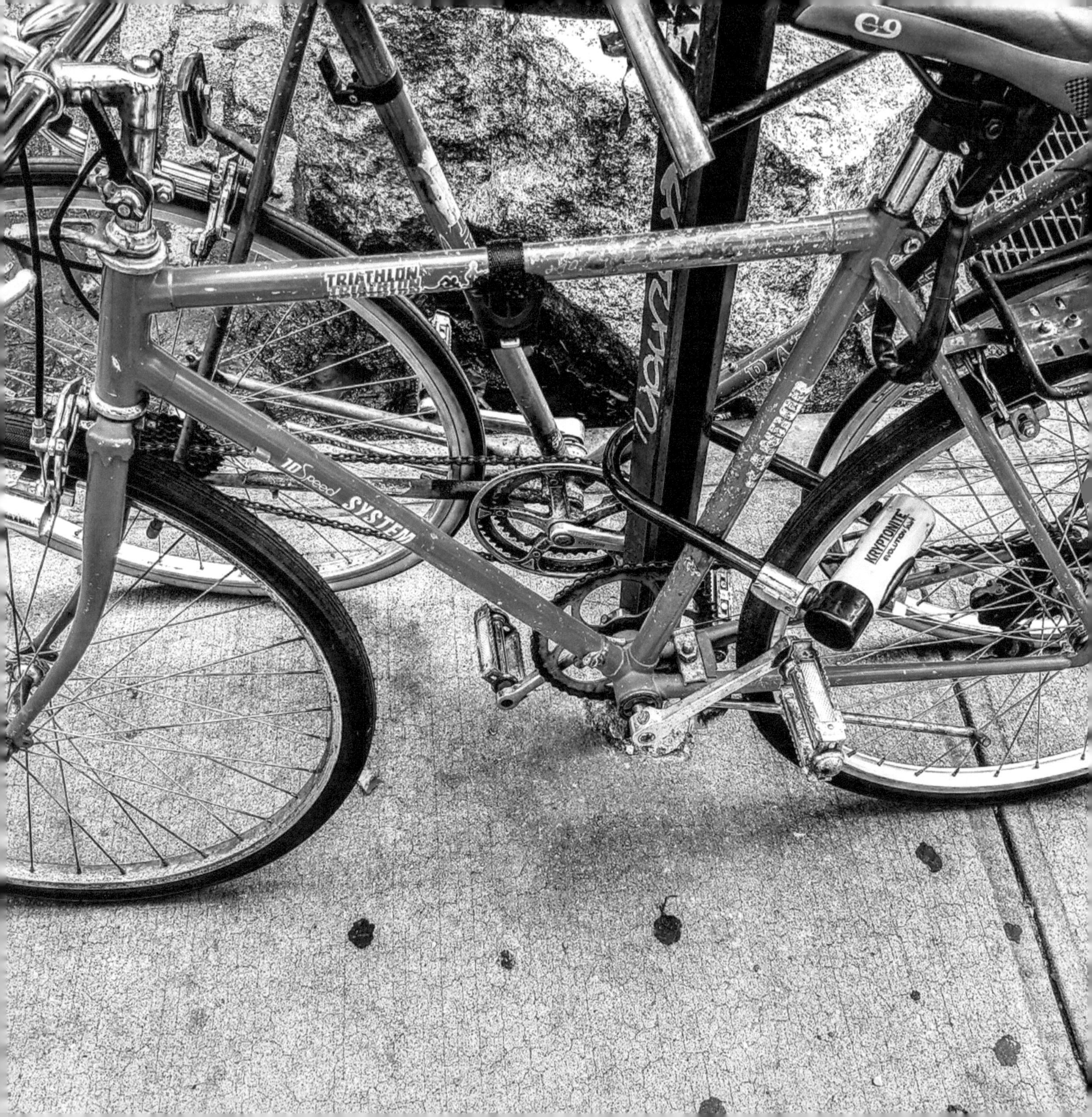
TRIATHLON
10Speed
SYSTEM
KRYPTONITE

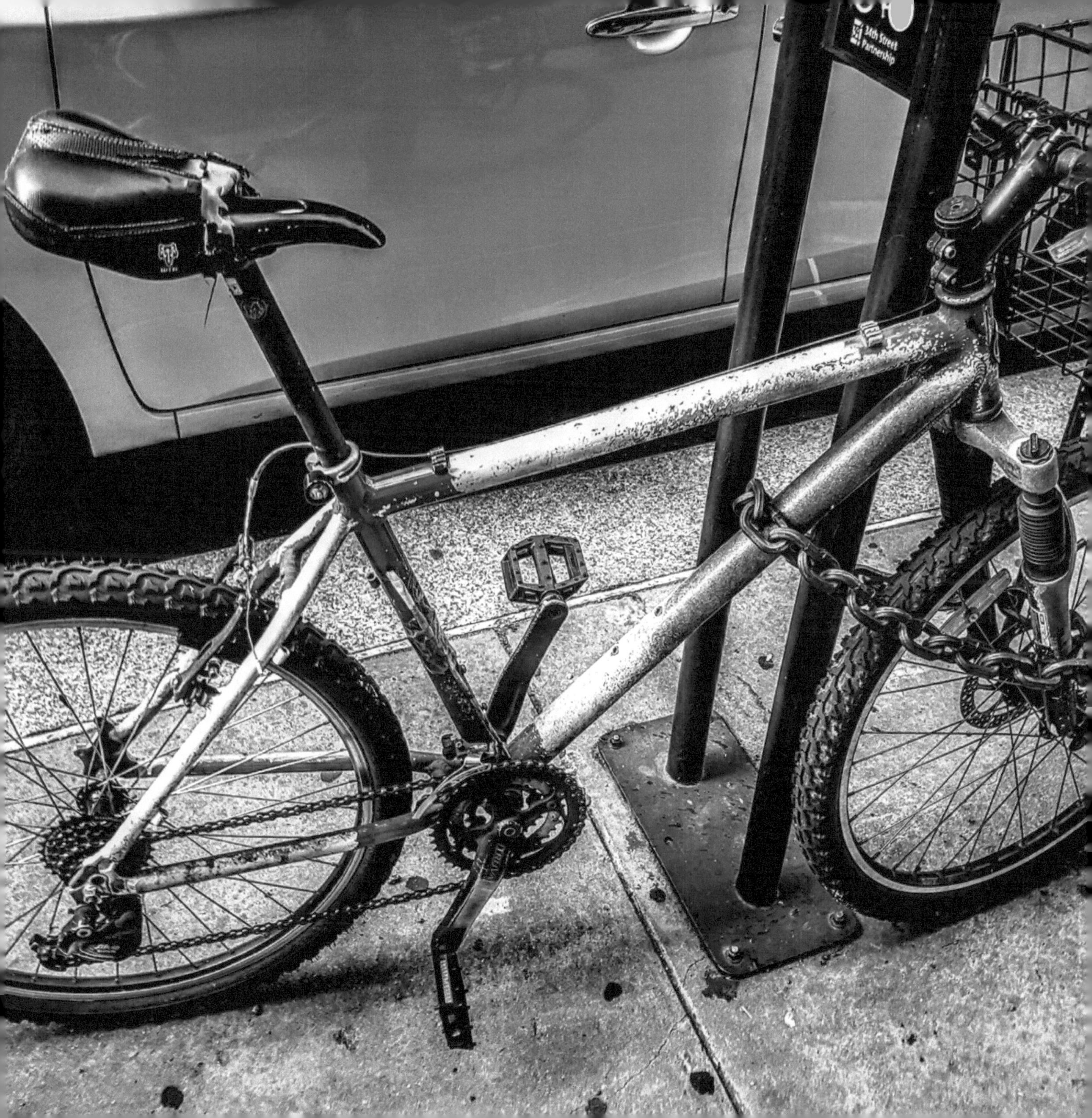
34th Street
Partnership

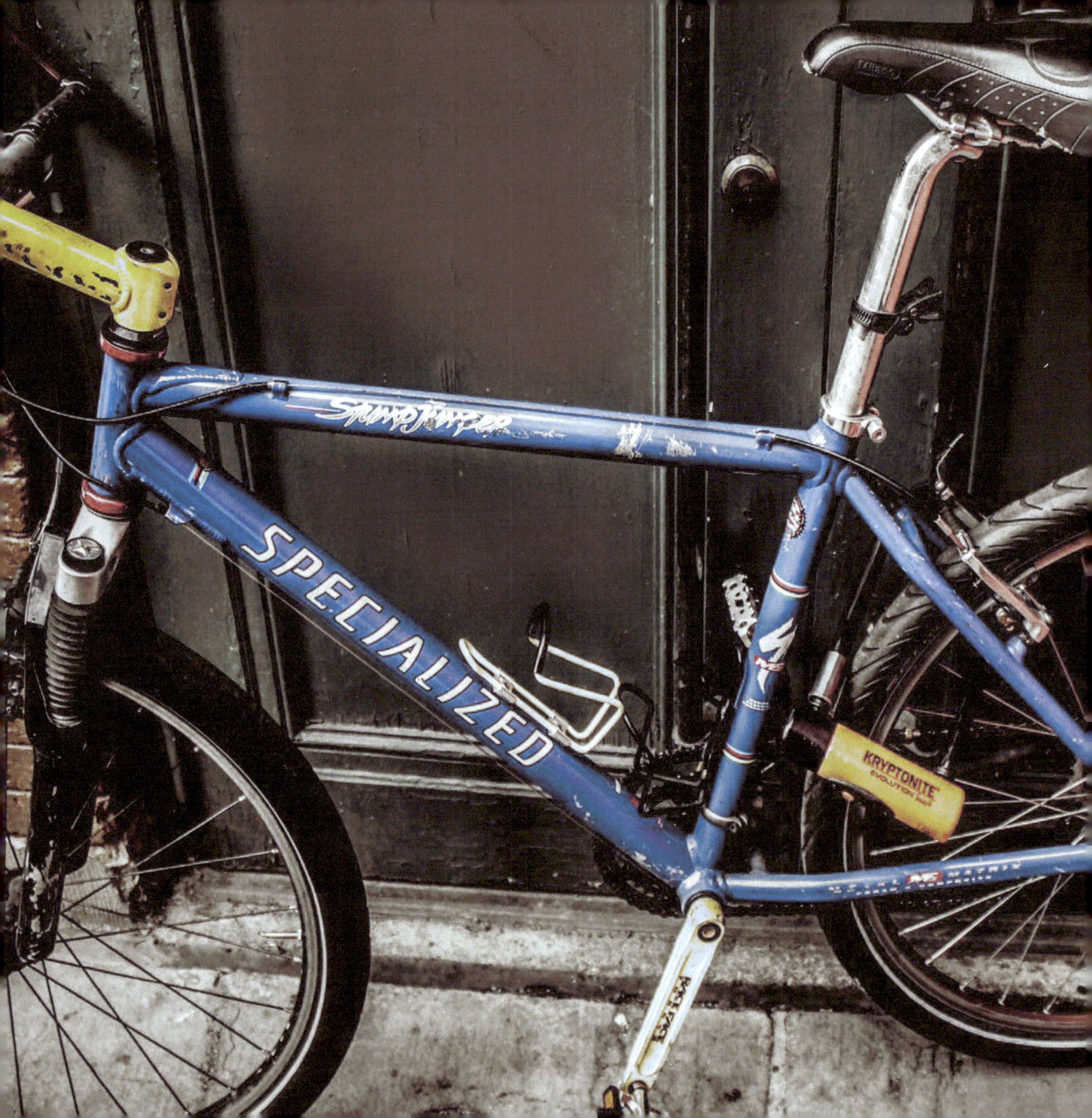
SPECIALIZED
KRYPTONITE

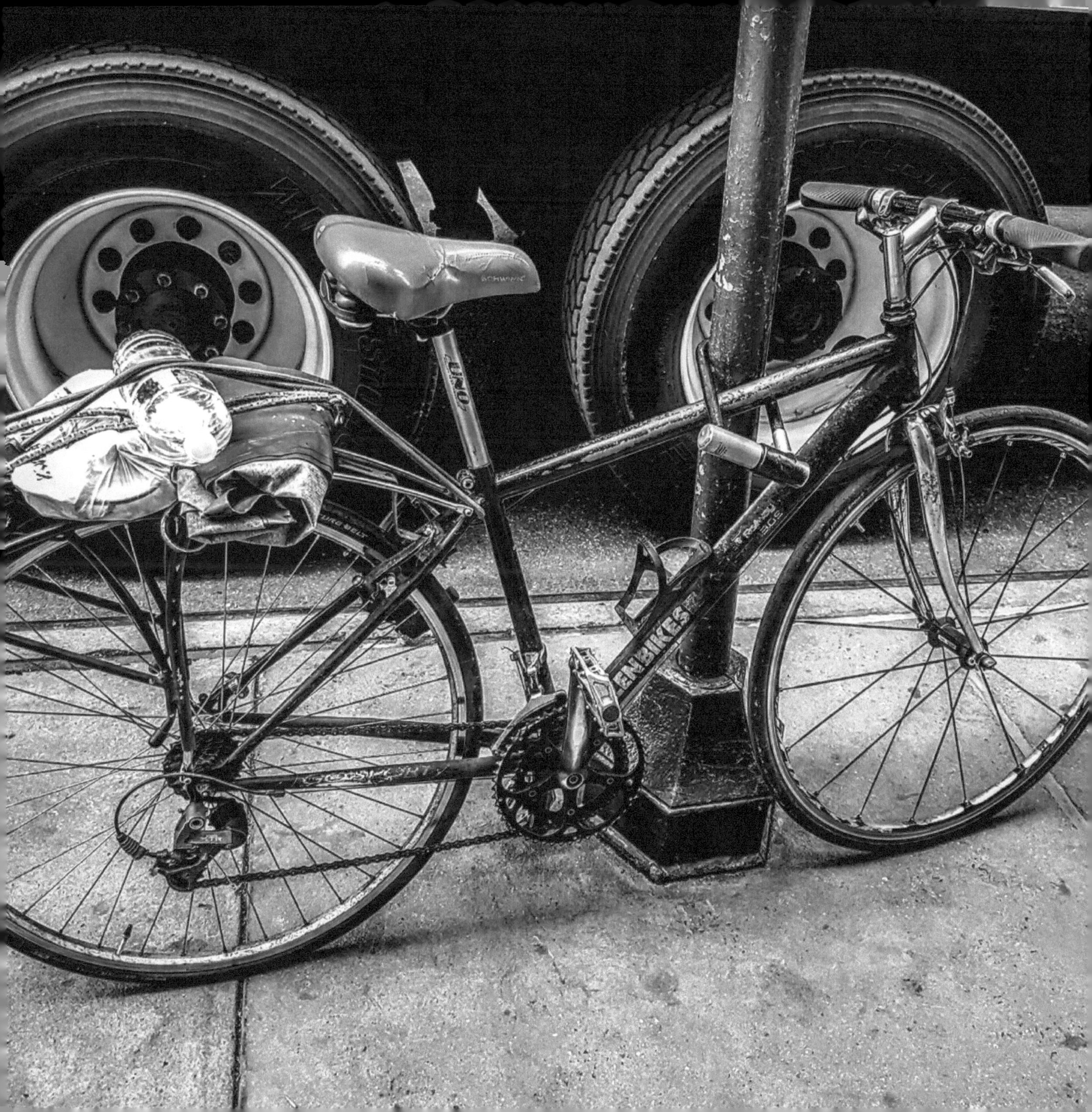
SCHWINN
UNO

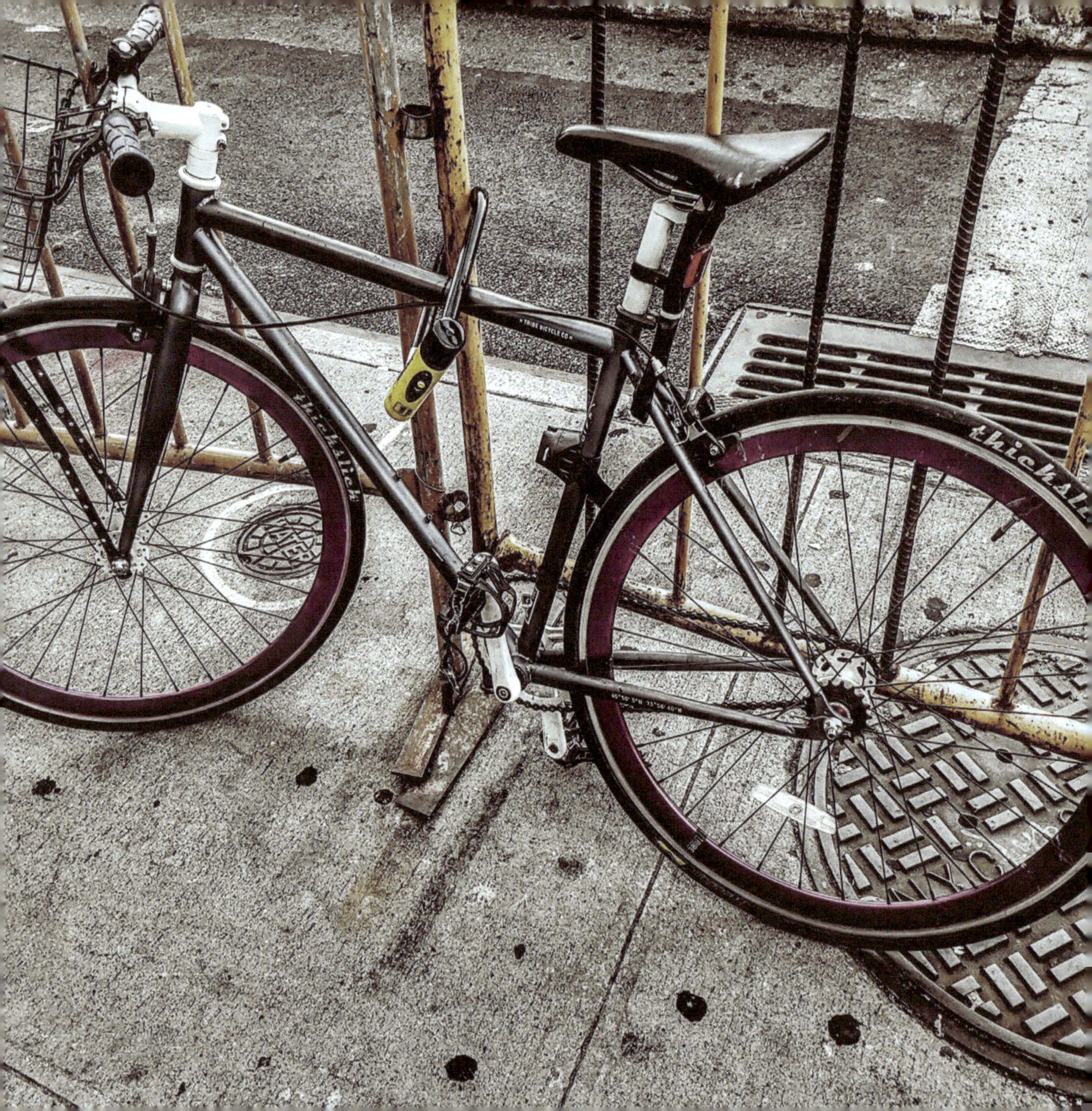
TRIBE BICYCLE CO
thickslick

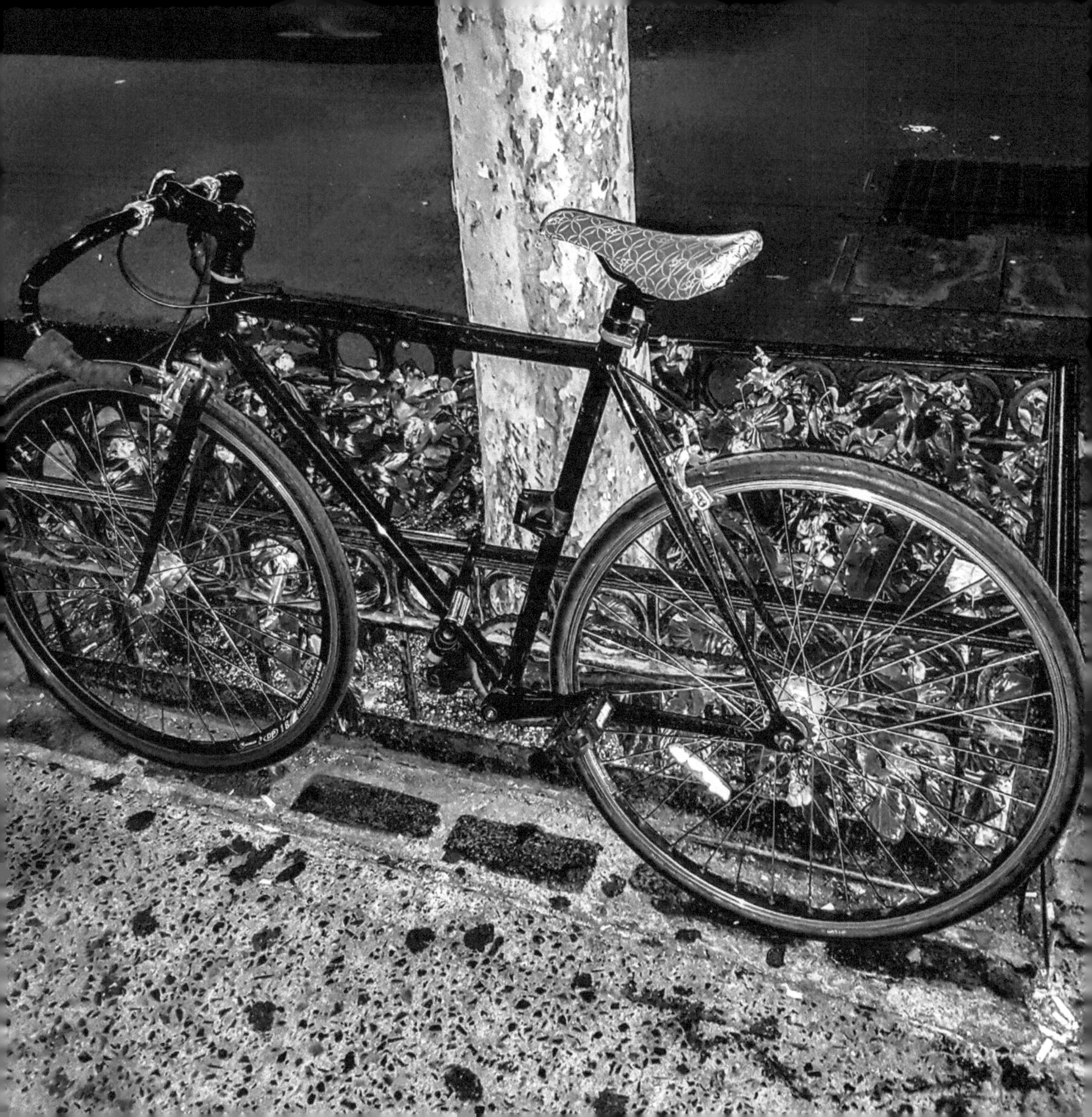

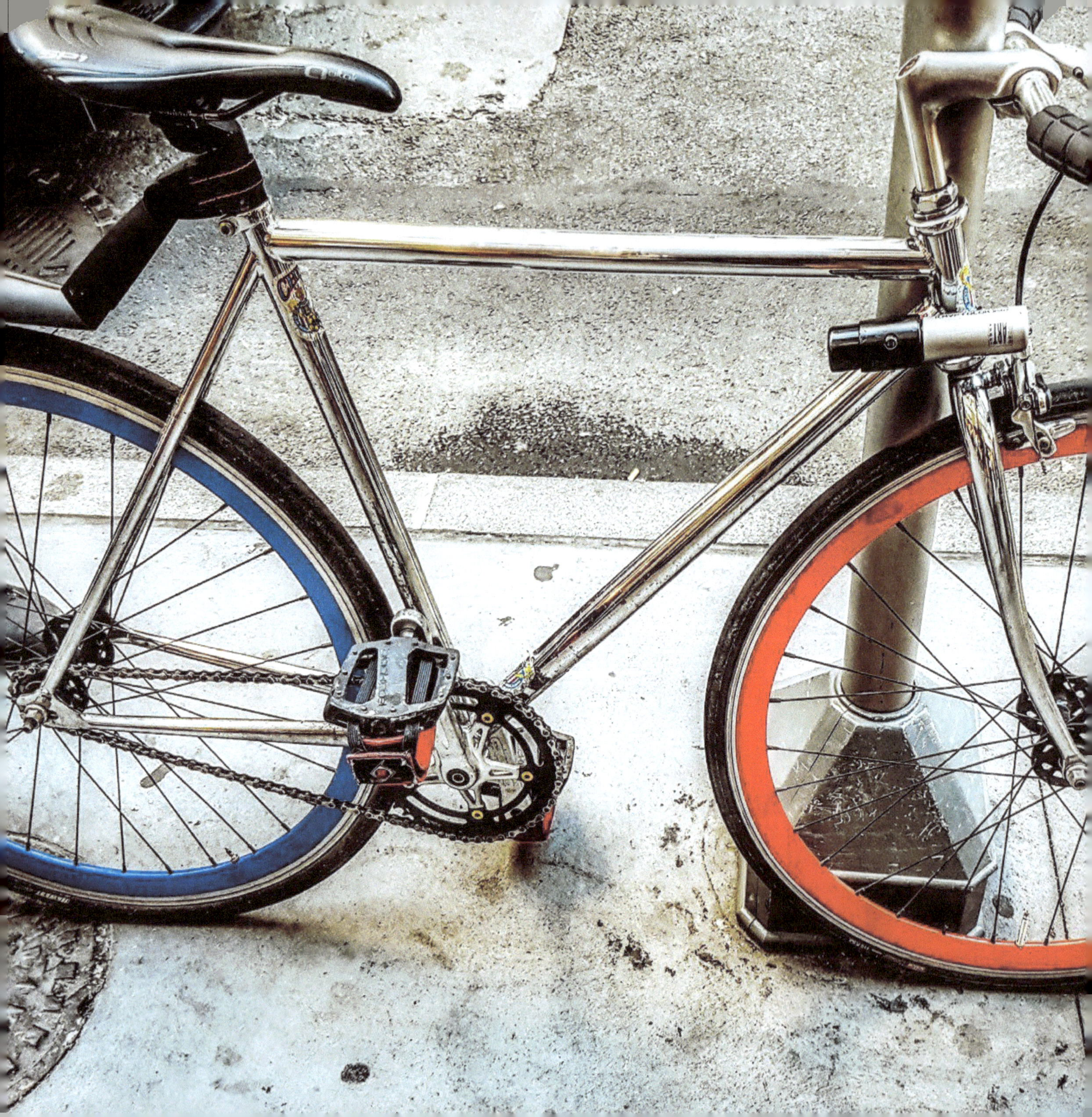

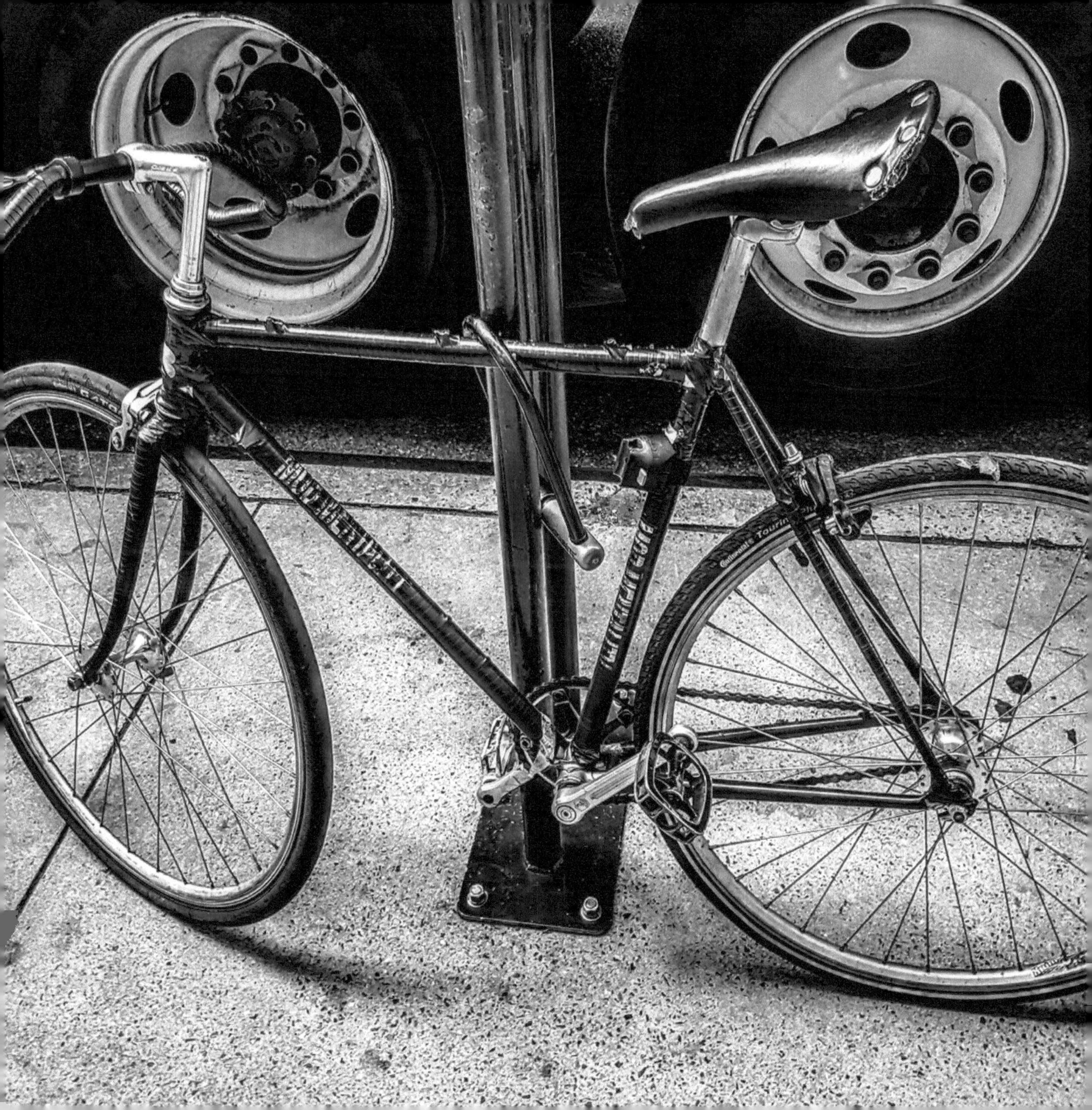

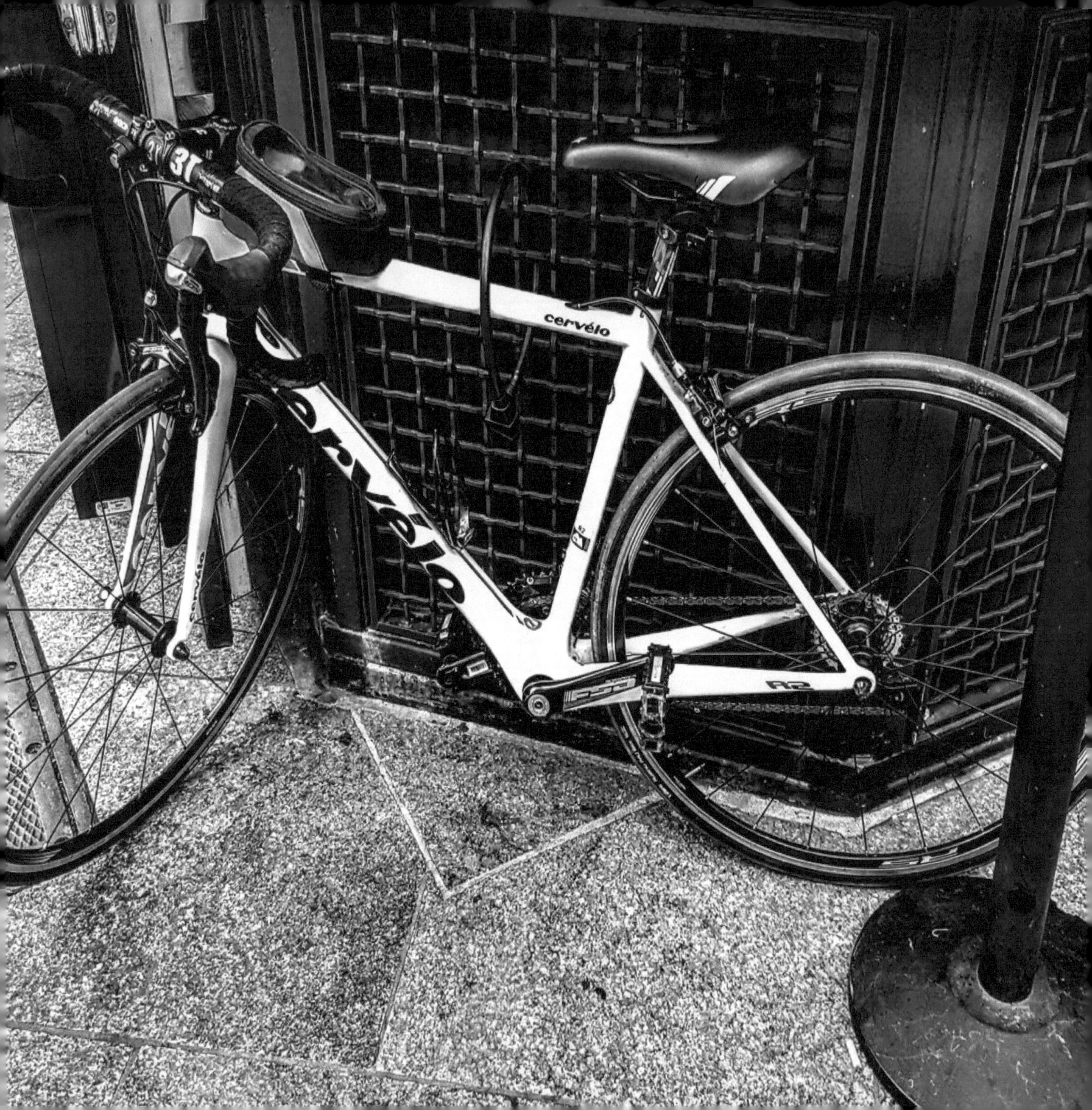
3T
cervélo
cervélo
R2
FSA

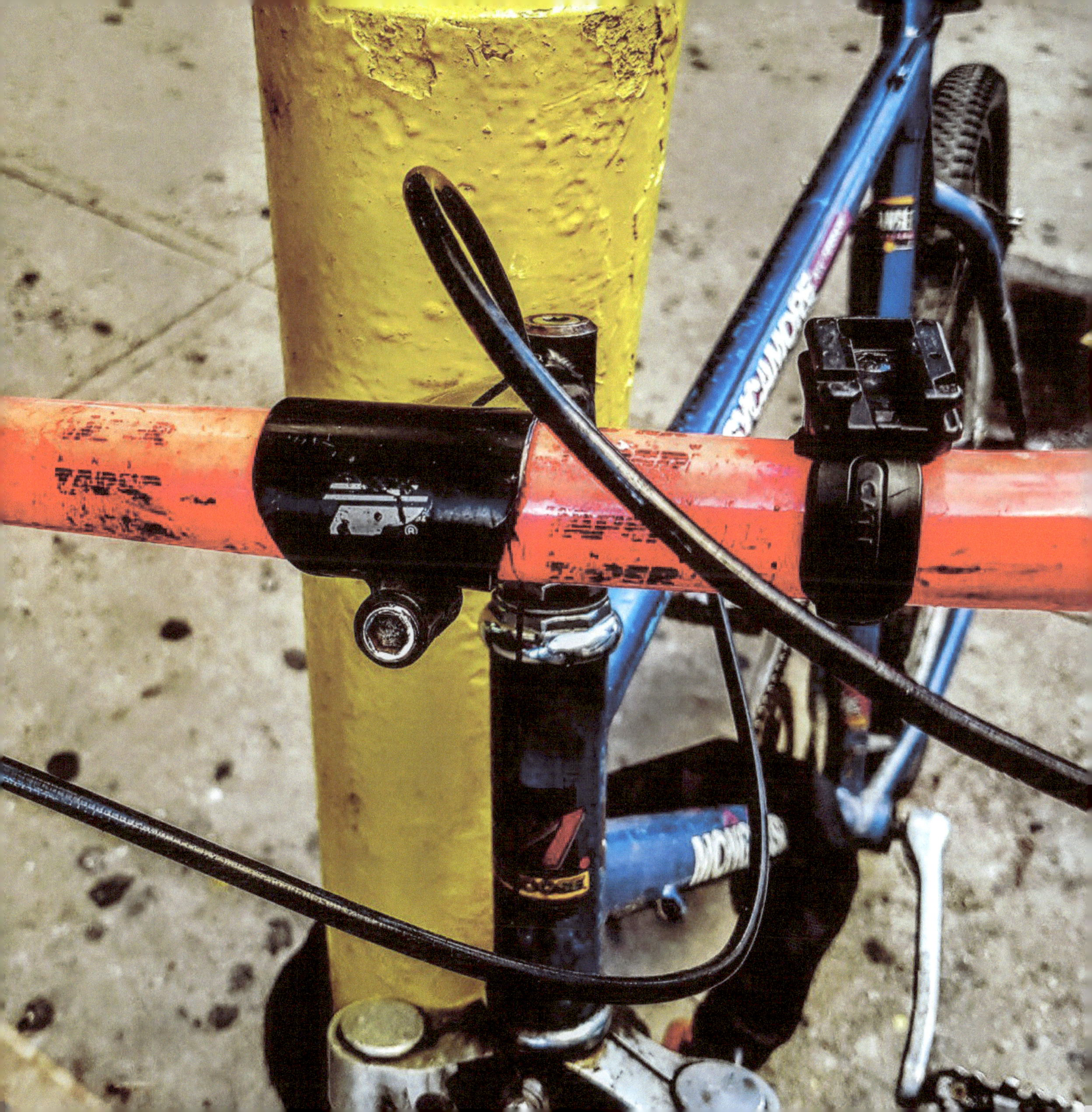

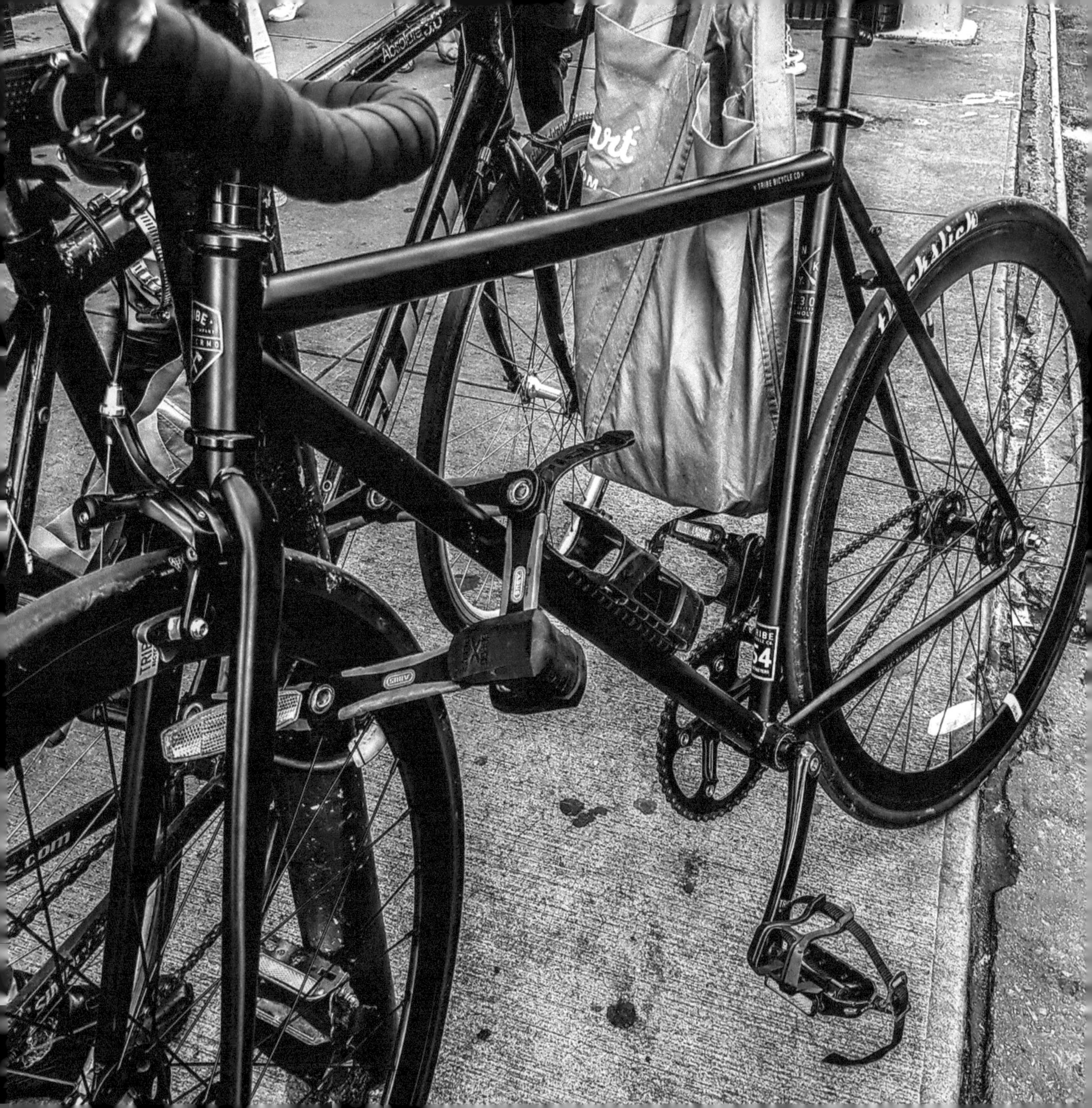
ABUS

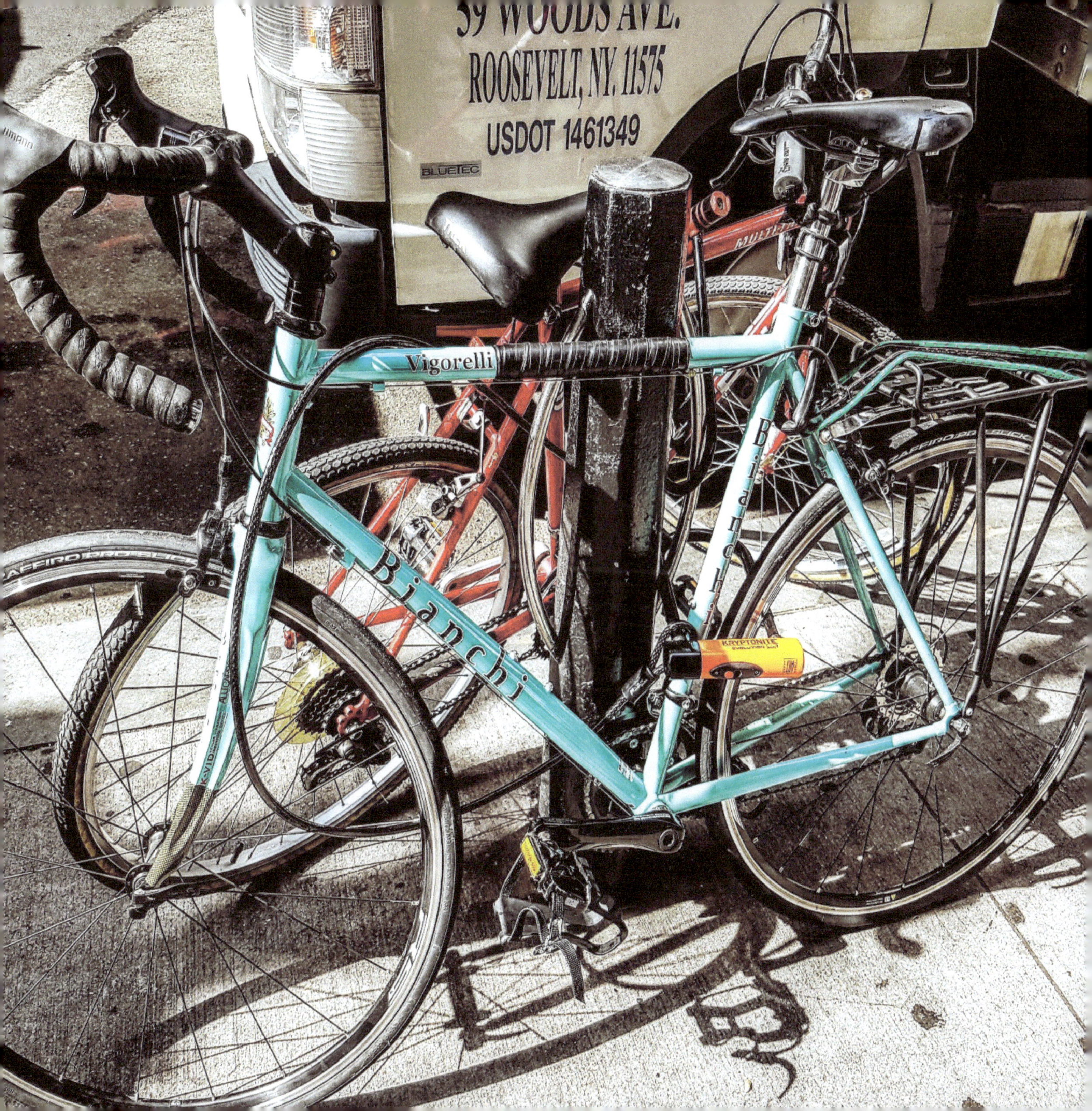
59 WOODS AVE.
ROOSEVELT, NY. 11575
USDOT 1461349
BLUETEC
Vigorelli
Bianchi
Bianchi
KRYPTONITE

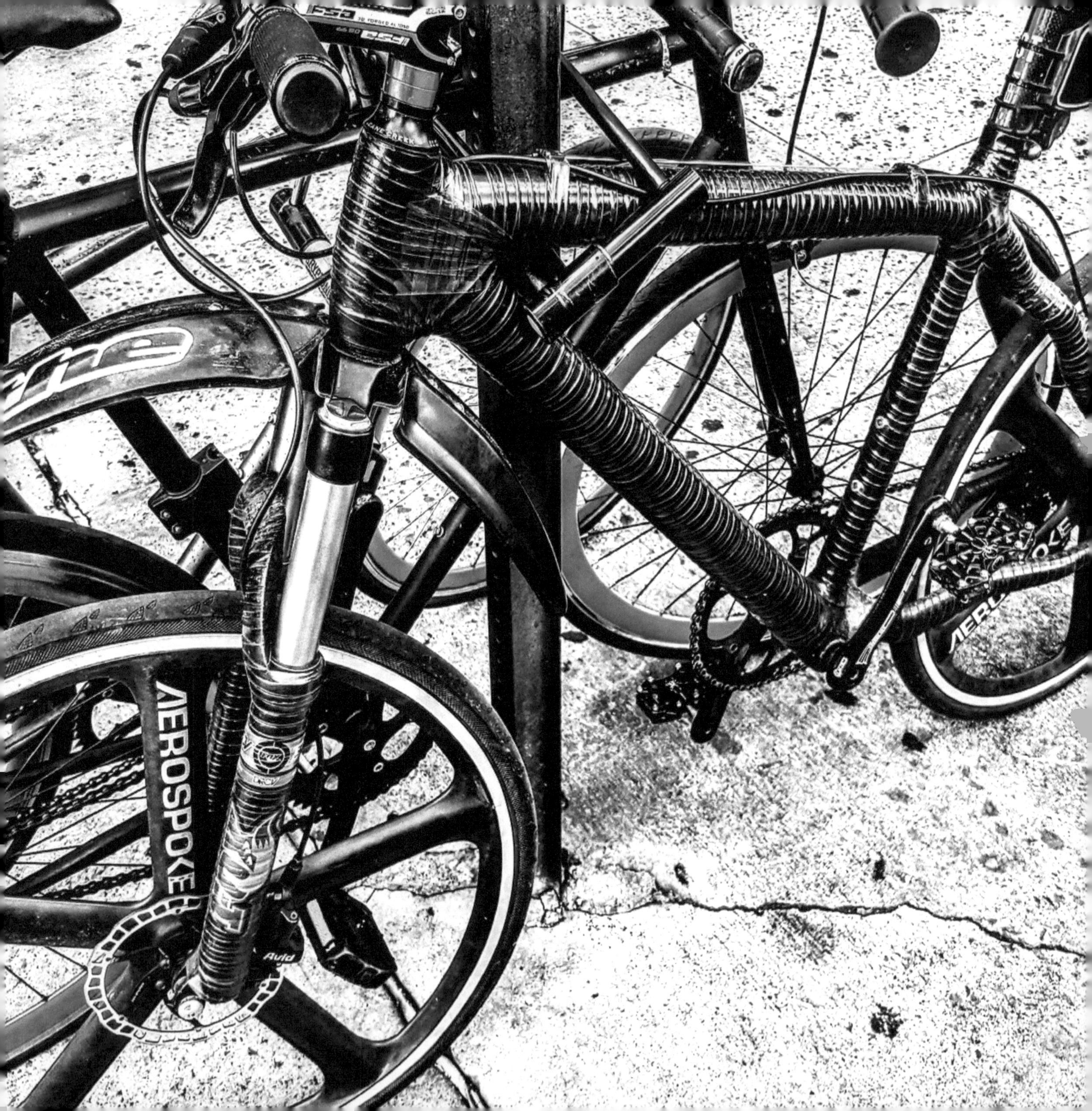
AEROSPOKE

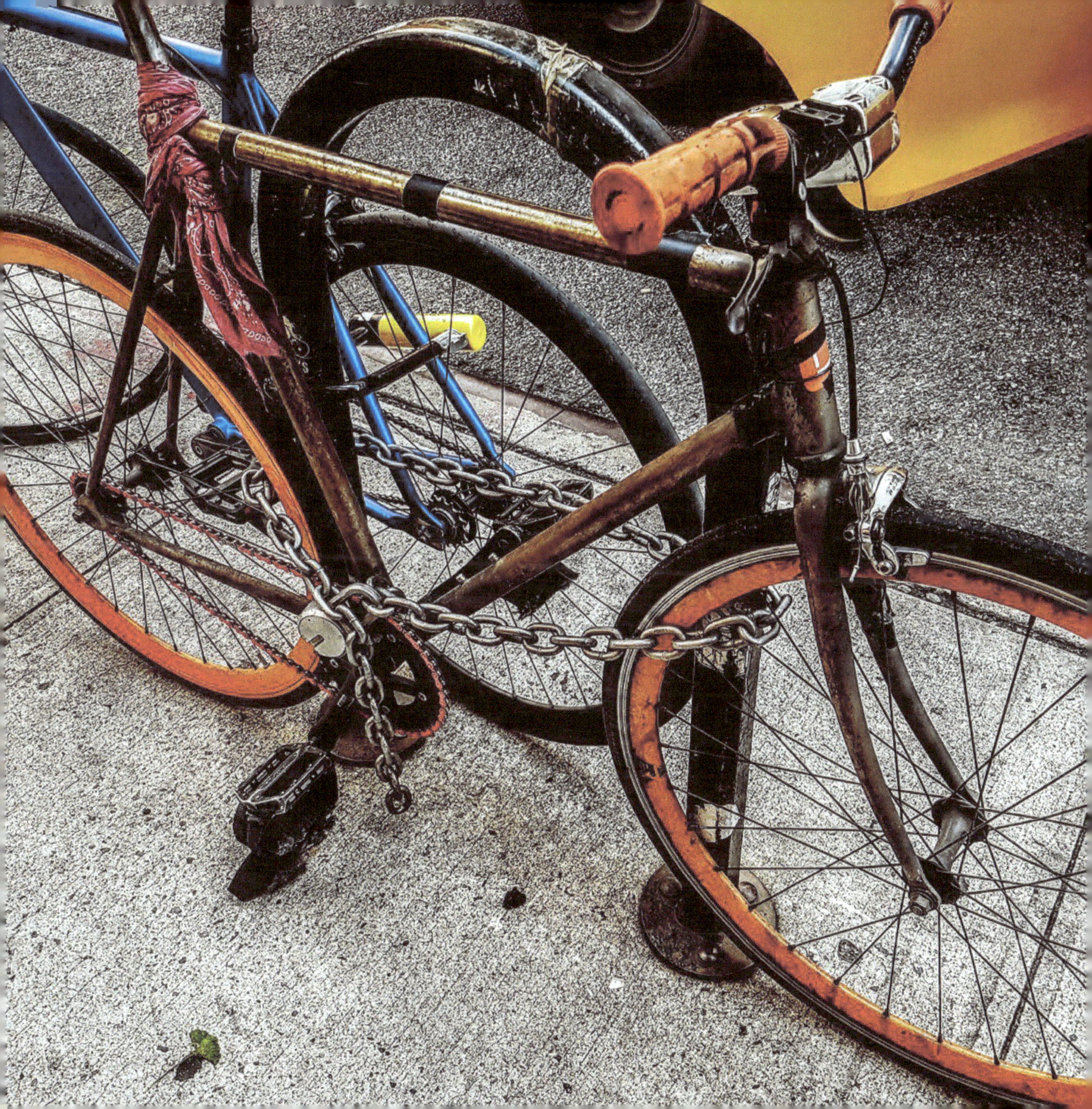

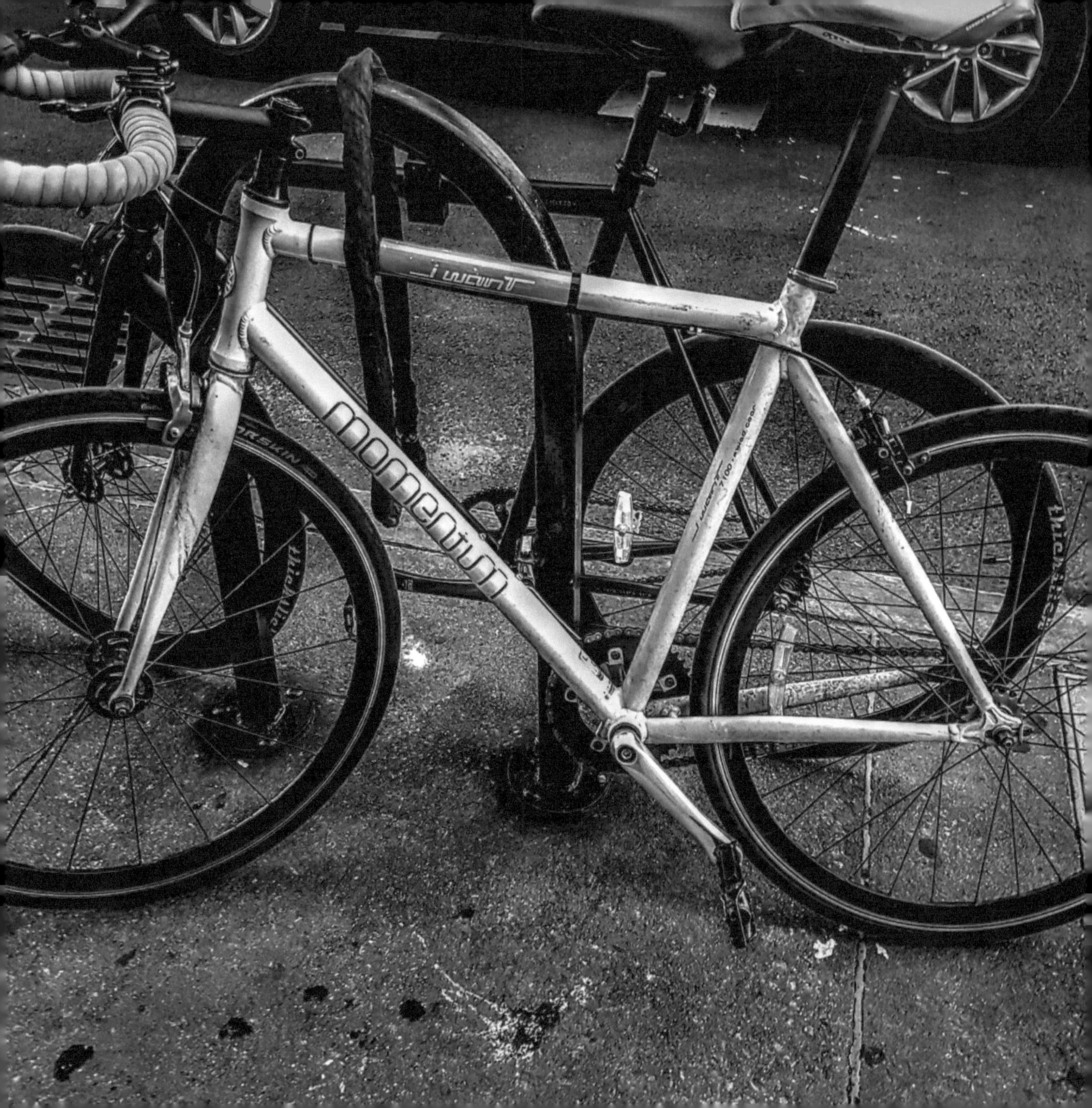
i want
momentum

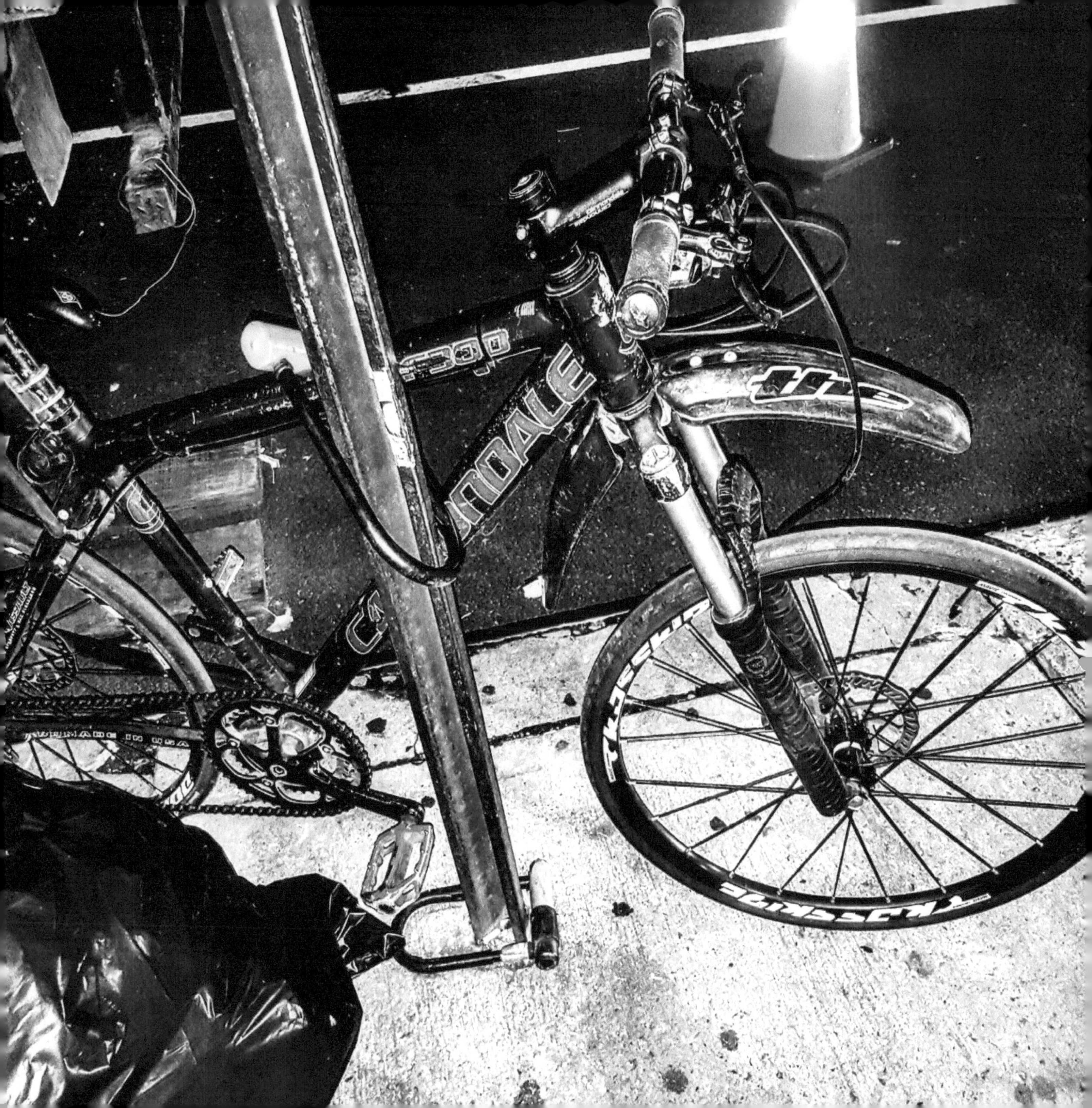

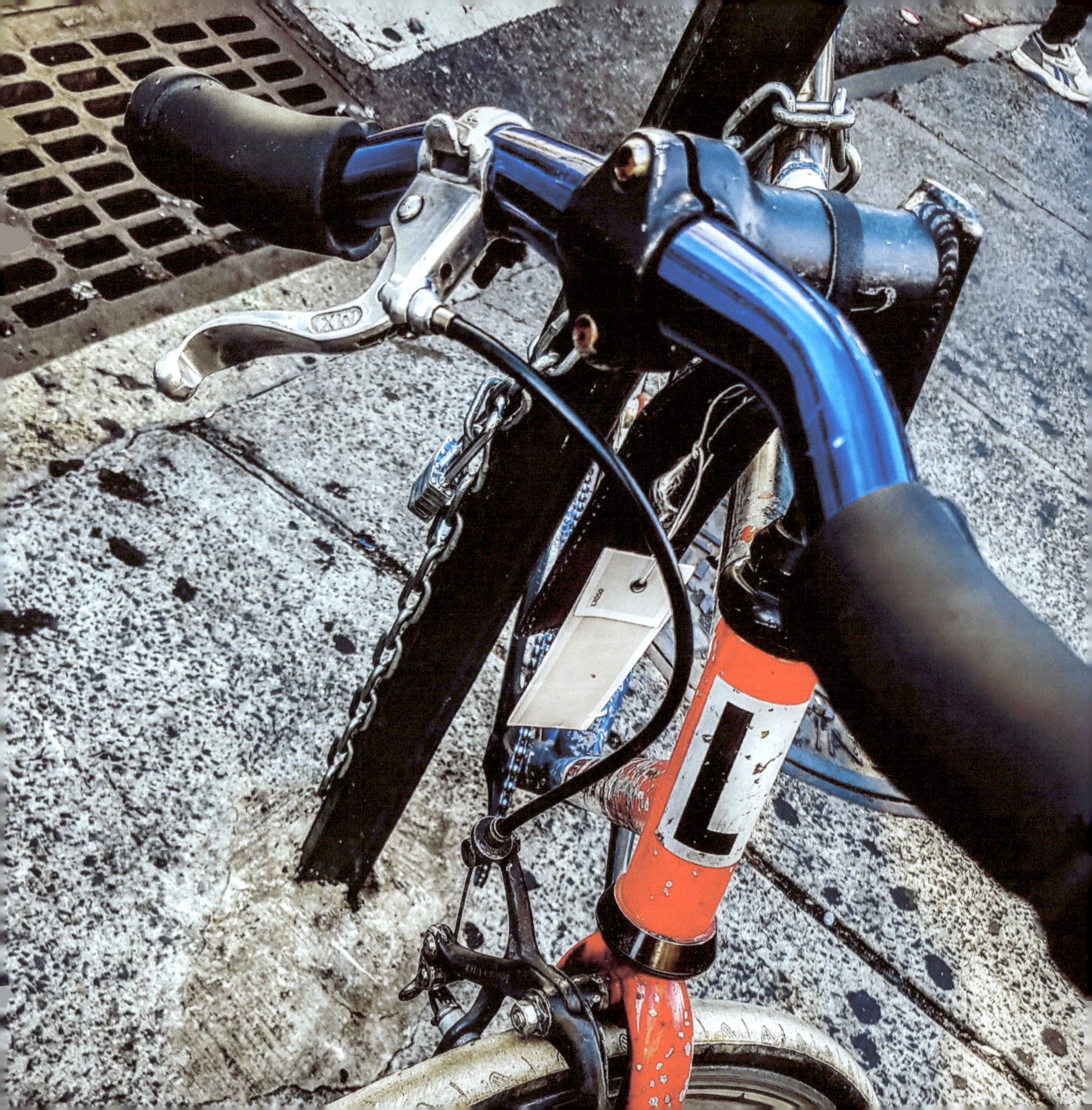

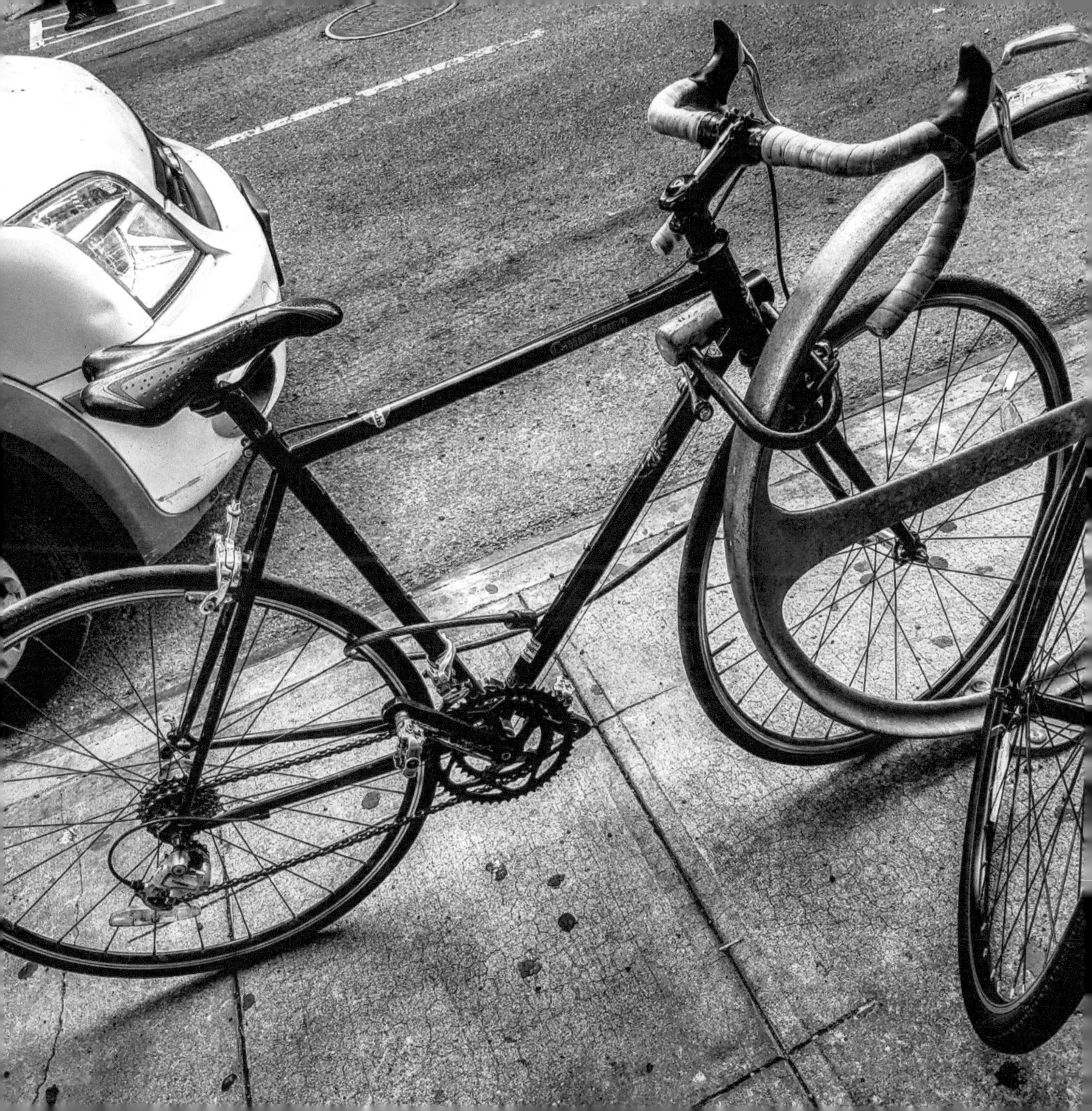

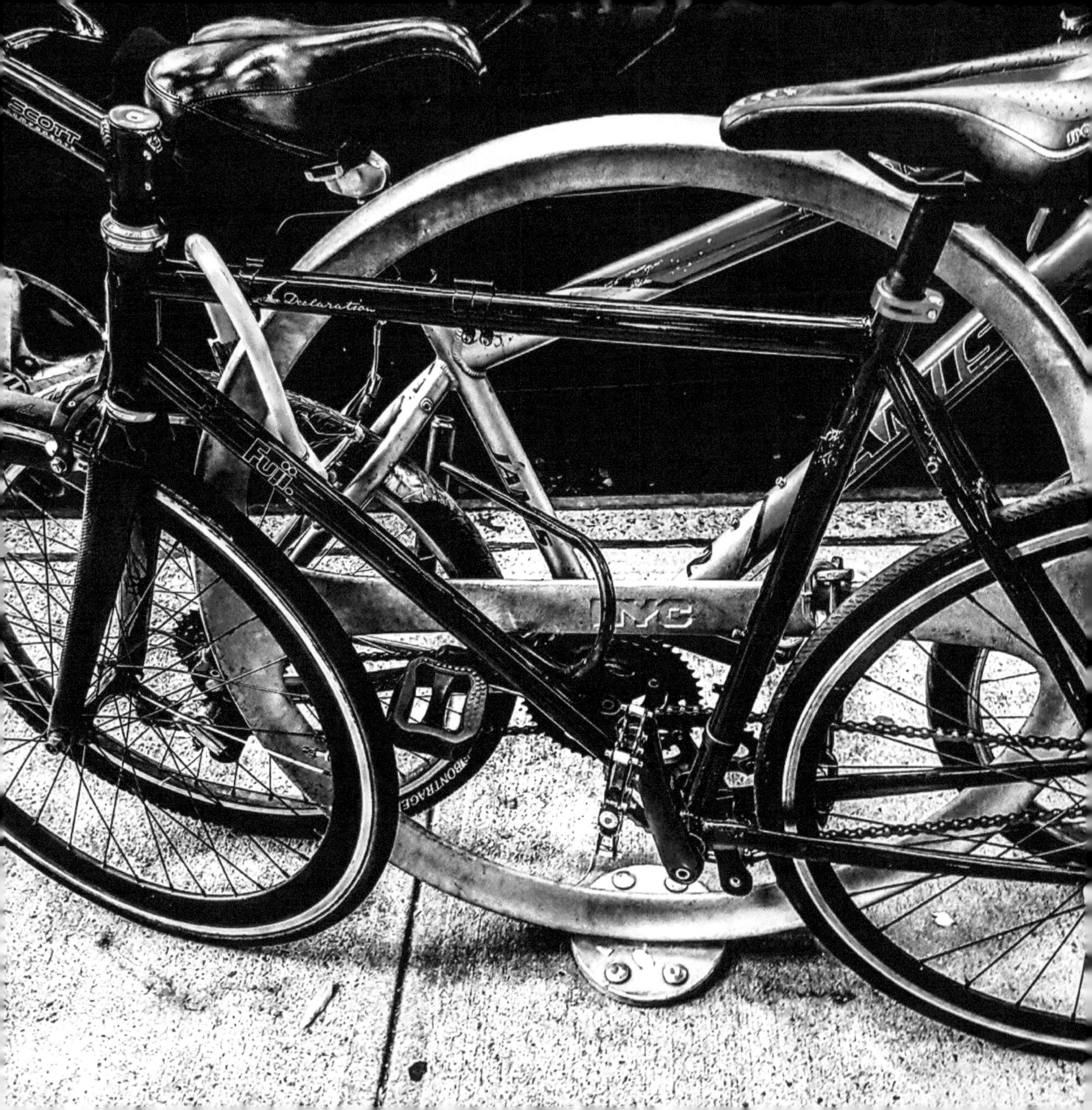
SCOTT
Declaration
Fuji
NYC

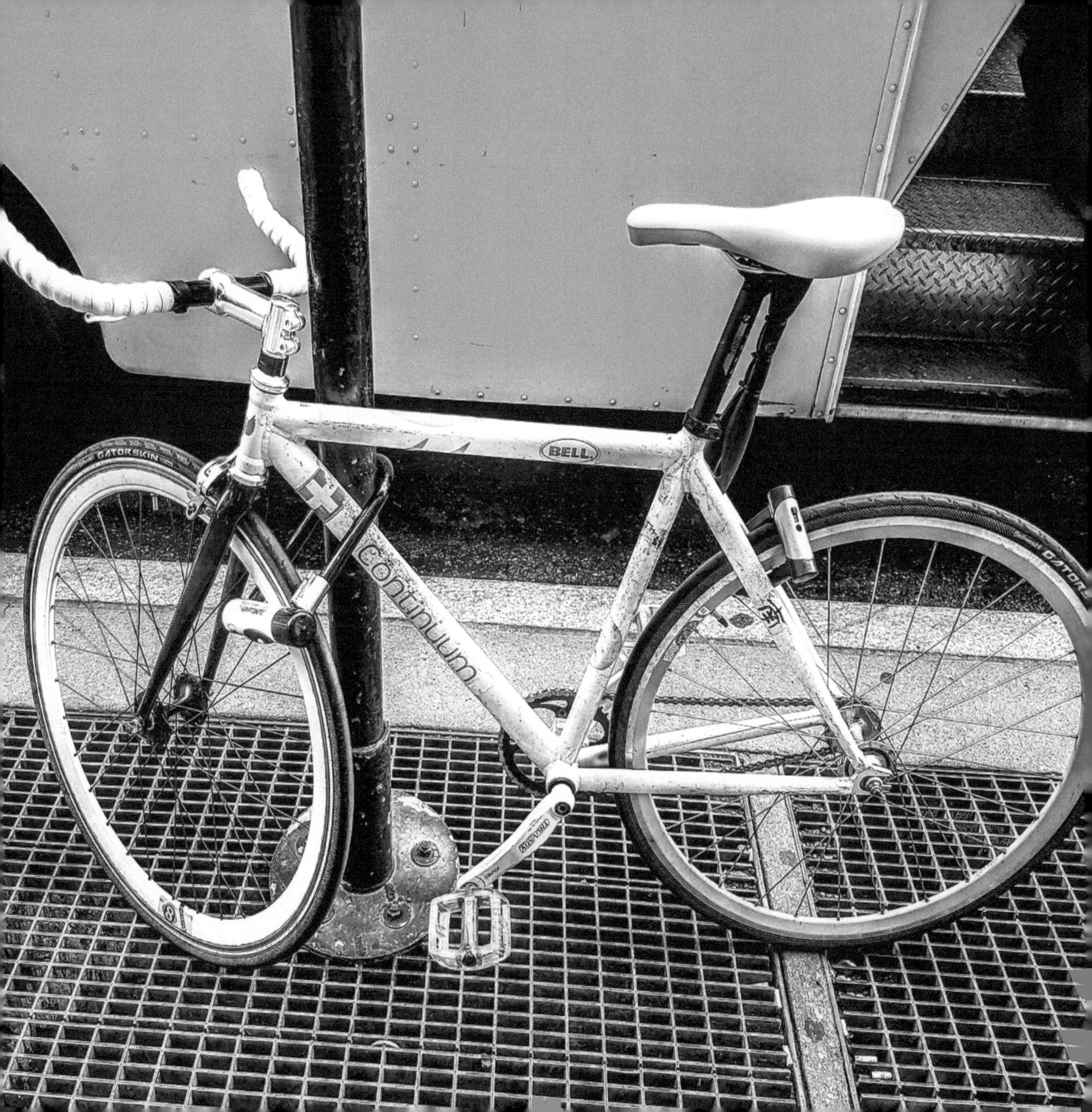
GATORSKIN
BELL.
continuum

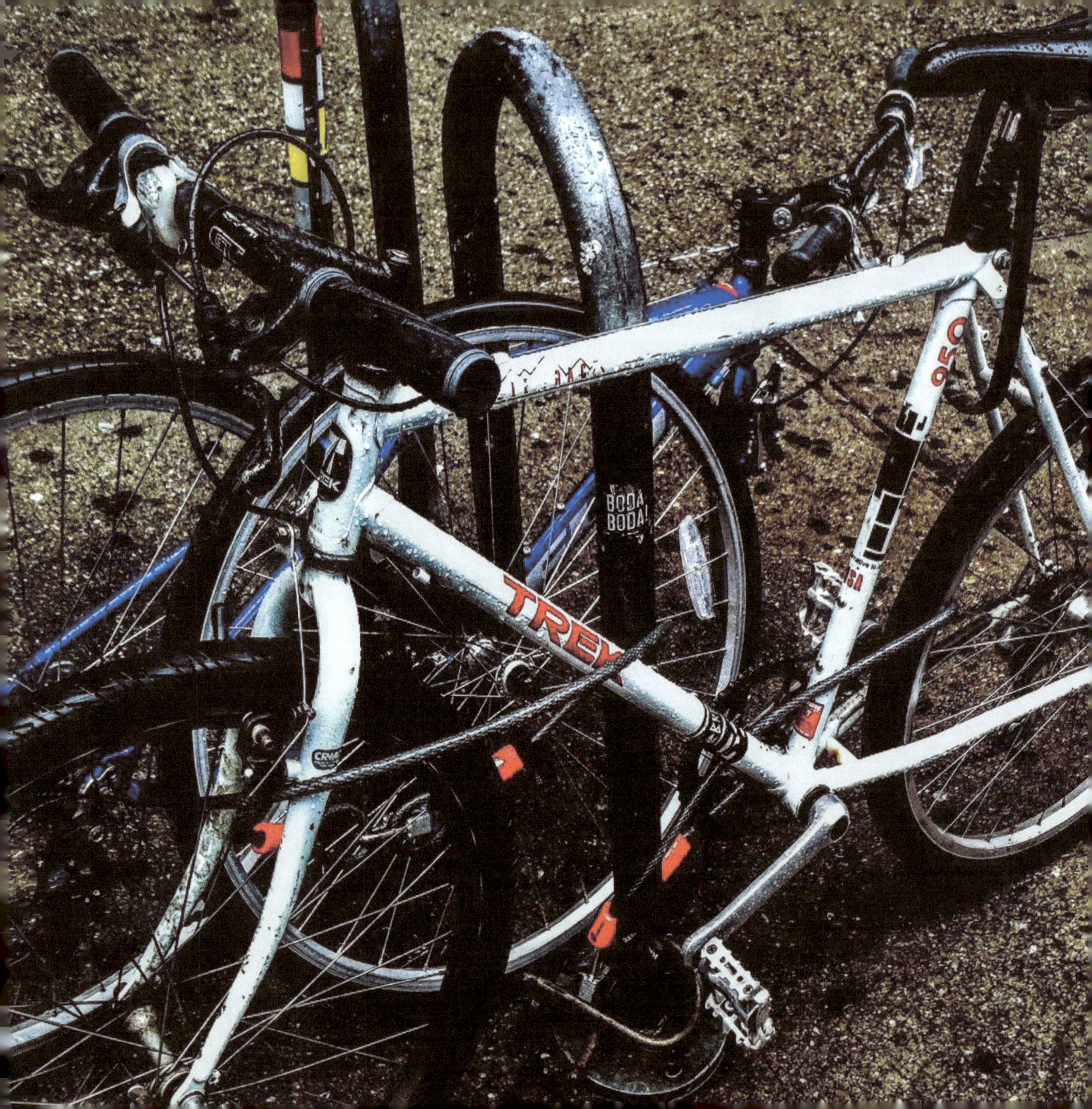
BODA
BODA!

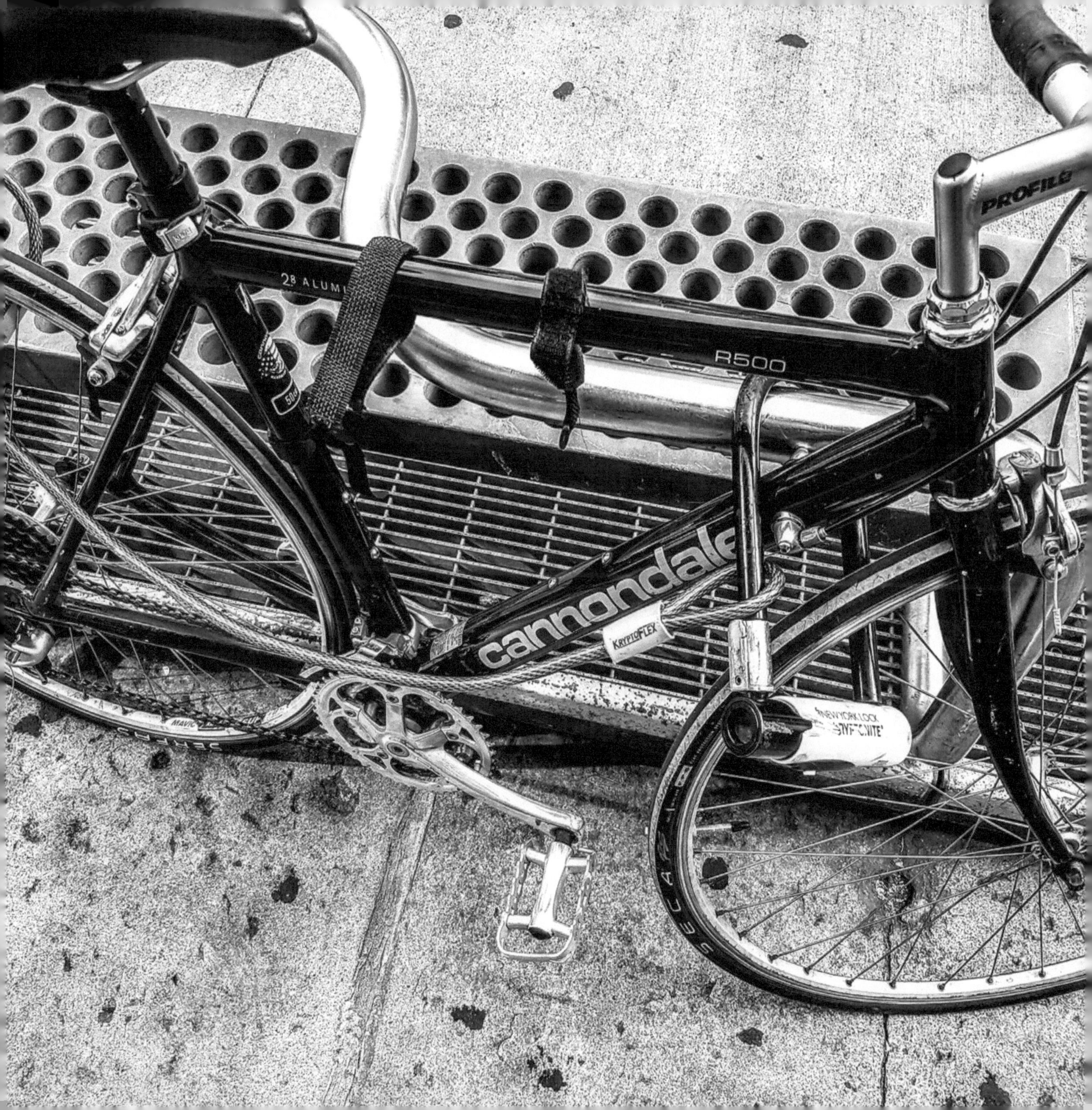
R500
cannondale
PROFILE
KRYPTOFLEX
NEW YORK LOCK

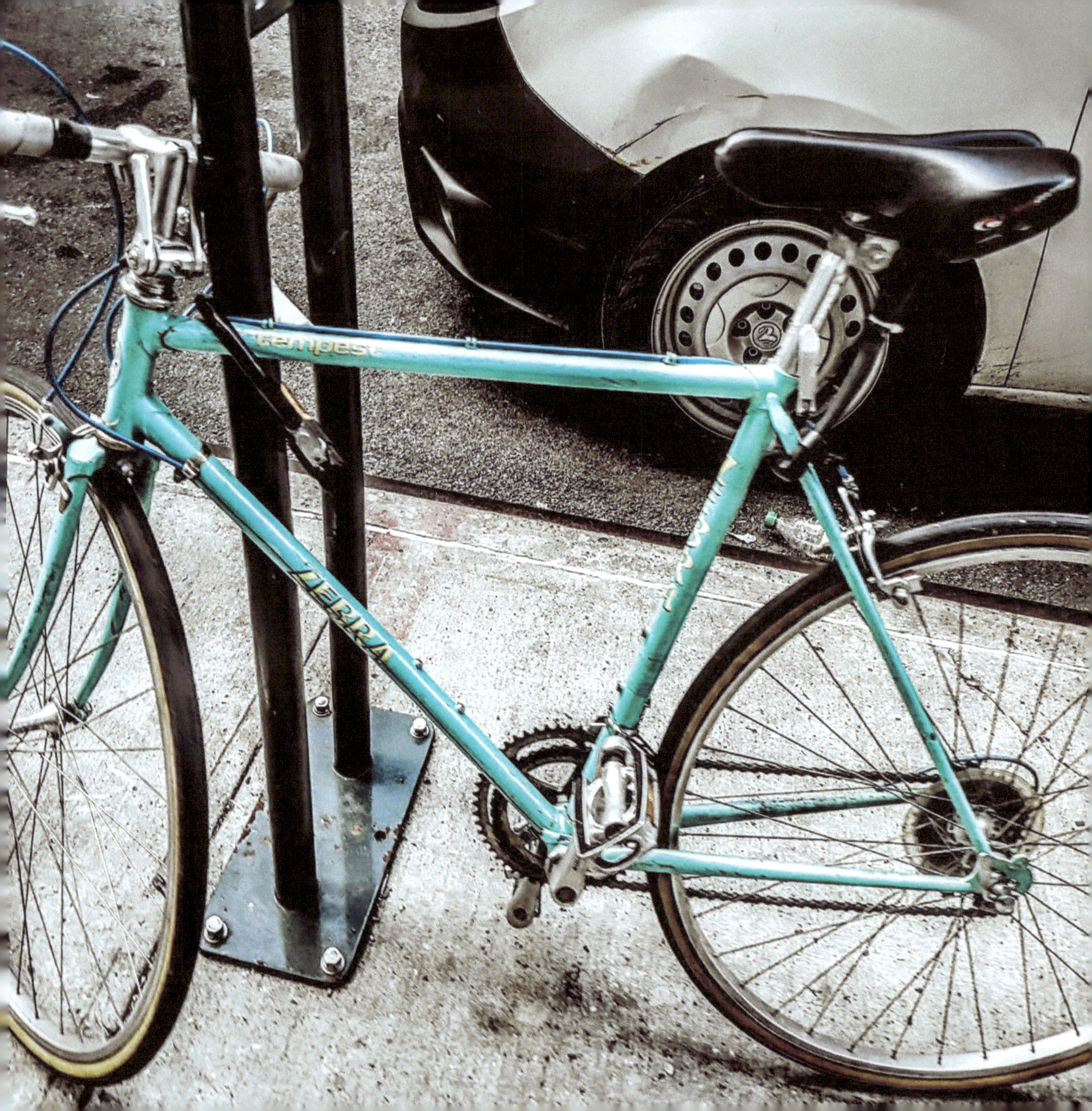
tempest
ZEBRA

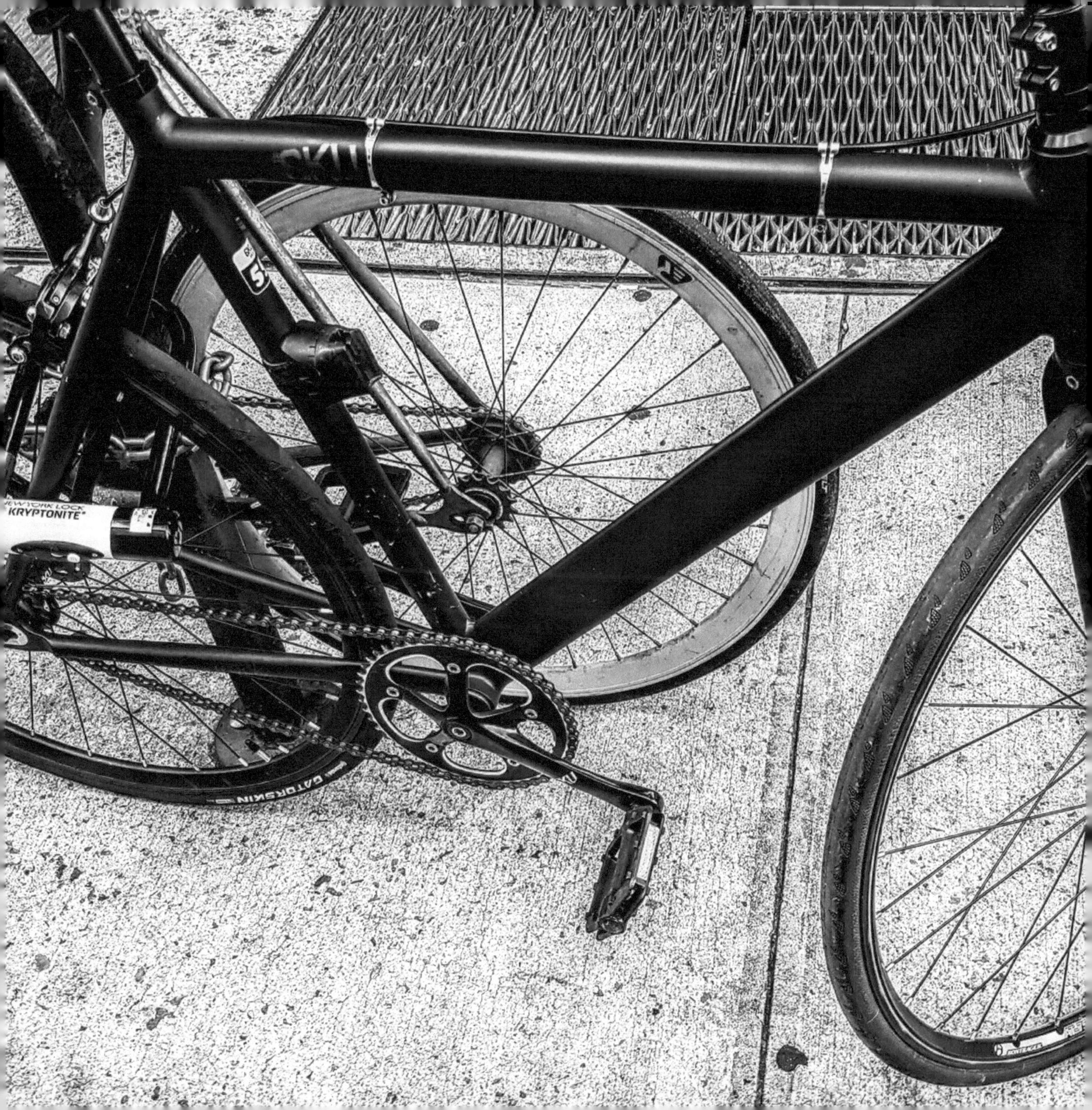
NEW YORK LOCK
KRYPTONITE

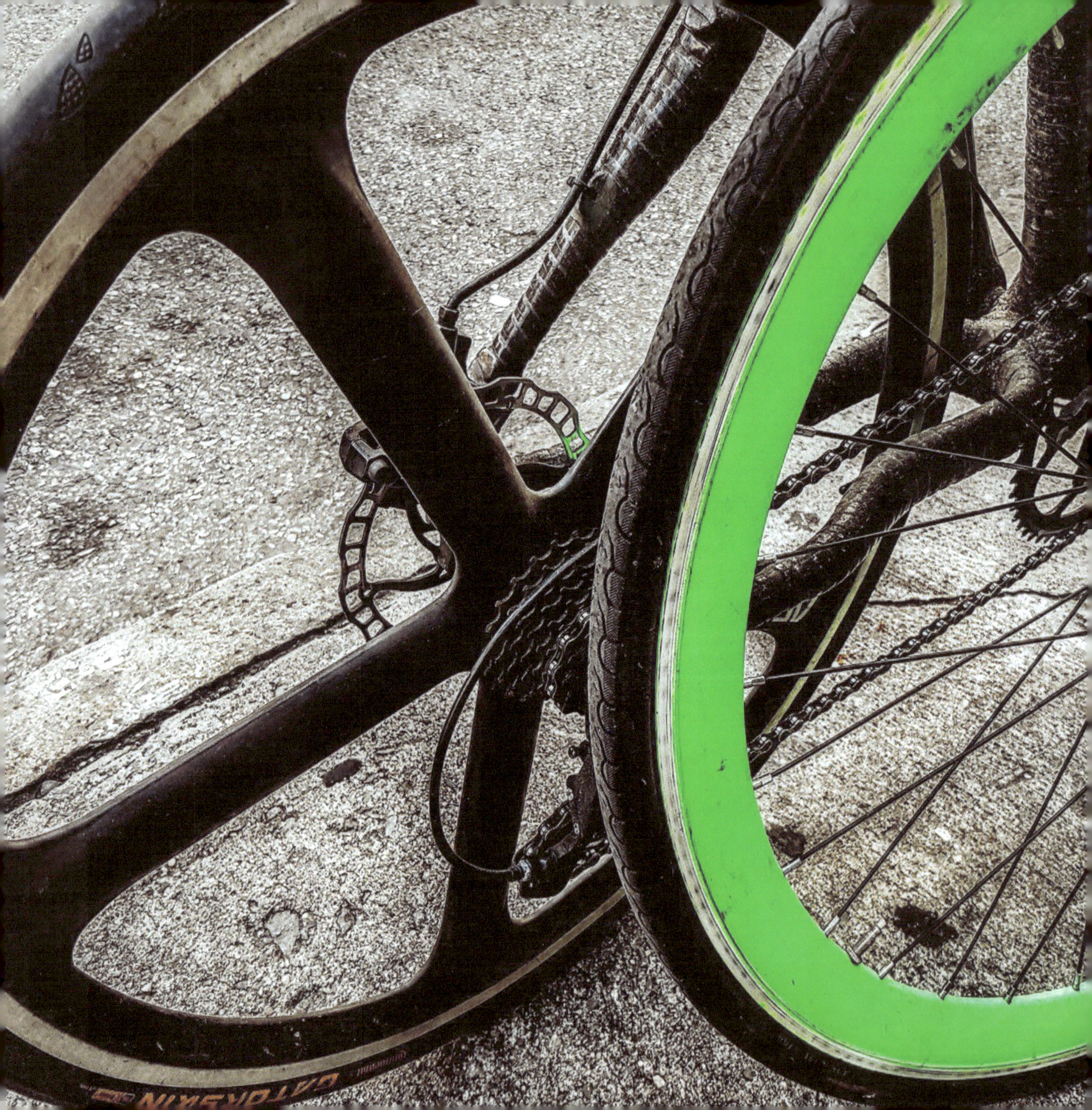
GATORSKIN

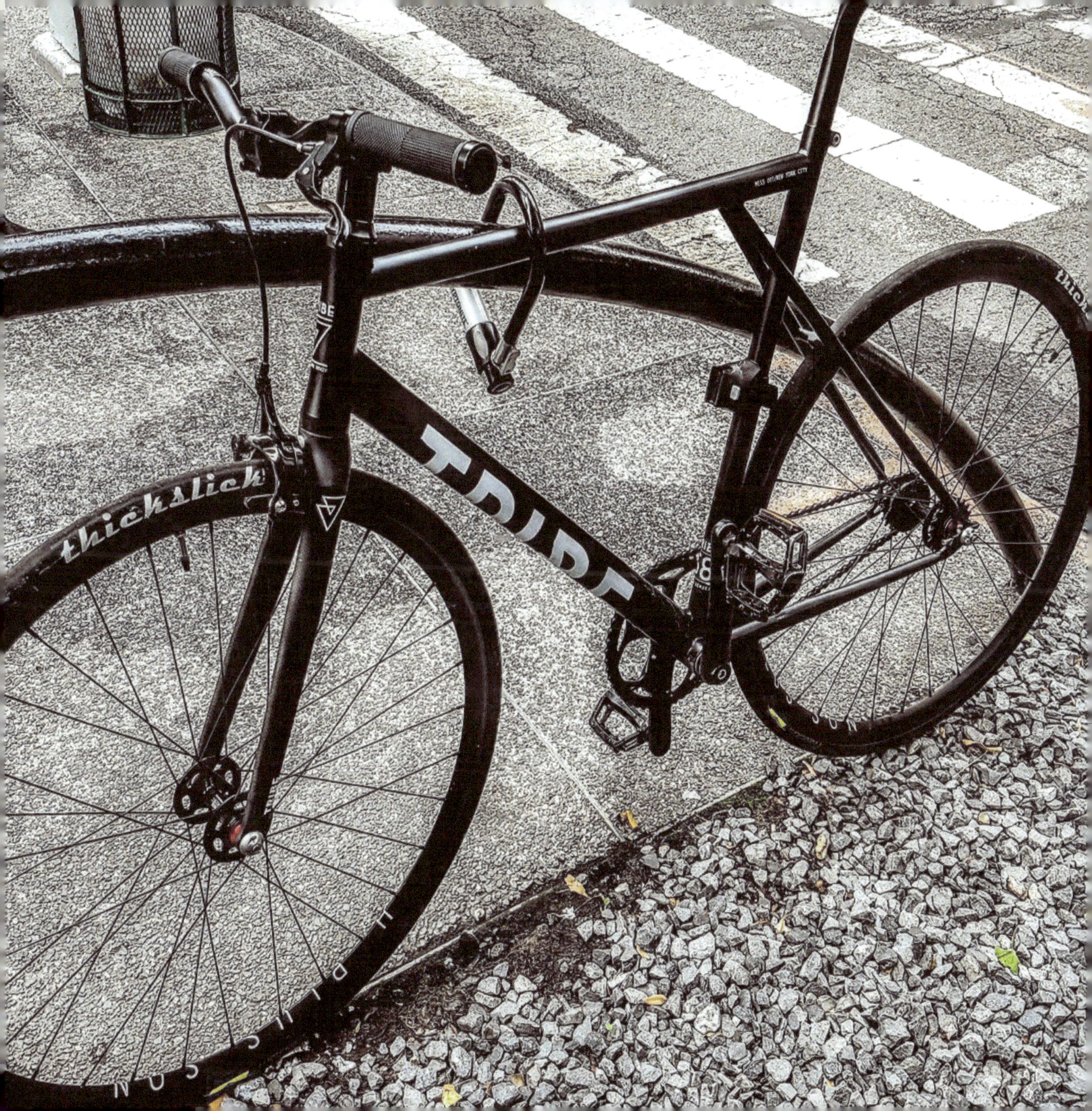
TRIBE
thickslick

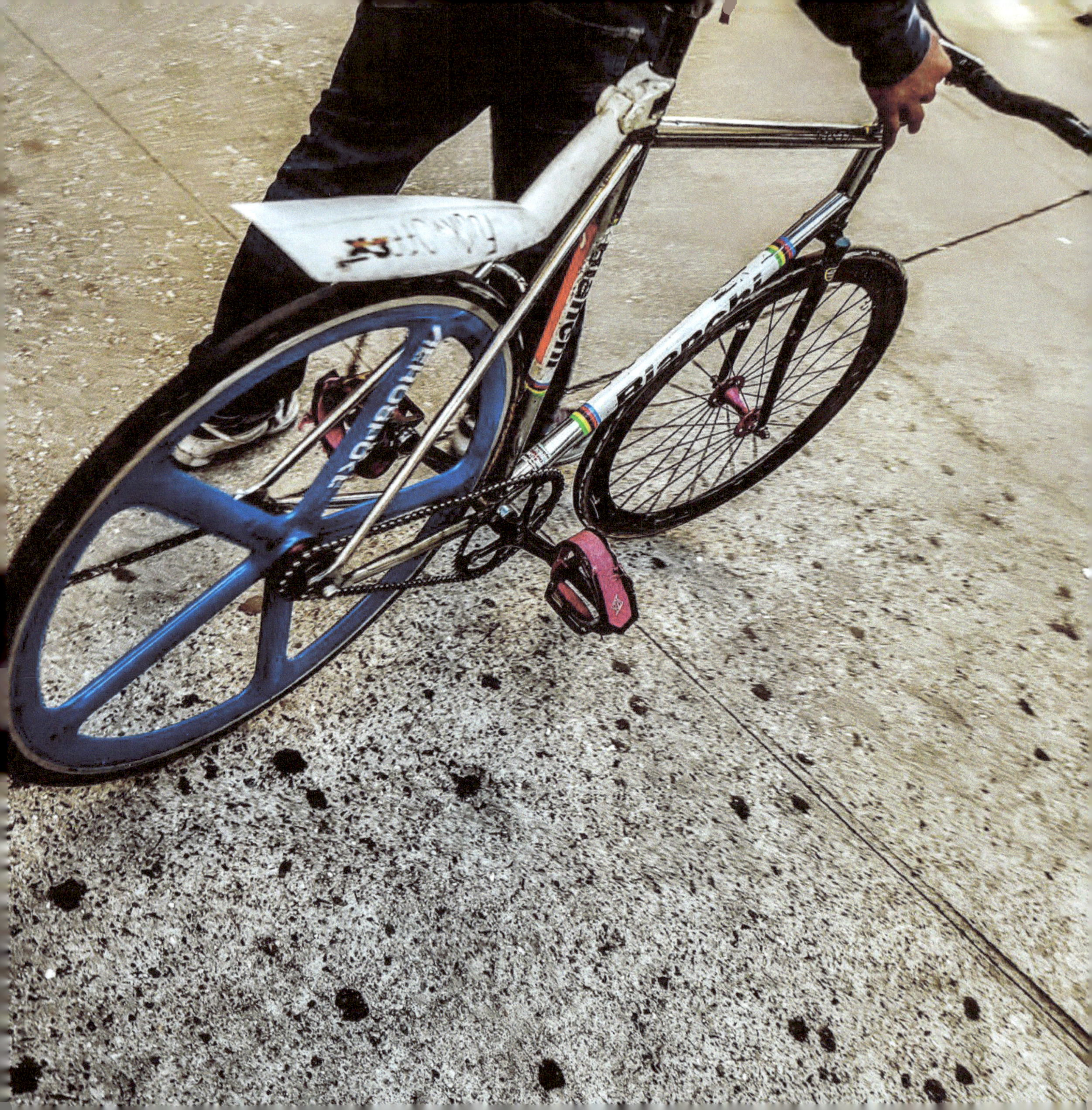

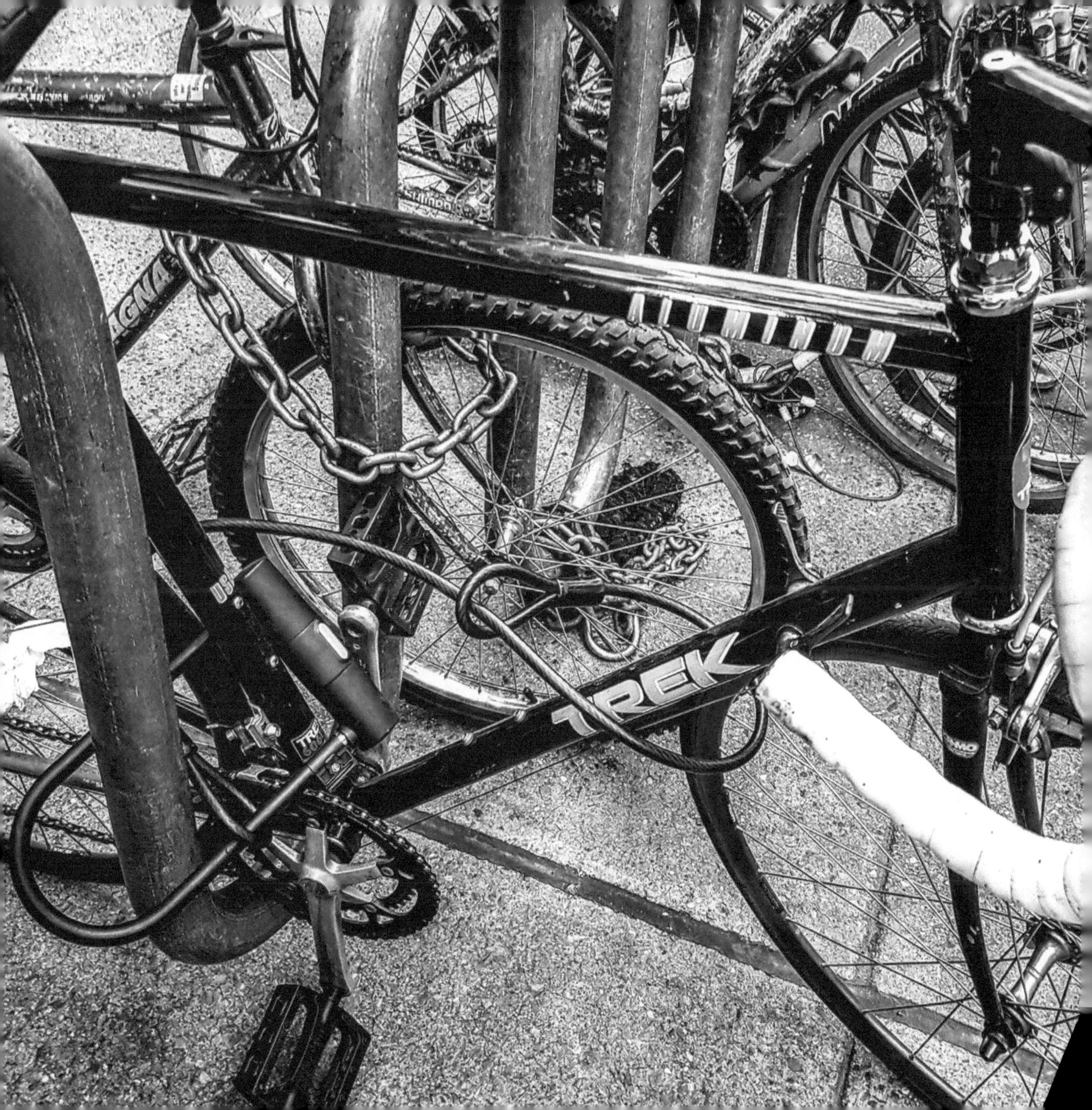
ALUMINUM
TREK

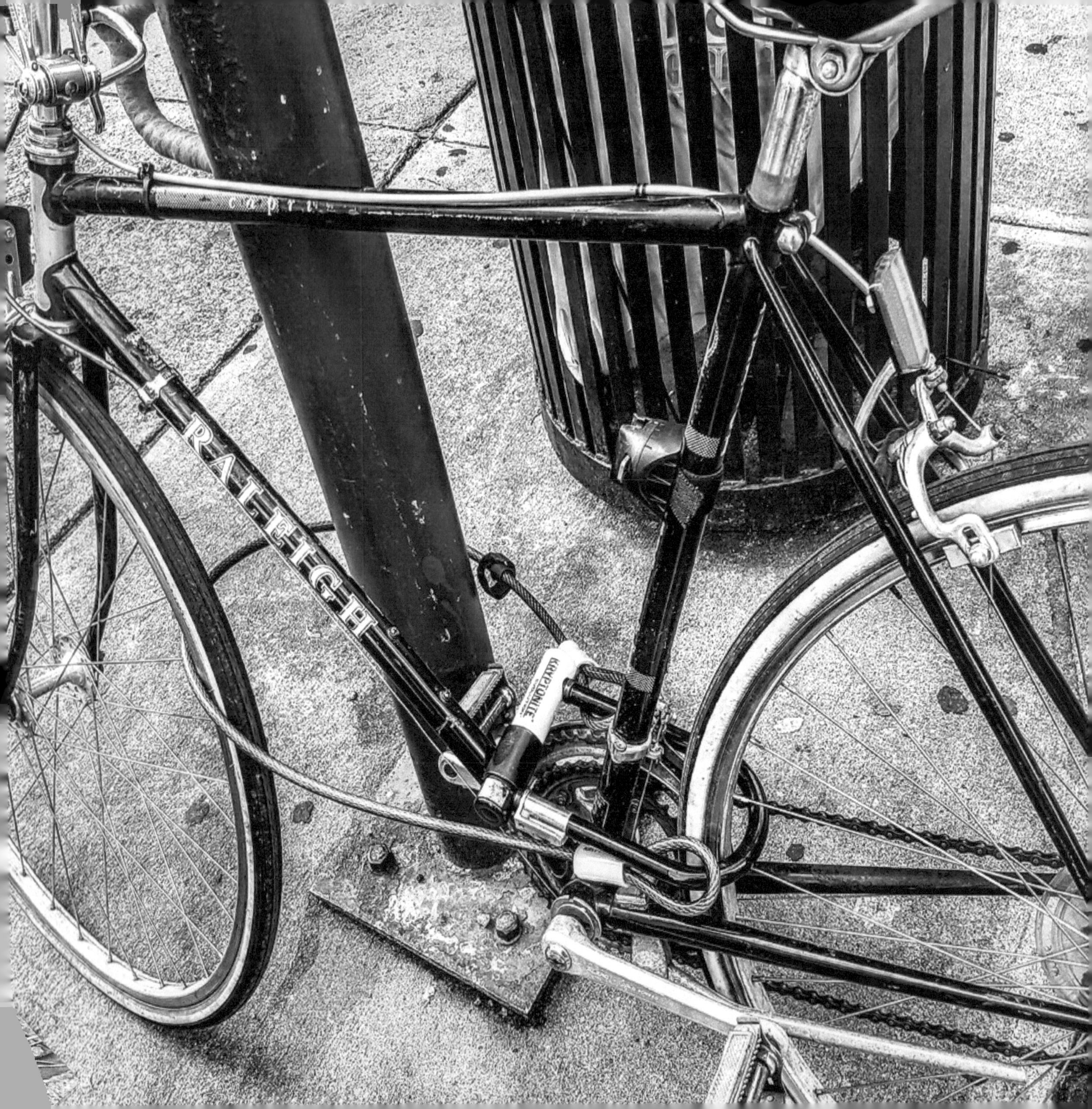
capri
RALEIGH
KRYPTONITE

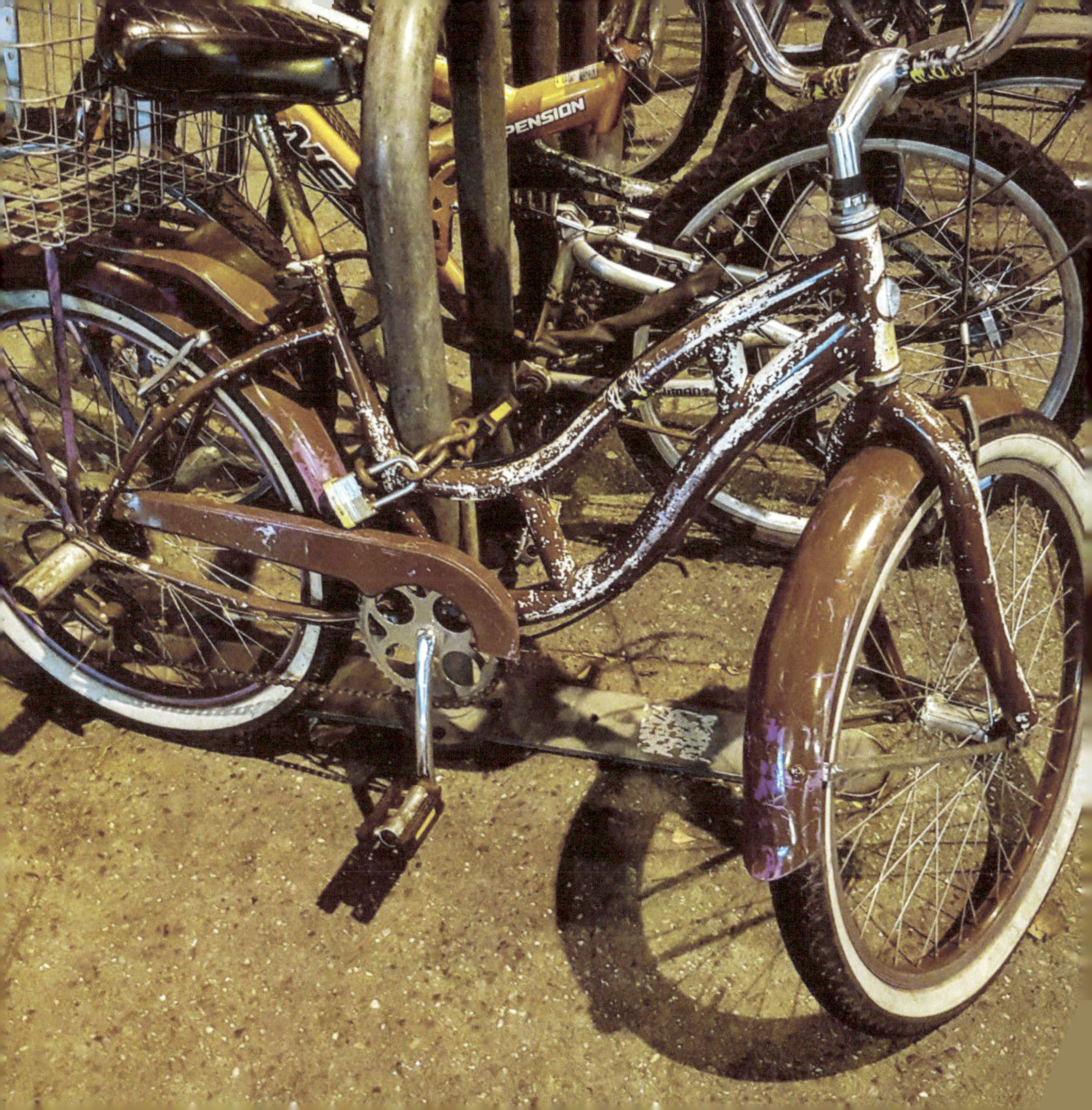
PENSION

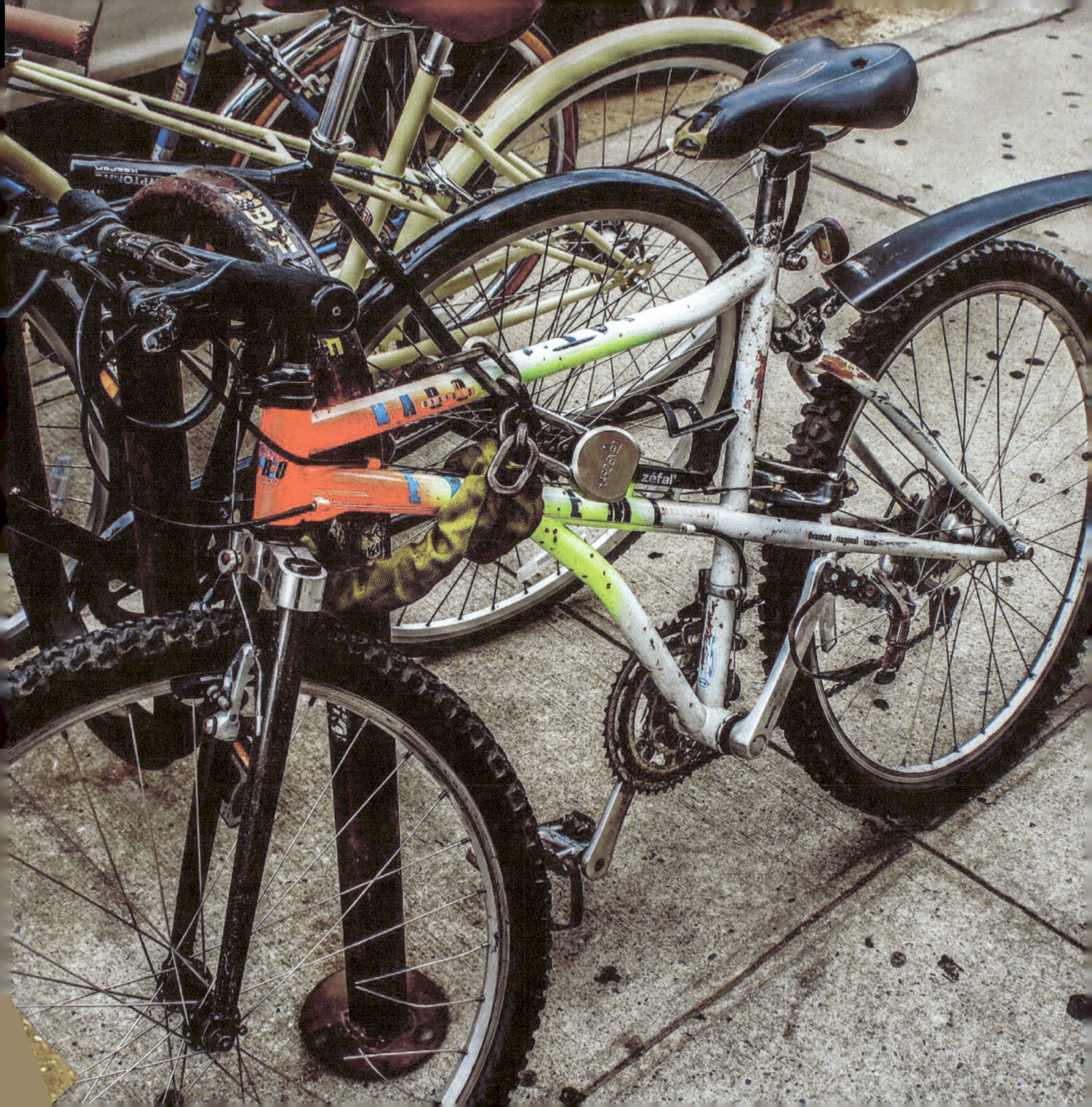
HARO
zéfal